THE SEA NEEDS NO ORNAMENT

EL MAR NO NECESITA ORNAMENTO

T0164044

THE SEA NEEDS NO ORNAMENT

EL MAR NO NECESITA ORNAMENTO

A BILINGUAL ANTHOLOGY OF
CONTEMPORARY CARIBBEAN WOMEN POETS

EDITED AND TRANSLATED BY

LORETTA COLLINS KLOBAH

AND

MARIA GRAU PEREJOAN

PEEPAL TREE

First published in Great Britain in 2020
by
Peepal Tree Press Ltd
17 King's Avenue
Leeds LS6 1QS
UK

ISBN 13: 9781845234737

Supported by
ARTS COUNCIL
ENGLAND

ACKNOWLEDGEMENTS

Loretta Collins Klobah and Maria Grau Perejoan wish to thank the English PEN organization for selecting our bilingual anthology project as a recipient of the 2018 PEN Translates Award. Your recognition and support encouraged us to complete the work.

A fellowship awarded to Maria Grau Perejoan by the Fulbright Commission, Spain, to be part of the Fulbright Visiting Scholar Program (2017-2018), made it possible for her to travel from Barcelona to Puerto Rico and reside on the island for months, facilitating our many work days of face-to-face collaboration during the translation process. Subsequently, she was awarded a travel grant by the Centre for Australian and Transnational Studies at the Universitat de Barcelona (2018-2019).

We are grateful to the Puerto Rico Science, Technology and Research Trust, in San Juan, for providing us with a temporary co-working space and access to electricity, an internet connection, and a coffee machine in the aftermath of Hurricane María. Nicole Marie Marrero Vázquez made us feel welcome every day, assisting with our facility and equipment needs.

We thank professor and linguist Alma Simounet for assistance with final line edits. We also thank the writers who have contributed poems to the collection for their comments and suggestions. Our appreciation to Vahni Capildeo, for their permission to use the line "The sea needs no ornament" from their poem "Shell" for the title of the anthology (*Utter*, Peepal Tree Press, 2013). Poet and editor of Ediciones Aguadulce, Cindy Jiménez-Vera, and poet and editor of printing workshop La Impresora, Nicole Cecilia Delgado, gave us invaluable recommendations and resources related to writers of Cuba, the Dominican Republic and Puerto Rico. Poets and colleagues Zaira Pacheco and Melanie Pérez, professors of Hispanic Studies and literature at the University of Puerto Rico, Río Piedras campus, suggested anthologies of Cuban literature during our early research phase. Damaris Cruz gave us permission to use her original artwork *Fuerza y Maña* on the book cover.

Loretta Collins Klobah thanks her family, Wenmimareba, Jeremy, and Meganne, for encouragement during the project; and Marcia Douglas, Leslie McGrath, Marty Williams, Charles and Diane Hanzlicek, and Lorilee Cabrera-Donovan for post-hurricane aid.

Maria Grau Perejoan thanks the support of her family at home, her parents, Antonieta and Joan, and Oriol, Lola, Nil and Joel, *gràcies per ser sempre al meu costat*. She also thanks Camilo, Albert, Andrea and Ivette *por tratarme como una más de la familia*.

Finally, Loretta and Maria both fondly thank Jeremy Poynting and Hannah Bannister of Peepal Tree Press for their enthusiasm and support for the anthology project, as well as their quick replies to queries throughout our process of preparing the manuscript. We appreciate all that Peepal Tree has done and continues to do for Caribbean and Black British literature.

CONTENTS

INTRODUCTION

The Sea Needs No Ornament/ El mar no necesita ornamento is titled after a line of poetry by one of our contributors, Vahni Capildeo. It represents, in a marvellously understated fashion, the full-on audacity, strong themes, thoughtful meditations, skilled vibrancy, and innovative verse forms of the thirty-three Caribbean women writers gathered together in these pages. Both monolingual readers of English or Spanish and bilingual readers can read and enjoy the book since all poems are presented in both languages.

It is the first bilingual anthology of contemporary poetry by women writers of the English- and Spanish-speaking Caribbean and its Diasporas to be published in more than two decades. Some of the writers may have published prior to the turn-of-the-century, but most contributors have published books, received awards, and become established during the first two decades of this century. All have published at least one or two significant collections, and several have also published fiction, essays, served as editors of anthologies or journals, been judges for literary competitions, and actively participated in literary culture on local and international scales. These are writers who will undoubtedly continue to publish and be leading literary voices in the decades to come. Although there are exceptions (especially among the Cubans, a few of the Puerto Ricans, and a Trinidadian), most of the selected poets have not previously been translated or included in a bilingual anthology of this scope. We have chosen some of the very best, but there are many other excellent women poets of the English- and Spanish-speaking Caribbean whom we admire and who also could have been included had our energies, resources, and time as translators and available page-count been limitless.

The poems speak to women's experiences in gripping, powerful, and radical ways, challenging gender, racial, ethnic, cultural, class, historical, and societal orthodoxies and proscriptions of all sorts. We wanted to suggest the breadth of the poets' concerns and writerly approaches, to include poems on an array of subjects, written in a diversity of moods, tones, and poetic styles. For this reason, we have included three to five poems by each author. We hope that readers will be inspired to look for and read the poetry collections of all of the authors. Many of the poets have recordings of their readings available on YouTube or elsewhere on the internet. The poems, whether originally written in Spanish or English, have been translated by the two editors, Loretta Collins Klobah and Maria Grau Perejoan. A poem is first presented in the language in which it was originally written and then, on opposite pages, the translated version.

The plurilingual context of the Caribbean archipelago and sites of Caribbean migration is a by-product of multiple campaigns of conquest and colonisation by the British, French, Spanish, Dutch, and Kingdom of the Netherlands; the presence and partial genocide of various indigenous peoples; the forced transshipment and enslavement of African peoples of diverse heritages and languages; the forced transportation of Irish and British political prisoners, and those who fell afoul of the law, as bond servants in the 17th century; the indentureship of East Indians, Madeirans and Chinese; the settlement of Arab, Sephardic Jewish and Syrian persons (among others); inter-island migration within the region; and relocation to metropoles abroad. This brief and incomplete sketch of the historical context doesn't begin to fully represent the cultural admixture and linguistic complexities of the Caribbean as creole societies, the larger circum-Atlantic Caribbean (including the Bahamas, the Caribbean coast of Central America, Guyana, and Surinam), and sites of migration. The historical trauma of the region is still very much a part of our reality and continually impacts the challenges faced by Caribbean societies and peoples, as well as the topics addressed by writers in the current era.

For any contemporary writer, the plurilingualism of the region is both an extraordinary creative potential and, at times, a barrier to fully knowing the work of writers from neighbouring islands and mainland localities, who may publish in another language. English-lexifier and French-lexifier Lesser Antillean Creole with island variants, English, Dutch, French, Haitian Creole, Garifuna, Hindi, Jamaican Creole (Patois/ Patwa), Papiamento, Sarnami, Spanish, Sranan Tongo, and Urdu are just some of the literary languages available to Caribbean writers, but every geographical location of the Caribbean has its own specific idiom, vocabulary, and shared set of references. Both editors of *The Sea Needs No Ornament/ El mar no necesita ornamento* revel in the region's linguistic diversity, hoping that this anthology will promote multilingualism and more solidarity between women writers and their readers, who have been separated by geography and language barriers but who share global histories and the urgencies of the contemporary moment. We regret that we have not been able to include poets from the Antillean Creole-, French-, and Haitian Creole-speaking islands of Guadeloupe, Martinique, and Haiti; nor have we included writers who may write in English, Dutch or Papiamento from the islands of Aruba, Bonaire, Curaçao, or St. Martin. Our contributors, whatever their birthplaces or current homes, have close connections to Barbados, the Bahamas, Cuba, the Dominican Republic, Grenada, Guyana, Jamaica, Puerto Rico, St. Lucia, Trinidad and Tobago, the U.S. Virgin Islands.

Poems included here are written in myriad forms and styles – lyric and narrative, realist and boldly experimental or purposefully minimalist. They draw on the blues, nursery rhymes, marketplace vendor songs and other oral traditions; on myths, and textual allusion, they personify the natural world, and create memorably-voiced personas. The writing is fierce, fresh, incisive, inventive, humorous, thought-provoking, and tender.

Some of the poems revisit childhood roots, where all is not the innocence of playing marbles and dandy shandy, riding bicycles, running in white sneakers or gold sandals, hair-braiding, go-karting, church-singing, leaping across rooftops, and kite-flying on the green grounds of a colonial fort. Powerful poems meditate on memories of the quiet mystery of grandmother's attic, (mis)education by history lessons, and many daily occurrences that impact a child's sense of self and the world. Poems visit barbershops, bedrooms, bulldozed or gated communities, churches, corner shops, hospitals, fruit and fish markets, train stops, and the seaside. Imaginative play and self-discovery mix with abuse by relatives, gender socialisation, and the patrolling or punishment of both girls' and boys' bodies. Concern about the vulnerability of children in societies where people feel the need to protect their homes with burglar bars is a strong theme of some poems, as is lamenting parental and random public violence and the killing of children.

The poetry scrutinises, reinterprets, and inscribes, from the authors' various perspectives, the history of the societies of the Caribbean archipelago and the experience of familial or individual migration. Political and social issues such as the increasing inequalities of late capitalism, popular culture, misogyny, racialism, the position of refugees, class oppression, resistance, revolution, and dictatorship are explored. The lives of enslaved African women mentioned in a Jamaican plantation overseer's diary are honoured in outrage and solidarity. Poems challenge and rebel against ideologies and paradigms that have shaped society and still seemingly overdetermine the contemporary parameters of social life, culture, justice, interpersonal relationships, and the lived experiences of women, elders, mothers, fathers, persons who identify as LGBTTIQ, non-binary, or cisgender heterosexual, teenagers, boys, and girls.

Authors who have experienced migration or are second generation children of migrants write about living between cultures or with multiple ethnic heritages, the loss of and search to regain family knowledge and connections, missing foodways of home islands, and estrangement from Caribbean mother tongues.

Poems take readers to urban scenes of bars, cheap hotels, conversations with strangers, domestic violence, drug-trafficking, graffitied streets, murder, music clubs, porn, prostitution, tourist dives, or prisons. Some are carnivalesque and transgressive, delighting in sensual pleasures at Phagwa and fighting racism at rock concerts. Some delve into, celebrate or critique the spirituality of island communities and families, referring to Kumina, Hinduism, Roman Catholicism, Christianity and Rosicrucianism. Other works focus on rites of passage, memorialising the lives of those who cross over, burial arrangements, wakes, and the phenomena of religious pilgrimages.

Several of the poems re-purpose wondrous myth and ride out wild weather. Pages are inhabited by exuberant flora and fauna: fish, goats, bees, boas and other snakes; fabled beings like duppies, soucouyants and douens; the natural forces of earthquake, flood and hurricane; the human diversity of women on the loose, healers, gossipers, priestesses, sistren of Caliban, mermaids, scarlet women, sirens, song divas, space aliens, virgins, writers, maroon women rebels who fought slavery with fire, women pirates, and rural farmworkers.

Poems consider mothers and fathers, or other close, foundational family, paying homage to their love and care, or exposing their unfortunate acts of cruelty and neglect. Poems include women who told stories, loved, educated, groomed, or fiercely defended their children; and those who had only a brittle, stony love or searing pepper to pass down; those who were complicitous with a family abuser; or those who scared, scarred, and hurt their girl children. Poems try to understand mothers and female relatives who had been traumatised by their own childhoods, history, mental illness, society's codes, or their men. Manhood is a theme of some poems that discuss boys, men who love men, men as allies, lovers, and fathers. Fathers are denied or searched for in a distant karaoke bar, a ballet studio, a hospital, a reggae recording session, or under the bonnet of a Cherokee Jeep.

Poems focus on the female body, its orifices and secretions, its invasion by others, rape, desire, sexual pleasure, its womb, menstrual blood, pregnancy, vaginal examinations, sonograms, abortion, birth-giving, skin-colour, hair, and women loving women. The body's times of solitude are portrayed – those seasons of the crossing of "well-trafficked legs/ into the form of a withered lotus" (Delgado). The poignancy and pain of doomed affairs, of playing the prescriptive roles of baby mama, "wifey" (Yanique) or wife are creatively contextualised.

Rather than organise the anthology by identifying the writers by island(s), the language(s) that they write in, their birthplaces, their current homes, or other descriptors of identity, we have chosen to present the poets in alphabetical order and leave the process of identification to the writers themselves. Some mention in their biographies or poems their Caribbean heritage or connections, or where the poems are enacted, and some do not. Several of the writers selected consider themselves persons of multiple origins, locations, and affiliations. Some identify as non-binary, bisexual, lesbian, or heterosexual, as allies or, from time to time, as critics of men, or speak to life experiences related to sexuality and sexual identity, societal pressures, and issues of justice. Most address questions of political and societal agency, discrimination, and the traumas of history in one manner or another. All have shown in their oeuvre a commitment to writing poems that address women's experiences in the most intimate and public realms and Caribbean cultural and social imperatives.

As avid readers and university teachers of Caribbean literature, we have focused on writers who started to publish book-length works mainly during the first two decades of the 21st century. We know, greatly appreciate, and acknowledge the continuing work of generations of women poets who are already well-established and associated with traditions of Caribbean and Latin American literature. We have not included often-anthologised and, in some cases, deceased writers. In our desire to foreground writers whom we feel should be much more widely read and recognised internationally, the anthology doesn't include some of the major poetic voices among such living writers as Lillian Allen, Caridad Atencio, Julia Alvarez, Yolanda Arroyo Pizarro, Ruth Behar, Dionne Brand, Jean 'Binta' Breeze, Merle Collins, Afua Cooper, Christine Craig, Sandra María Esteves, Lina de Feria, Lorna Goodison, Claire Harris, Ángela Hernández Núñez, Jane King, Lelawatee Manoo-Rahming, Jeanette de los Ángeles Miller Rivas, Pamela Mordecai, Nancy Morejón, Grace Nichols, Opal Palmer Adisa, M. NourbeSe Phillips, Velma Pollard, Soleida Ríos, Mayra Santos-Febres, Olive Senior, Lynn Sweeting, Luz María Umpierre, Jael Uribe, Enid Vian, and Sherezada Chiqui Vicioso, among many others who could be mentioned. Our respect to these forerunners.

As the editors and translators, we consulted a number of anthologies and individual poetry books of English- and Spanish-speaking Caribbean writers during the research, selection, and translation process. Our project builds on, is indebted to, or is in conversation with the work of previous anthologisers of writing by Caribbean women, a few of whom we will mention, noting our convergences with and differences from their significant work.

In 1996 the ambitious multilingual anthology *Sisters of Caliban: Contemporary Women Poets of the Caribbean* (1996), edited by M. J. Fenwick, presented over ninety poets who wrote in English, Creole, Dutch, French, Spanish, and Sranan Tongo. Although Fenwick worked on several of the translations herself, she collaborated with six other translators. Some of the strongest poems by the major Caribbean women writers of the day were included. Poems originally written in a language other than English were published in both the original version and the English translation; however, poems originally published in English were not translated into another language. The imagined readership was, it seems, monolingual English-speaking, with perhaps some interest or skills in other Caribbean regional languages. Monolingual Antillean or Haitian Creole, Dutch, French, Spanish, and Sranan-speaking readers would have had access only to the poems composed in their own languages.

We readily acknowledge the continuing relevance and importance of Fenwick's work towards multilingualism in Caribbean letters, and her insistence on critically promoting poetry that spoke eloquently to "women's experiences in patriarchal, colonial, post- and neocolonial societies" (xxii). Our project recognises the urgent need for also translating the English-speaking women writers to other languages and facilitating more cross-cultural dialogue between writers and readers with differing mother tongues. We hope that our anthology will be read widely in both the larger English- and Spanish-speaking worlds, and that the book will encourage others to translate individual books by our contributors.

We see *The Sea Needs No Ornament* as distinct from but in conversation with other recently published anthologies featuring women writers of the African Diaspora (*New Daughters of Africa: An International Anthology of Writing by Women of African Descent*, ed. Margaret Busby, 2019), women writers of Cuba (*The Oval Portrait: Contemporary Cuban Women Writers and Artists*, ed. Soleida Ríos, trans. Margaret Randall, 2018), and women writers of the English-, French-, and Spanish-speaking Caribbean (*Border Crossings: A Trilingual Anthology of Caribbean Women Writers*, eds. Nicole Roberts and Elizabeth Walcott-Hackshaw, 2011).

New Daughters of Africa: An International Anthology of Writing by Women of African Descent follows an earlier anthology edited by Busby, *Daughters of Africa: An International Anthology of Words and Writings by Women of African Descent, from the Ancient Egyptian to the Present* (1992). The new book anthologises two hundred women writers of Africa and many locations of its Diaspora, starting with the 18th and 19th centuries and moving to the present. Arranged in order of the authors' birthdates and identifying the writer's geographic affiliations, the anthology includes non-fiction prose, journalism, short fiction, excerpts from longer works of fiction, and poetry, among other genres. Its range of voices, concerns, writing styles, and societal contexts is vitally important, as is its attempt to promulgate black women's perspectives across language boundaries. It includes as many of the major women writers establishing themselves during the 21st century as possible. As Busby states in her introduction, no writers are duplicated from the first anthology to the new one. Though several of the women anthologised in *New Daughters of Africa* mainly publish in languages other than English, and their backgrounds are acknowledged in the biographical notes, all texts are in English.

Although we have selected different works, *The Sea Needs No Ornament/ El mar no necesita ornamento* has published some of the same authors to be found in *New Daughters of Africa* and shares with that project a profound interest in and commitment to African Caribbean women's writing. Our bilingual anthology additionally prioritises sharing the writer's original text along with the translation, and includes Caribbean-related writers of diverse racial, ethnic, cultural, class and sexual-identity backgrounds.

The Oval Portrait: Contemporary Cuban Women Writers and Artists, edited by the Cuban writer Soleida Ríos and translated by the experienced translator and anthologiser of Cuban literature, Margaret Randall, published one 5-7- page work by thirty-four women writers who were asked to take on a mask and write a persona piece: a prose essay, short story, or poem in the voice of another. An important text founded on an intriguing concept, it introduces English-speaking readers to a broad selection of contemporary Cuban women writers. The original Spanish texts are not included; all work is presented in

English. A separate Spanish version of the text was previously published by Ríos. Our anthology publishes different works by a few of the Cuban writers included in *The Oval Portrait,* but we also include Cuban writers who do not have work in the anthology by Ríos and Randall.

In *Border Crossings: A Trilingual Anthology of Caribbean Women Writers,* editors Roberts and Walcott-Hackshaw published short fiction by Caribbean women writers. Unlike *The Oxford Book of Caribbean Short Stories* (1999; 2002), edited by Stewart Brown, which published fifty-two stories (in English) by men and women writers from various language contexts, or *The Peepal Tree Book of Contemporary Caribbean Short Stories* (2018), which published over thirty stories, Roberts and Walcott-Hackshaw limited their scope to six women fiction writers from Jamaica, Trinidad, Puerto Rico, Cuba, Guadeloupe, and Haiti who were born in the 1940s or 50s. However, one story by each of the six writers is presented in English, Spanish, and French. Like the editor-translators of *Border Crossings*, we appreciate that there are many confluences between the literatures of Caribbean societies, despite language differences. Similarly, our project intends to encourage plurilingual abilities, collaboration and communication, or the "ability to speak to each other" (vii). In the first sentence of their introduction, Roberts and Walcott-Hackshaw say, "When we started this trilingual anthology, we could not have imagined the length of time" (ibid.) required to complete the work. We certainly understand what they mean by that. When we conceptualised our project, we too could never have foreseen the many hours over a period of two years that it would take two of us, working nearly full-time, face-to-face and by long distance, to complete this project. More translation work is needed in Caribbean literature. It is an intensely satisfying, but time-consuming and strenuous endeavour.

As readers of translated work, we realised that some translators of poetry (including Caribbean) have tended to, maybe inadvertently, write their own lines that creatively diverge significantly from the original text in meaning or register. Whilst a translation is always a new and different poem, a version of the original, we have sought to recreate the poet's voice, images, and ideas in the target language by carefully considering all aspects of the poem, such as meaning, sound, rhythm, order, punctuation, spacing, and choice of words. To find the best equivalent word, we have sometimes discarded the most straightforward option and searched for other words, discussing them at length, even if we ultimately decided that the most obvious was, indeed, the right choice in that particular line. In the process, we have many times asked ourselves what the poet really meant and, when we had different word options, which one she would prefer. When the poet was familiar with both languages, we have simply asked her; and, when that was not the case, we have explained to her the implications of the different words we were considering in the target language in order to find the word that best translated hers. All poets received drafts of our translations and were invited to give us feedback, suggest changes, or respond to our doubts and questions.

This relationship with the poets has helped us enormously, particularly taking into account that translating a whole collection from a single author is not the same as translating a selection of poems by thirty-three different authors. At times, we found we could easily adapt to the idiosyncrasies of the poet and relatively quickly produce translations that felt and sounded right, but in other instances, poems required a lot of work, time, research, the reading of our translations aloud over and over again, and multiple – it felt never-ending – revisions.

Hence, the collaborative nature of our project lies not only in having direct contact with the authors. All translations have been conducted jointly by both editors, mainly co-translating in-person (in a university office, a renovated prison, restaurants, coffee shops, and even a parking lot equipped with electricity and WIFI after Hurricane María hit Puerto Rico). Finally, we have been very lucky to count on the collaboration of Dr. Alma Simounet, a bilingual linguist and professor who teaches in both the Spanish-language graduate program in Linguistics and the doctoral program of Literatures and Languages of the English-speaking Caribbean at the University of Puerto Rico, main campus. She assisted us with the last proofreading round of line edits.

We hope that our translations can be transformative. As Maria Tymoczko argues, translations can participate in "shaping societies, nations, and global culture in primary ways" (20). In this sense, we have pinpointed knowledge of the linguistic contexts of the region as crucial to translating Caribbean poetry in English, in particular an understanding of the use of different island Creoles. In our research, we saw that the presence of Creole – a distinguishing feature of West Indian literature – has for the most part gone unnoticed or unattended to by the literary translator. And here we speak not of two distinct linguistic mediums (English vs. Creole), but of a continuum in which overlapping between the two codes frequently occurs. As Barbara Lalla argues, only the Creole speaker can distinguish what items (words, phrases or sentences) are identical in form and function and which ones share the same form but differ in function (179). As a consequence, texts may be ambiguous or nuanced with multivalence for the reader with a knowledge of written Creole or Caribbean spoken languages and intonations, whilst, as Lalla explains, ambiguity might not be registered by a reader who is only competent in English (180). In the case of the Spanish-speaking Caribbean, even though there are no Spanish-based Creole languages, there exist varieties, as John H. McWhorther explains, that lack the radical grammatical restructuring seen in Creoles, but which may display certain phonological and morphological reductions and African lexical borrowings (9).

As translators, we were aware of working within these different linguistic and cultural contexts. Two fundamental principles helped us find the best solutions to translate Creole into Spanish. Throughout the process, we learnt that when translating Creole, no single strategy can be implemented in all contexts. As Tymoczko explains, the strategies necessary to accomplish engaged and committed translations are to be "selected, invented, and improvised for their tactical values in specific situations, contexts, places and times" (230). However, regardless of the different strategies used, we have tried to resist the pull towards standardisation and effacing difference.

Here are two examples of different strategies used to recreate Creole into Spanish. In the narrative poem "Dictionary" by Tiphanie Yanique, part of a line that reads "My woman vex with me" is translated into "Mi mujer está enfogona' conmigo". The adjective "vex", which in its Caribbean use means annoyed or very angry, finds its equivalent in the adjective in Puerto Rican Spanish "enfogona'". Both adjectives have very close meanings, belong to Caribbean varieties, and share a certain tone. Even though, in general, we have tended not to adapt the spelling to accommodate Caribbean Spanish or Creole phonology unless the poet has opted to do so, "enfogona'" is one of the rare cases in which we have decided to use an apostrophe to represent Caribbean Spanish pronunciation. In using the shortened form of "enfoganada", – "enfogona'" with an ending apostrophe – we opted for the commonly-used scribal representation of spoken Caribbean Spanish of some locations. In this way, we have sought to compensate for another trait of Creole languages, the zero copula – that is the fact that in Creole the copulative verb is not necessary. The zero copula does not, as Velma Pollard explains, affect comprehension by the non-Creole speaker (69), and as Richard Allsopp describes, it is "most likely a reflection of the substratum influence of the predication syntax of many African languages" (86). In using the apostrophe, we have thus sought to compensate for this African-based syntactic feature of Creole languages, which does not have a direct correspondence in Caribbean Spanish.

Another example is to be found in the poem "Reader, I Married Him" by Dorothea Smartt. This excerpt: "and chop-he/widda a machete!" is translated as "iy a él le cayeron/a machezatos!". In this case, we decided to use the form "caerle a (alguien)" used in the Caribbean and other Latin American regions to refer to attacking somebody, as its tone fits perfectly with the original, followed by the word "machete" in its augmentative form, that is, "machetazo".

Idiomatic phrases, cultural references, popular slang, and vocabulary vary geographically within Spanish-speaking territories. Thus, the challenges that a Creole-inflected West Indian literary text might present to a reader unfamiliar with the full range of possibilities of language aren't exactly equivalent when reading Spanish-Caribbean literary texts. However, writers may use local vernacular forms of oral Spanish, code-switching between Spanish and English, Espanglish phrases, or "Spanish-ification" or shortened-forms of adopted English words (such as "biuti" instead of "beauty shop"). Respecting language choices on the part of our contributors and the creative richness of Caribbean languages ranked high in our objectives and recognition of the transformative potential of our work.

Sometimes there are no direct equivalents between English and Spanish words. This is the case with some of the poems that use elements of Caribbean English(es). At times we have been surprised at how well and natural a poem with a first-person speaker who uses a markedly-Caribbean lexicon – say, with a Jamaican voice – reads when translated from English to Spanish. At other times, however, after starting to translate a very dynamic poem heavily based in Creole registers, we had to stop midway and ask ourselves if we were flattening the poem out in the target language – what was being gained and what lost through translating the poem. In the case of one poem by a Trinidadian contributor, we decided that it would do too much damage to the poem to try to translate it, and so we selected another. In other cases, we were able to maintain some of the original language phrasing through code-switching, keeping the English or English Creole references in the Spanish translation, or the Spanish vocabulary in the English translation – this only when appropriate and the meanings would be clear from the context or could be clarified in an endnote. Three examples from our Spanish translations of phrases that we maintained in English were "a jolly good chap" (Bethel), "whitey gal" (McCallum), and "*nuff*" ("a lot of") (Weir-Soley). In our English translations, we maintained the Spanish and included an immediate in-text translation of the idiomatic phrase "*pa' quedar acicalao'* – to be fly" (Antonetty Lebrón).

A translation of Safiya Sinclair's "Crania Americana" presented an interesting dilemma, provoking discussion because of one basic difference between English and Spanish. The latter distinguishes masculine and feminine nouns (even for inanimate objects), which are in agreement in grammatical gender with determiners and adjectives that refer to them. Moreover, in Spanish, the masculine is the unmarked gender. The plural masculine form can refer to a group of men and women (for example, "maestros" – "teachers"), whilst the plural feminine form refers only to women or feminine-gendered objects ("maestras" – "teachers"). As a result, Spanish has been deemed a sexist language, as it effaces women on a linguistic level.

Certainly, Spanish-language writers and speakers from different geographical regions have, in the last decade, or so, tried to propose inclusive, non-binary solutions, choosing to replace feminine (often "a") or masculine (often "o") gender-marking vowels or suffixes by chosing collective nouns when possible ("ciudadanía" instead of "ciudadanas" or "ciudadanos" – "citizenry" rather than "citizens"); with "x" ("todxs", instead of "todas" or "todos" – "all"); with the "@" sign, representing "a" and "o" simultaneously ("Latin@s"); or with an "e" ("amigues", instead of "amigas" or "amigos" – "friends"). Not all of these gender category-defying experiments have caught on, are commonly used in all regions – nor are officially recognised by the Real Academia Española (The Royal Spanish Academy), a cultural institution that makes standardising determinations about the Spanish language and its rules.

Sinclair's poem is gender-bending in that it constructs a sense of womanhood in response to Caliban. The poem re-appropriates all of the words spoken by Caliban and the lines spoken about him in Shakespeare's play *The Tempest*. Sinclair distils the feminine from the "impolite body" of Caliban and his rebellion. Scientific racism is a referent in the poem, as well. Some of the language in the poem is intentionally gender-neutral although the poem generally refers to a female subject/ speaker, without unambiguously marking gender. Words that were not gendered in English in her poem, had, in several cases, translations that mark gender in Spanish. We worked with her to arrive at a translation that expresses both her intended meanings and preserves the poetic sound-structures of the original, but at times, in selecting certain words, the three of us opted for translations that varied marginally from the original.

The best example of this is when the poem uses the nonspecific, non-gendered, generic term "sibling", which has no direct equivalent in Spanish. Rather it is translated as the gender-specific "hermana" (sister) or "hermano" (brother). While "hermanx" or "herman@" were possibilities, their use would lose the sonic resonances, the consonance, that Sinclair was striving for in the stanza, which uses the words "sibling", "Sisyphean" and "simian". No matter how we might alter "hermano/a", the word is still inescapably marked by its specific semantic gender associations. The lines in English also refer to "us", a plural subject; whereas the noun "sibling" and adjective "sisyphean" are descriptors in the singular form. So we had decisions to make about masculine, feminine, or non-binary words, and singular/plural forms. Ultimately, we agreed upon the Spanish equivalent of the word "consanguineous" (an adjective) to translate "sibling" (a noun) and used the plural, masculine form, per the preference of the author, who made the decision as much for sound as for sense. Other stanzas with a singular referent (Caliban transmogrified to the female subject) use the feminine word forms. Although the Spanish "consanguíneos" is a word more elevated in register than "sibling", it fits perfectly with the register and semantic associations of the vocabulary in the poem overall, allusions to scientific racism, and the poetic sound structures. The gender work is represented in the Spanish version, but we didn't break free entirely of the restraints imposed by a language with grammatical gender.

This anthology of poems, read all together, provides a cultural and linguistic frame of reference. We debated and deliberated over whether or not we would include endnotes about the cultural content – fauna, flora, historical events, persons, or other potentially unfamiliar details or vocabulary in the poems. In the end, we chose not to foist textbook-style informational notes on the poems or add overmuch to the kind of contextualisation originally given to the poems by the authors. If the writers included endnotes to a poem in their own poetry books, then we maintained their endnotes, providing them in both English and Spanish. We didn't encumber or pin-down the poems by providing our own notes on cultural aspects or events. If the authors didn't include in their books an endnote on content for one of the poems that we selected, then we didn't endnote it either, unless we agreed with the writer to do so. Those cases were rare.

Respecting our contributors' intentions, we chose to leave it to readers to have the pleasure of looking up any unfamiliar references. Even the most experimental poet is not usually trying to obscure meaning, but poetry makes use of spoken and unspoken meanings, direct expressions and purposeful omissions, the subtleties of image and fresh language, and sometimes bold and energetic experimentation in poetic form and words. The poems in this anthology certainly speak for themselves. We didn't want our notes to be an awkward apparatus that would unintentionally detract from the force of truly remarkable poetry. We do provide some endnotes in English and Spanish in separate sections. The individual notes differ according to what information a reader of each language might need to know.

Some of the poets engage in wordplay, selecting words with multiple meanings, all the layers of which might not even be understood in a neighbouring island of the same language grouping. We tried as much as possible to maintain that multiplicity in the text rather than in explanatory endnotes. This aspect of the project was both challenging and enjoyable, requiring consultation with the writers. Jamila Medina Ríos excels in wordplay of this kind. In her poem "Fur(n)ia," for example, the word "damajuana" gave us homework because the Spanish word commonly means a large ceramic, clay, or glass jug, a meaning that would seemingly fit well in a poem with many biological references to a woman's bodyscape and land formations. Inside the word, one can see "dama" and "juan-a", suggesting female/male resonances. Actually though, as Jamila told us, the word "denomina en Cuba también una semilla gris pequeña con la que se hacen collares"; the word "damajuana" refers to a small, round, grey seed that is used to bead necklaces in Cuba. We sent her a photograph of the seed that we thought she was referring to and received her surprised response; "Síiiiii, no sé cómo lograste hallarla". She was amazed that we knew of the seed, but the same seed is also used for beadwork in some of the other islands where we each have lived. We just didn't know that it was called "damajuana" in Cuba. In our translation, we kept her multiple meanings. In other instances, we used a slash and two words to translate her single words with double-meanings, her own stated preference for our approach and a stylistic feature that fits with her experimental poetic technique. Maintaining consistency in our translation methodology of her work, we didn't need to explain her frequent wordplay and our choices in endnotes.

Overall, we only provided a minimum of translation notes about regional differences when, for example, we selected one term from a list of other possible commonly used terms within the Caribbean context (i.e., the choice of the English "flamboyant tree" rather than "poinciana" for the Spanish "flamboyán").

We dealt with questions about cross-cultural understanding by carrying out searches and exploring regional differences in vocabulary when deciding which vernacular of Spanish (Cuba, Puerto Rico, or the Dominican Republic, and Diaspora locations) or English (the various islands, the Creole continuum, and Diaspora locations) we were going to use to arrive at the best equivalent translation of a word or phrase for a particular poem. For fauna, flora, and food, there are regional variants within languages, for instance, in the daily parlance of Barbados, the Bahamas, Jamaica, St. Lucia, and Trinidad and Tobago. The beloved "dilly" fruit of the Bahamas, which appears in one of Marion Bethel's poems, is a "sapodilla" in Trinidad and Tobago and a "naseberry" in Jamaica. Only when deemed most necessary, did we choose to gloss in the endnotes regional differences of the names of things.

We began this project just a few weeks before Hurricane Irma and Hurricane María ravaged the Caribbean and left an apocalyptic landscape in Puerto Rico and many of our sister islands. Because we knew how phenomenal these women are as persons and writers and how vital it was that their work crossed language divides, we remained focused and full of hope during the aftermath of having no electricity, water, internet, and communication systems, scarcity of basic necessities, university closure, and the unexpected health challenges and surgeries that we both underwent. We completed the book at an equally historic Caribbean moment when the island that has served as our project base had risen up in massive, intensely creative street protests to challenge the political system, see a governor resign, denounce corruption and public expressions of misogyny, homophobia, and racism, and defend the right to a better future. Women were protagonists in initiating a social revolution. As we prepared the text for publication, Puerto Rico was dealing with damage and displacement caused by a series of earthquakes and aftershocks. Women again played a vital role in organising community-based relief efforts. We are excited and joyful that this book, crafted in such a charged atmosphere and comprised of the work of our sistren, has found its way into your hands.

For reasons of space, we provide the introduction and contributor biographies only in English in this edition.

The thematic and stylistic ground covered in *The Sea Needs No Ornament/ El mar no necesita ornamento* is broad and varied, but the women's voices and poetic imperatives come across dazzlingly throughout. We hope that you enjoy their work and ours.

Works Cited

Allsopp, Richard, editor. *Dictionary of Caribbean English Usage*. University of the West Indies Press, 1996.

Busby, Margaret, editor. *New Daughters of Africa: An International Anthology of Writing by Women of African Descent*. HarperCollins, 2019.

Fenwick, M. J., editor. *Sisters of Caliban: Contemporary Women Poets of the Caribbean – A Multilingual Anthology*. Azul Editions, 1996.

Lalla, Barbara. "Creole Representation in Literary Discourse." *Exploring the Boundaries of Caribbean Creole Languages*. Edited by Hazel Simmons-McDonald and Ian Robertson, University of the West Indies Press, 2006, pp. 173-187.

McWhorter, John H. *The Missing Spanish Creoles: Recovering the Birth of Plantation Contact Languages*. University of California Press, 2000.

Pollard, Velma. "'To Us All Flowers are Roses': Writing Ourselves into the Literature of the Caribbean." *Sargasso 2001: Concerning Lorna Goodison*, 2001, pp. 65-74.

Roberts, Nicole and Elizabeth Walcott-Hackshaw, editors. *Border Crossing: A Trilingual Anthology of Caribbean Women Writers*. University of the West Indies Press, 2011.

Tymoczko, Maria. *Translation, Resistance, Activism*. University of Massachusetts Press, 2010.

Gloriann Sacha Antonetty Lebrón

LA CAJITA

después de tu despedida
descubrí un tesoro
Canoso,
Grueso
Fuerte…
Eran mechones desprendidos de tu cuero
por la terapia
combatiendo
los monstruos alojados en tu piel.
No dijiste nada,
no me dejaste cumplir la promesa
dispuesta a sacrificar
mi maranta
para que no te sintieras sola;
despojada de tu cabellera.
Allí en aquella cajita
llena de cabellos y secretos
te vi como la que tanto guardó,
tanto aguantó,
hasta que dejó el pellejo
pero que nunca, nunca dejó
de tener
su pelo bello…

Gloriann Sacha Antonetty Lebrón

THE LITTLE BOX

after your send-off
I discovered a treasure
Grey,
Thick
Strong...
They were locks detached from your scalp
because of the therapy
battling
the monsters lodged in your skin.
You didn't say anything,
you didn't let me carry out the promise,
my willingness to sacrifice
my curly hair
so that you wouldn't feel alone;
dispossessed of your head of hair.
There in that little box
full of hair and secrets
I saw you as one who kept much to herself,
one who endured so much,
until she let go of her skin,
but who never, never gave up
on having
her beautiful hair...

Gloriann Sacha Antonetty Lebrón

GLORIA

madrugaba la noche
me separabas los cabellos
hasta trenzarlos
mientras me contabas
de bailes de sociedad, vestidos y costuras en francés
sombreros Pra-prá y serenatas.
Me cantabas
sones cubanos, boleros y danzones;
fascinada no dolían los jalones
que sanabas con bálsamos de coco.
Me escondiste tus pesares
fue un secreto
ser la amante.
Dama matriarca de barrio
centenaria.
Hacía tiempo que no me peinabas
ya me hacía falta vivir en tus manos arrugadas
la sabiduría
sentirte nostálgica.

Amanecía
abrí los ojos
con mi pelo listo
renovada.
Mientras tanto se derramó la sangre
debajo de tus canas.

Gloriann Sacha Antonetty Lebrón

GLORIA

predawn hours of night
you parted my hair
to braid it
while you told me in French
of society dances, dresses and sewing
Pra-Prá straw boater hats and serenades.
You sang to me
Cuban *sones*, *boleros* and *danzones*;
fascinated, I wasn't hurt by the pulling,
which you healed with coconut balms.
You hid your sorrows from me –
it was a secret
to be the mistress.
Centenarian
matriarch *Dama de barrio*
It had been a long time since you'd combed my hair
I'd missed living in your wrinkled hands
the wisdom
feeling your nostalgia.

Dawn
I opened my eyes
with my hair finished
renewed.
Meanwhile blood seeped
underneath your grey hairs.

Gloriann Sacha Antonetty Lebrón

BARBERÍA

cerquillo
de secretos desnudos
disfrazados en chismes de "biuti"
polvo
con olor a macho
"Pásame, la uno, no, la dos"
o mejor "Hazme un *fade*, o un *blow out*"
que suene a *hip hop* o a soneos de Maelo
pa' quedar acicalao'
y hoy
poderme llevar
una jeva
a la cama.

Gloriann Sacha Antonetty Lebrón

BARBERSHOP

shape-up trimmed
hairline
of naked secrets
disguised in gossip of the *"biuti"*
powder
with a macho scent
"Give me the number 1 haircut, no, the 2"
or better yet, "Give me a fade, or a blowout"
sounding like hip hop or improv *soneos* of Maelo
pa' quedar acicalao' – to be fly
and able to take
a babe
to bed
today.

Marion Bethel

SUNDAY IN FORT CHARLOTTE

why on earth in heaven's name
would paradise need a fort?

I didn't know then of slave-trading forts
in Gorée Gold Coast & Gambia
hell holes and grottos blasted in rock

growing up in Fort Charlotte
a colonial coloured christian child
I was Columbus' girl all the way
sailing with him from Canary Islands
to Guanahani every night on the *Nina*

I learned forts on earth were for bonfires
of a straw terrorist Guy Fawkes
protection from pillage piracy and plunder
crisped celebrations of royal family visits
& flying kites where angels dwelled

after a uniform week of red & white tan & brown
green & grey blue & white walking to school
after Saturday's salt-parched skin on Long Wharf
& sand-filled hair were washed & greased
wooden go-karts & bicycle rims defied death

the handsaw wheezed to a stop & sawdust settled
Mr. Dan stopped bruising his missus
fisherman parked his bicycle
policyman tucked his book on the shelf
the numbers runner put on his Sunday shoes

leading the charge Fr. Holmes a jolly good chap
marched us the Bahamian grenadiers

Marion Bethel

DOMINGO EN EL FUERTE CHARLOTTE

¿a santo de qué en el nombre del cielo
podría el paraíso necesitar un fuerte?

entonces no sabía de los fuertes de la trata de esclavos
en Gorée Costa de Oro y Gambia
hoyos infernales y grutas detonados en la roca

al crecer en Fuerte Charlotte
una prieta colonizada cristiana
era completamente la chica de Colón
navegando con él cada noche en la *Niña*
desde las Islas Canarias hasta Guanahani

aprendí que los fuertes en la tierra eran para hogueras
de Guy Fawkes un terrorista hecho de paja
protección del pillaje la piratería y el saqueo
celebraciones almidonadas de visitas de la familia real
y volar cometas donde moraban ángeles

después de una semana caminando a la escuela de uniforme rojo y blanco
caqui y marrón verde y gris azulado y blanco
después de un sábado de piel reseca de sal en Long Wharf
y cabello lleno de arena lavado y untado
go-karts de madera y llantas de bicicleta que desafiaban la muerte

el serrucho jadeó hasta parar y el serrín se asentó
el Sr. Dan dejó de dar moretones a su señora
el pescador estacionó su bicicleta
el agente de seguros colocó su libro en el librero
el corredor de números se puso sus zapatos de domingo

encabezando la carga el Padre Holmes *a jolly good chap*
nos hizo marchar, los granaderos de Bahamas,

up & down the church aisles singing
We are soldiers of Christ who is mighty to save
would our saviour ever come?

during the march the most irreverent of prayers
Bonny Read & me firing cannons for heaven
before church ended & rescued us from itself
we sang *Hold the fort for I am coming!*
the only pirate in sight was holy father himself

later we fluttered & flapped
over Fort Charlotte
high as kites on tails of cotton
gliding with gods dressed in gingham

why on earth for heaven's sake
would Eden need a fort?

pasillo arriba pasillo abajo de la iglesia cantando –
Somos soldados de Cristo quien es poderoso para salvar
¿vendría alguna vez nuestro salvador?

durante la marcha las más irreverentes oraciones
Bonny Read y yo disparando cañones para el cielo
antes de que acabara el servicio religioso y nos salvara de sí mismo
cantábamos ¡*Defiendan la fortaleza que ya vengo*!
el único pirata a la vista era el mismo padre santo

más tarde ondeábamos y aleteábamos
sobre Fuerte Charlotte
altos como cometas con colas de algodón
planeando con dioses vestidos de guinga

¿a santo de qué por el amor de dios
podría el Edén necesitar un fuerte?

Marion Bethel

IN THE MARKETPLACE

Don't mind the noise in the market
only mind the price of the fish

I

to market to market
to buy a new tongue
home away home away
brigidum brum

the part of me
I share
with you
was not bought
in the marketplace

my father borrowed
pounds sterling
to buy me
a new tongue
at the age of ten
in Canada
one that could speak
in the same breath
the language of Descartes
and Strauss
with the accent
sugar-milled and refined
of a lady
lips soft and pursed

Marion Bethel

EN LA PLAZA DEL MERCADO

No hagan caso del ruido del mercado
hagan caso del precio del pescado

I

al mercado al mercado
a comprar una lengua nueva
a casa a casa
brigidom brom

la parte de mí
que comparto
contigo
no fue comprada
en la plaza del mercado

mi padre cogió
libras esterlinas prestadas
para comprarme
una lengua nueva
a los diez años
en Canadá
una que pudiera hablar
en el mismo aliento
la lengua de Descartes
y Strauss
con el acento meloso
molido y refinado
de una dama
labios suaves y fruncidos

II

his sister pregnant
at sixteen in the '30s
he swore
to divert the movement
of his daughters' hips
reroute rotation
of their pedalling motion
bend the logic of
interrogatory hips
and pubescent exclamations
question marks
in his house

I think
therefore I am not
about to calypso
in the labour market
of any kind
at the age of sixteen

He thinks
therefore he is not
about to change
his market ideas
of all kinds
of accents and hips

III

no more licking up
truppence cups
of frozen cherry koolaid
from Mr. B's pennystore
on the way home from school

44

II

su hermana embarazada
a los dieciséis en los años 30
él juro
desviar el movimiento
de las caderas de sus hijas
cambiar la ruta de rotación
de su meneo con pedaleo
doblar la lógica de
caderas interrogatorias
y exclamaciones pubescentes
signos de interrogación
en su casa

Yo creo,
por lo tanto… no estoy
a punto de bailar calypso
en ningún tipo
de mercado laboral
a los dieciséis años

Él cree
por lo tanto… no está
a punto de cambiar
sus ideas de mercado
de todo tipo
de acentos y caderas

III

ya no más lamer
vasitos de dos centavos
de koolaid de cereza congelado
de la tiendita de Mr. B
en Meeting Street en Nassau

on Meeting St. in Nassau
no more cotton shorts
of thin pink gingham
made by Miss Maura
on Maura's Lane

in Toronto I do
what they do
put on a lead-grey coat
the distance of a cold sun
leaves hailstones whole
in my veins

I step into the navyblue
of bloomers on schooldays
to dress down
make uniform
the imperative shape
of hips

I leave the skin
of my tongue
hanging on an icicle
a stalactite dagger
outside the dormitory window

IV

did my father ever dream
what sweet things
I would long for
besides pure maple syrup?
what I would profess
inside the Nicene Creed
& Hail Mary
with this new tongue?
and the how of it all?

al volver de la escuela
ya no más pantalones cortos
de algodón, de liviana guinga rosa
hechos por Miss Maura
en Maura's Lane

en Toronto hago
lo que hacen
me pongo un abrigo gris plomo
la distancia de un frío sol
deja granizos enteros
dentro de mis venas

meto las piernas dentro del azul marino
de los calzones bombachos los días de escuela
para vestir acorde a las normas
hacer del uniforme
la forma imperativa
de las caderas

dejo la piel
de mi lengua
colgando de un carámbano
una daga de estalactita
fuera de la ventana de los dormitorios

IV

¿soñó alguna vez mi padre
qué cosas dulces
yo anhelaría
además del jarabe de arce puro?
¿qué yo profesaría
dentro del Credo Niceno
y el Ave María
con esta lengua nueva?
¿y el cómo de todo?

he had taught my tongue
to suck to straw
waterlessness
the rum-streaked sugar cane
he stripped the cane
for me

he had trained the tongue
to sip and savour
throw back without a choke
the water of a soft coconut
he saw the tongue
roll the jelly round
and round
cheeks and lips pulling
like the sucking of fuel
from a full tank
he husked the coconut
for me

V

did my father ever guess
that because of his purchase
this tongue was shame
to say *guh mornin?*
the tongue would tell
my eyes to look beyond
a West Indian immigrant
walking on Bloor St.
in Toronto in the '60s

the tidal current
of another tongue
the currency of it
sucked me
under

él había enseñado a mi lengua
a chupar a sorber
sin agua
la caña de azúcar manchada con ron
él pelaba la caña
para mí

él había entrenado mi lengua
para beber y saborear
apurar sin ahogarme
el agua de un coco verde blandito
vio mi lengua
enrollar la gelatina
una y otra vez
mejillas y labios tirando
como la succión de combustible
de un tanque lleno
él descascarilló el coco
para mi

V

¿adivinó alguna vez mi padre
que debido a su compra
a esta lengua le avergonzaba
decir *guh mornin*?
la lengua decía a
mis ojos que miraran por encima de
un inmigrante caribeño
caminando por Bloor Street
en el Toronto de los años 60

la corriente de la marea
de otra lengua
la aceptación de ella
me envolvió

and my father coloured
colonial and christian
existed somewhere
between somethingness
and nothingness
and somethingmoreness
a putative son
of the enlightenment
and the namesake
of Marcus Garvey

VI

and you
you always smile
at the part of me
I share with you
uncolonized
you would say

let me tell you, man
I aint buy that
the truth is
I borrowed...
no... stole it
from my mother
on her knees
I stole all of it
at the age of twelve

what was the value
of her prayer
in the marketplace
her smile-to-please?
what price did she pay
for my new tongue?

y mi padre persona de color
colonial y cristiano
existía en alguna parte
entre ser algo
y ser nada
y ser algo más de algo
un hijo putativo
de la ilustración
y tocayo de Marcus Garvey

VI

y tú
tú siempre sonríes
a la parte de mí
que comparto contigo
no colonizada
tú dirías

déjame decirte, hombre
no compré eso
la verdad es que
lo tomé prestado...
no... lo robé
de mi madre
en sus rodillas
me lo robé todo
a los doce años

¿cuál era el valor
de su oración
en la plaza del mercado?
¿su sonrisa-para-agradar?
¿qué precio pagó ella
para mi lengua nueva?

VII

to market to market
to buy a new tongue
home again home again
brigidum bram

I discovered the new market
had no pumpkin cassava peas corn
breadfruit dilly okra grits
this market had no grunts
and goggle-eye fish
and I had no stomach
for trout bass and sweet pears

God! there was too much noise
too many sounds
signals and signs
I could not make out
in the market place

and in my first year
abroad in Toronto
at the age of ten
I could not hear
did not know
when I lost
my accent
and the idiomatic
vernacular swing
of my hips

VII

al mercado al mercado
a comprar una lengua nueva
a casa a casa
brigidom bram

descubrí que el nuevo mercado
no tenía calabaza yuca gandules maíz
pana níspero quimbombó sémola
este mercado no tenía roncos
ni jurel de ojo grande
y yo no tenía estómago
para truchas róbalos y peras dulces

¡Dios! había demasiado ruido
demasiados sonidos
señales y signos
que no podía descifrar
en el mercado

y en mi primer año
fuera en Toronto
a los diez años
no pude oír
no supe
cúando perdí
mi acento
y el contoneo
idiomático y vernáculo
de mis caderas

Marion Bethel

VINEGAR, BEES & GOATS

I

at the southern gate
of church
honeycombs of wax
and blood
tiny craters deep and dark
seething
like a malevolent tumour
under his left armpit
down his pierced side
a hive of bees fixed
absolute command
on a marble statue
of the crucifixion

we were not afraid
of the hands and breath
of sperrits jumbeys and haints
on our way to church
every Saturday every Sunday
jumping across graves
in the Western Cemetery
playing catchers around tombs
and crypts
on our way home from church

nor were we all-a-buzz-buzz
with Father's satursunday faith

Marion Bethel

VINAGRE, ABEJAS Y CABRAS

I

en el portón sur
de la iglesia
panales de cera
y sangre
pequeños cráteres profundos y oscuros
hervideros enfurecidos
como un tumor malévolo
bajo su axila izquierda
por su costado abierto
una colmena de abejas fijó
comando absoluto
en una estatua de mármol
de la crucifixión

no nos asustaban
las manos y aliento
de espíritus *jumbeys* y espectros
de camino a la iglesia
todos los sábados todos los domingos
saltando de un lado a otro de las tumbas
en el Western Cemetery
jugando a pillapilla entre las tumbas
y criptas
cuando volvíamos de la iglesia

ni estábamos zumbando
con la fe del sába-domingo de padre

II

but at this cross-road
of the beehive
I was a kid-goat
weak-kneed & wobbly
always
a newborn she-goat
transfixed
at birth
by beehive business

most times I scrambled
goat-footed
and a jumbled unsign
of the cross
across my tummy
a quick genuflection
eyes goatwide
and unblinking

III

one time
at noon on Saturday
the true hour
of my christening
I offered up
on a stick
a native sponge
swollen
with vinegar
(left from Mother's douche)
I offered it up
upon hyssop
(no – I lie)

II

pero en esta encrucijada
de la colmena
yo era una cabra jovencita
de rodillas débiles y tambaleante
siempre
una cabra-hembra recién nacida
paralizada
al nacer
por el zumbido de la colmena

la mayoría de las veces trepaba
con patas de cabra
y una señal confusa
de la cruz
sobre mi barriga
una rápida genuflexión
anchos ojos abiertos de cabra
y sin parpadear

III

una vez
el sábado al mediodía
la hora verdadera
de mi bautizo
ofrendé
en un palo
una esponja nativa
hinchada
con vinagre
(el que quedó de la ducha vaginal de mi madre)
Lo ofrendé
sobre hisopo
(no — miento)

it was upon poison ivy
an offering
to the queen
of bees

the sky darkened
a corona of bees
circled my head
bee buzz on my lips
and eyes
a buzzing light
dizzibeeness

IV

in bed
I turn my face
to the wall
my back
to the drone of my father
the hum of my mother
the murmur of neighbours

I overhear
gossip of seraph and cherub
angel busyness
and one kid of the goats
for a sin offering
also offer one she-goat
as a sin offering

beeziness on bloated lips
a baptism by bees
I confess
to being born
again

fue sobre hiedra venenosa
una ofrenda
a la reina
de las abejas

el cielo se oscureció
una corona de abejas
rodearon mi cabeza
zumbido de abeja en mis labios
y ojos
una luz zumbadora
abeja-vertiginosa

IV

en la cama
giro la cara
hacia la pared
doy la espalda
al sonsonete de mi padre
al tarareo de mi madre
al murmullo de los vecinos

oigo
chismes de serafines y querubines
ángeles bulliciosos
y una cabra jovencita
para una ofrenda por el pecado
ofrendan también una cabra-hembra
como ofrenda por el pecado

laborezzzz en labios hinchados
un bautismo oficiado por abejas
confieso
haber renacido

Jacqueline Bishop

SNAKES

All those years when my mother knew exactly
what my grandfather was doing, she knew,
and she let it continue. Her excuse: *It happened to me too.*
After my grandmother had left him, had packed her things
and moved out, he complained of being lonely,
said he wanted a girl to help about the house.
I begged her not to send me, peed on myself, hollered,
rolled in the dirt, told her how he spooned-up
against me at night, his hot breath quickening
around my neck. How frightened
I was of his darkened contorted face. Then the touch
of those rough, callused hands, reaching for
my breasts – the shame of them –
the revulsion of them – I wished they would stay buried
within my body. Then the sudden sharp pain
of those large knobbed fingers between my legs. It was then
that I learnt to hate myself, to feel different,
to know that something was wrong
with me. She taught me to take it, to forgive my grandfather
and take it. She taught me that this was what it meant
to be a woman. I did not know how to name
what my mother and my grandfather had done to me,
until that day at the zoo when I saw them, a family,
curled around each other, saw the venomous tongues that darted
and flickered, the evil intent in their glowing red eyes.

Jacqueline Bishop

SERPIENTES

Todos esos años mi madre sabía exactamente
qué hacía mi abuelo, lo sabía,
y dejó que continuara. Su excusa: *también me pasó a mí.*
Después de que mi abuela le dejara, empacara sus cosas
y se mudara, él se quejó de sentirse solo,
dijo que quería una chica que le ayudara en la casa.
Le supliqué a ella que no me mandara, me mee encima, grité,
me tiré por el suelo, le dije que él se acostaba
pegado a mi por la noche, su aliento caliente acelerándose
en mi cuello. Qué aterrada
estaba de su oscura cara desencajada. Entonces al sentir
esas manos duras, encallecidas tratando de tocar
mis pechos – la vergüenza de tenerlos –
la repulsión hacia ellos – deseaba que se quedaran enterrados
dentro de mi cuerpo. Entonces el dolor punzante repentino
de esos largos nudos de sus dedos entre mis piernas.
Fue en ese momento que aprendí a odiarme a mí misma,
sentirme distinta, saber que algo estaba mal
en mí. Ella me enseñó a aguantarlo, perdonar a mi abuelo
y aguantarlo. Ella me enseñó que esto era lo que significaba
ser una mujer. No sabía cómo llamar a
lo que mi madre y mi abuelo me habían hecho,
hasta aquel día en el zoo cuando los vi, una familia,
enroscados los unos con los otros, vi las lenguas venenosas que disparaban
y titilaban, la maléfica intención en sus ojos rojos encendidos.

Jacqueline Bishop

IXORA

Why must you pout like that?
Why must you put on that showy red dress,
go down to the Bay where the men will gape at you?

Why can't you be the good Catholic girl,
the flower in white,
all that your mother wanted you to be?

Or, if you insist on that bright red colour,
why can't you be more like red ginger –
hide your true flowers within?

Do you know what they say about you
Behind your back? Do you know the names
They call you?

Flame-of-the-Wood, Jungle Flame, Jungle Geranium.

I have been sent by the good women
of the church to ask of you:
Be done with the drinking, the swearing,
the staggering home at night.

Put away those shimmering emerald earrings
you call leaves.
Tame that brick-red hair.

Come back
from living by yourself
at the edge of the woods.

Jacqueline Bishop

IXORA

¿Por qué tienes que hacer esos pucheros?
¿Por qué tienes que ponerte este vestido rojo chillón,
bajar a la bahía donde los hombres te mirarán boquiabiertos?

¿Por qué no puedes ser una buena niña católica,
una flor vestida de blanco,
todo lo que tu madre quiso que fueras?

O, si insistes en ese color rojo brillante,
por qué no puedes ser más como jengibre rojo –
esconder tus verdaderas flores a dentro?

¿Sabes qué dicen de ti
a tus espaldas? ¿Sabes qué nombres
te llaman?

Flama del Bosque, Flama de la Jungla, Geranio de la Jungla.

Me han enviado las buenas mujeres
de la iglesia para pedirte:
Deja de darle a la bebida, de ser malhablada,
de volver tambaleándote a casa por la noche.

Guarda esos pendientes vistosos de esmeralda
que tú llamas hojas.
Amansa ese pelo rojo ladrillo.

Vuelve
de vivir sola
en la linde del bosque.

Your kind – our kind, Ixora,
prefer being bunched together, forming
a large spherical head, all of us

whispering.

Tu tipo – nuestro tipo – Ixora,
preferimos estar juntas en un pomo, formando
una gran cabeza esférica, todas nosotras

susurrando.

Jacqueline Bishop

HASAN TALKING TO HIMSELF IN
THE MIRROR OF A CHEAP HOTEL ROOM

You think only of your cock.
Your father is sick at home; your mother is worried.

And again you are out with the American.
At least this room is better than the others.

This girl, the one naked on the bed, the one who looks
like some lush exotic flower on the crumpled white sheets,

she asks too many questions.
Your cock cannot stand the questions.

You are sorry you told her you are a Kurd.
Now she wants to know what it all means, being Kurdish.

Not even you have an answer to this question.
You tell her time and time again: you were born in Istanbul,

first and foremost you are a Turk.
Still, her many questions.

She wants to know if she can meet your parents?
She wants to know if you can marry her?

She collapses into tears when you answer truthfully.
There is still so much she does not know –

this girl who took herself half way across the world –
even as she knows war is trembling in the not-too-distant future.

This time, really, you are done.
Until the next time, she says from the bed, *until the next time*.

Jacqueline Bishop

HASAN HABLANDO CONSIGO MISMO
EN EL ESPEJO DE UN HOTEL BARATO

Solo piensas en tu pinga.
Tu padre está en casa enfermo; tu madre está preocupada.

Y de nuevo saliste con la americana.
Al menos esta habitación es mejor que las otras.

Esta chica, la que está desnuda en la cama, la que parece
una exuberante flor exótica encima de las arrugadas sábanas blancas,

hace demasiadas preguntas.
Tu pinga no puede soportar las preguntas.

Te arrepientes de haberle contado que eras kurdo.
Ahora quiere saber qué significa todo esto, ser kurdo.

Ni tan siquiera tú tienes una respuesta para esta pregunta.
Le dices una y otra vez: tú naciste en Estambul,

ante todo, tú eres turco.
Aún así, sus muchas preguntas.

Quiere saber si puede conocer a tus padres.
Quiere saber si te puedes casar con ella.

Se deshace en lágrimas cuando le contestas sinceramente.
Aún hay tanto que ella no sabe —

la chica que cruzó medio mundo —
aun sabiendo que la guerra tiembla en un futuro no muy lejano.

Esta vez, de verdad, no puedes más.
Hasta la próxima vez, dice ella desde la cama, *hasta la próxima vez.*

Danielle Boodoo-Fortuné

PORTRAIT OF MY FATHER AS A GROUPER

The weight is too much to carry, even underwater.

You lie in a bed of silt and algae,
wait for the lord of sunken things
to call your name and raise you home.

When I come to see you, I forget how to breathe.
There is ash on your forehead, your silver mouth
cracked with thirst and too much salt.

Here is no place for the living.
In the cot beside you lies a hollowed eel,
still sparking faintly with the charge
of what was.

Barred windows keep out an unchanging sea,
but all the doors here are broken.
You say there have been gunshots
in the ward next door, that the drowning
cry out at night for mercy, young men caught
between teeth, old men tangled in nets.

I show you photos of what my life looks like.
I have chosen only the bright things,
left out the spiny years of pain. Oh, Father,
look at the face you have given me to live with.

You have pulled our lives,
soft and impermanent as polyps,
into your crushing mouth,
but as you once were, I am a fish unwilling to drown.

Danielle Boodoo-Fortuné

RETRATO DE MI PADRE COMO MERO

El peso es demasiado para cargar, incluso bajo agua.

Yaces en una cama de sedimentos y algas,
esperas que el señor de las cosas hundidas
llame tu nombre y te levante para que vuelvas a casa.

Cuando voy a verte, olvido cómo respirar.
Hay ceniza en tu frente, tu boca plateada está
agrietada por la sed y demasiada sal.

Esto no es lugar para vivos.
En la camilla de tu lado yace una anguila ahuecada,
todavía reluciente con la tenue carga
de lo que era.

Las ventanas enrejadas no dejan pasar un mar que no cambia,
pero aquí todas las puertas están rotas.
Dices que ha habido balaceras
en la sala de al lado, que de noche los que se están ahogando
claman pidiendo misericordia, hombres jóvenes capturados
entre dientes, viejos atrapados en redes.

Te enseño fotos de cómo se ve mi vida.
He escogido solo las cosas luminosas,
he dejado de lado los espinosos años de dolor. Ay, padre,
mira la cara que me has dado, con la que vivo.

Has arrastrado nuestras vidas,
blandas y efímeras como pólipos,
hasta tu boca que muele,
pero tal como tú fuiste una vez, yo soy un pez que se niega a ahogarse.

So I sit at your undersea bedside as you pray,
and I wait,
boning knife clutched in hands
in case your god does not come.

Por eso me siento al lado de tu cama bajo el mar, mientras rezas,
y espero,
con el cuchillo deshuesador agarrado en mano,
por si tu dios no viene.

Danielle Boodoo-Fortuné

BOA GRAVIDA

When we were new,
our love still minnow-soft
and silver, you set their names
like nets along the water's edge.

Now the first, a son,
surfaces, a great fish writhing
in the basket of my hips.

These last gravid days of rain
we digest the remains of years.

You speak of everything to come,
how you long to cradle the lotus-bud
of his skull in the broad leaf of your hand,
to swim in with him from the other side.

Until then, let us wait here in the restless earth,
whisper to each other in mangrove tongues.

Tell me I am beautiful and cold.
I will tell you how thirsty I am
for a mouthful of light.

At night I ache. Veins purple and rise
with this sudden season of blood.
Pelvic plates shift, bones shudder.

I am the great mother boa
turning the soft egg of the world
beneath my ribs. I will tear myself in two
and heal before morning.

Danielle Boodoo-Fortuné

BOA GRÁVIDA

Cuando éramos nuevos,
nuestro amor aún suave y plateado
como pececillo, desplegaste sus nombres
como redes a lo largo de la orilla del agua.

Ahora el primero, un hijo,
sale a la superficie, un gran pez revolcándose
en la cesta de mis caderas.

Estos últimos grávidos días de lluvia
digerimos lo que queda de los años.

Hablas de todo lo que viene,
como deseas mecer el pimpollo de loto
de su cráneo en la amplia hoja de tu mano,
nadar con él desde el otro lado.

Hasta ese momento, esperémonos aquí en la tierra inquieta,
susurrémonos unos a otros en lenguas del manglar.

Dime que soy bella y fría.
Te diré cuán sedienta estoy
por llenarme la boca de luz.

De noche, siento dolor. Las venas se vuelven purpuras
y crecen con esta repentina temporada de sangre.
Las placas pélvicas se desplazan,
los huesos se estremecen.

Soy la gran madre boa
dando vueltas al huevo blando del mundo
bajo mis costillas. Me desgarraré en dos
y sanaré antes de la mañana.

Danielle Boodoo-Fortuné

A HAMMER TO LOVE WITH

On her sixteenth birthday
you gave her a hammer,
told her,
Here, love with this.

Love has been hard
since then, and brittle.

You've gone ten years
without sleep, five years
without silence.

Today she lets you in,
mines the cracks in her bones
with the point
of her tongue
and listens.

You straighten the sheets, crush
fennel seeds in her tea
to keep the gods at bay.
How any man can survive her
is beyond your wisdom, but
in some way you are proud
of the thing she's become.

When did it happen,

she asks, as she always will,
her tongue bruised
from the night's work.

Danielle Boodoo-Fortuné

UN MARTILLO CON EL QUE AMAR

En su decimosexto aniversario
le diste a ella un martillo,
le dijiste,
Toma, ama con esto.

El amor ha sido duro
desde entonces, y quebradizo.

Has estado diez años
sin dormir, cinco años
sin silencio.

Hoy ella te deja entrar,
excava las grietas de sus huesos
con la punta
de la lengua
y escucha.

Tú arreglas las sábanas, machacas
semillas de hinojo para su té
para mantener a los dioses alejados.
Cómo puede sobrevivirla cualquier hombre
está más allá de tu sabiduría, pero
de alguna manera estás orgullosa
de en lo que se ha convertido ella.

Cuándo pasó,

pregunta ella, como siempre hará,
su lengua amoratada
del trabajo nocturno.

When did it start?

You remember, oh yes.
She must've been seventeen,
dragged him home bleeding from the mouth
and singing in god's tongue,
between her bone-sharp teeth,
the hammer, dark and glistening.

Or at least that's how you remember it.

You say nothing,
wipe the spilt marrow
from her breasts,
feed her, spoon idle talk
into her bitten mouth.

You do what you can.

Oh, this one is difficult;
you can tell by her eyes.
She is afraid he might undo her,
take her by the hips
too gently,

undress
the wound

too slowly.

But you smell the bones
buried shallow in the bed.
She will manage him,
like she always does.
There is no tenderness
here, not since
then.

Cuándo empezó?

Te acuerdas, sí, claro.
Ella debía de tener diecisiete años,
le arrastró a él a casa sangrando por la boca
y cantando en la lengua de dios,
entre los huesos afilados de sus dientes,
el martillo, oscuro y reluciente.

O al menos así lo recuerdas.

No dices nada,
le limpias el tuétano derramado
en los pechos de ella,
le das de comer, pones cucharadas de palabrería
en su boca mordida.

Haces lo que puedes.

Ay, esta es difícil;
lo ves en sus ojos.
Ella teme que él la deshaga,
la coja por las caderas
demasiado suavemente,

desnude
la herida

demasiado lentamente.

Pero hueles los huesos
enterrados a poca profundidad en la cama.
Ella le sabrá llevar a él
como siempre hace.
No hay ternura
aquí, no desde
entonces.

Tonight you will comfort yourself
with smoke and prayer.
When she licks her way
into him, you will wish
you hadn't heard the cry,

wish you hadn't said the words.

But it is finished, you tell yourself.
And it is not your doing.
After all, a heart too soft
will fail, collapse in the lung,
send you fumbling for a body
to breathe for you.

You know this better than most.

After all,
anything swung hard enough
will kill a man,
hammer and heart alike.

Esta noche te consolarás
con humo y rezos.
Cuando ella se adentre en él
lamiéndolo, desearás
no haber oído el llanto.

desearás no haber dicho las palabras.

Pero se acabó, te dices.
Y no fue cosa tuya.
Después de todo, un corazón demasiado blando
fallará, un colapso pulmonar
te mandará a buscar un cuerpo
que respire por ti.

Lo sabes mejor que muchos.

Después de todo,
cualquier cosa, lanzada con suficiente fuerza,
matará a un hombre,
sea martillo o corazón.

Malika Booker

MY MOTHER'S BLUES

My mother knows pain
a sorrowful gospel type of pain —

a slowly losing her eyesight,
eye-drops every night pain,

a headache worrying for her children overseas,
praying for their safety pain,

a stare through each night, eyes blackening,
hope they are alright pain.

Yes, my mother knows pain.

My children don't call,
do they still love me pain,

a worrysome dying grey hair black,
children too far away pain,

a will my daughter ever have children,
she is thirty-eight now pain,

a *your womb is becoming stone* sermon
for her only girl on her birthday pain.

Yes, my mother knows pain.

A what did I do wrong
bringing them up pain,

Malika Booker

EL BLUES DE MI MADRE

Mi madre conoce el dolor
un góspel triste tipo de dolor–

una lenta pérdida de visión,
unas gotas para los ojos todas las noches tipo de dolor,

un dolor de cabeza por preocuparse de sus hijos afuera,
rezar por su bienestar,

una mirada ausente cada noche, ojos oscureciéndose,
espero que estén bien tipo de dolor.

Sí, mi madre conoce el dolor.

Mis hijos no me llaman,
¿todavía me quieren? tipo de dolor,

un preocupante tengo que teñirme las canas de negro,
los niños están demasiado lejos tipo de dolor,

tendrá hijos mi hija,
ahora tiene treinta y ocho años tipo de dolor,

un sermón de *tu útero se está volviendo de piedra*
para su única hija el día de su cumpleaños tipo de dolor.

Sí, mi madre conoce el dolor.

En qué me equivoqué
cuando les crie tipo de dolor,

a my son has gone astray, someone put obeah on him
so I have to pray real hard pain,

a look how so-and-so children do so well,
I wish mine were like that pain.

Yes my mother knows pain.

It's the house now empty
no one to cook for pain,

and I can't let go, have to let go pain,
it's a let me tell you how to bury me pain,

I want a plain box, no fancy coffin,
or I will come back and haunt you pain,

a don't have no big set of people
coming around calling it a wake pain,

it's a let me tell you who will get what
after I am gone, so you don't fight pain,

it's a don't worry I go soon be dead and gone
and then you go miss me pain.

Yes my mother feels pain.

mi hijo está descarriado, alguien le hizo *obeah*
así que debo rezar mucho tipo dolor

mira qué bien les va a los hijos de fulano y mengano,
ojalá los míos fueran así tipo de dolor.

Sí, mi madre conoce el dolor.

La casa ahora está vacía
nadie a quien cocinar tipo de dolor,

no sé dejarme ir, debo dejarme ir tipo de dolor,
escucha como quiero que me entierren tipo de dolor,

quiero una caja sencilla, nada de un ataúd lujoso,
o regresaré para perseguirles tipo de dolor,

no vayan a invitar a mucha gente
que cuando vengan lo llamen un velatorio tipo de dolor,

escucha para quién será qué
cuando ya yo no esté, para que no peleen tipo de dolor,

no se preocupen pronto ya no estaré
y entonces me extrañarán tipo de dolor.

Sí, mi madre siente el dolor.

Malika Booker

PEPPER SAUCE

I pray for that grandmother, grinding her teeth,
one hand pushing in fresh hot peppers, seeds and all, turning
the handle of that old iron mill, squeezing the limes, knowing
      they will burn and cut raw like acid.
She pours in vinegar and gets Anne to chop five onions
      with a whole bulb of garlic,
      Chop them up real fine girl, you hear?
And Anne dicing, and crying, relieved that no belt has blistered her skin,
      no knife handle smashed down onto her knuckles
until they bleed for stealing money from she grandmother purse.

I hear she made Anne pour in the oil and vinegar
      and stir up that hot sauce, how she hold her down.
I hear she tied that girl to the bedposts,
      strung her out naked, like she there lying on a crucifix.
I hear she spread she out, then say,
      I go teach you to go and steal from me, Miss Lady.
I hear she scoop that pepper sauce out of a white enamel bowl,
      and pack it deep into she granddaughter's pussy,
I hear there was one piece of screaming in the house that day.
      Anne bawl till she turn hoarse,
          bawl till the hair on the neighbours' skin raise up,
          bawl till she start hiss through her teeth,
          bawl till she mouth could make no more sound,
I hear how she turn raw,
how that grandmother leave her there all day,

I hear how she couldn't walk or talk for weeks.

Malika Booker

SALSA PICANTE

Rezo por esa abuela, haciendo rechinar los dientes,
con una mano echando pimientos picantes frescos, las semillas y todo,
    haciendo girar
la manivela de ese molinillo viejo de hierro, exprimiendo las limas,
    a sabiendas
de que quemarán y cortarán como el ácido hasta dejar en carne viva.
Le echa vinagre y hace que Anne pique cinco cebollas
    con una cabeza entera de ajos,
        Pícalo bien finito, chica, ¿me oyes?
Y Anne trocea y llora, aliviada de que ningún cinturón le ha hecho
    ampollas en su piel,
ningún mango de cuchillo ha hecho trizas sus nudillos
hasta sangrar por robar dinero del bolso de su abuela.

Me dicen que hizo que Anne echara el aceite y el vinagre
    y mezclara la salsa picante, que la sujetó ahí.
Me dicen que la amarró a los postes de la cama,
    la ató desnuda, como si estuviera ahí tumbada en un crucifijo.
Me dicen que la abrió de piernas, luego le dijo,
        Voy a enseñarte a robarme a mí, Señorita.
Me dicen que sacó la salsa picante de la palangana blanca de esmalte,
y se la embutió bien adentro en el coño de su nieta,
me dicen que hubo tremendos gritos en la casa ese día.
    Anne gritó hasta quedar ronca,
        gritó hasta que a los vecinos se les pusieron los pelos
            de punta,
        gritó hasta que empezó a resoplar entre los dientes,
        gritó hasta que su boca ya no pudo hacer más sonidos,
me dicen que quedó en carne viva,
que la abuela la dejó ahí todo el día,

me dicen que no pudo caminar ni hablar durante semanas.

Malika Booker

CEMENT

Last week my tears were sucked out
with our aborted child. Yesterday
in the shower, pain contorted me,
I squatted, expelled a souvenir:

red, liver-textured, squeezed out.
I scooped it up and flushed it away.
You were not there. Your absence
no longer makes me cry.

My tears are gone, so I plaster my heart
against every grit-worried wound.
Now I understand older black women
like my aunts, their hard posture,

why I never saw them cry.
My father made my mother stony,
a martyr for her kids, brittle and bitter,
till my stepdad unbricked her wall;

layer by layer I watched it crumble.
My aunt, shattered by fists, blocked her heart;
stone cold, her tears dried up.
All my life, I never saw her cry, until foetal

in a hospital bed, wrapped in my mother's arms,
facing death, tears tracking her face,
she whispered, *I am scared*.
Crying for all her tear-barren years.

Malika Booker

CEMENTO

La semana pasada mis lágrimas fueron succionadas
con nuestro hijo abortado. Ayer
en la ducha, retorciéndome de dolor,
me agaché, expulsé un souvenir:

rojo, textura de hígado, estrujado.
Lo recogí y lo tiré al inodoro.
No estabas ahí. Tu ausencia
ya no me hace llorar.

Mis lágrimas se fueron, así que enyeso mi corazón
contra cada arenilla que empeore la herida.
Ahora, entiendo a mujeres negras mayores
como mis tías, su dura pose,

el por qué nunca las vi llorar.
Mi padre hizo que mi madre fuera dura como una roca,
una mártir para los niños, quebradiza y amarga,
hasta que mi padrastro rompió su muro ladrillo a ladrillo;

capa a capa lo vi derrumbarse.
Mi tía, destruida por puños, bloqueó su corazón;
fría como una piedra, sus lágrimas se secaron.
Toda mi vida, nunca la vi llorar, hasta que, en posición

fetal en una cama de hospital, envuelta en los brazos de mi madre,
afrontando la muerte, lágrimas dejando rastros en su cara,
ella murmuró, *Estoy asustada.*
Llorando por todos los años baldíos de lágrimas.

Washing water-diluted blood down the drain,
bleaching the bath tiles white, I want to bawl
my eyes out, but I have learnt my lesson well.
Each passing day hardens my voice.

Limpiando la sangre diluida en agua por el desagüe,
blanqueando las losetas del baño, quiero arrancarme
los ojos, pero he aprendido bien la lección.
Cada día que pasa mi voz se endurece.

Vahni Capildeo

INVESTIGATION OF PAST SHOES

INSIDE THE GATEWAY: 1970S RED CLOGS WITH SIDE BUCKLE

The forever shoe, which points homewards, belongs to my mother. When our house was being built, she stepped onto the driveway while the tarmac was still wet, still setting. Ever since that step, the driveway, which slants upwards, bears an imprint of her 1971 footwear. Her foot-print says, *Climb! Come with me*. Whoever steps into that impression becomes, for a moment, the leggy wearer of a fire-red clog with a piratical silver buckle on the side.

OUTSIDE THE TEMPLE: GOLD AND SILVER SANDALS

The sandals which will make a female of me belong to many women. The front of the temple entrance hides itself behind shoe-racks. Visitors enter barefooted, leaving behind the dung, dried frogs, spilled petrol and ketchup traces of the streets. Hundreds of pairs of gold and silver sandals wait here for the women who will re-emerge from the vigil with the taste of basil leaf and sugar in their deep-breathing mouths and carpet fibres between their toes. The sandals, gold and silver, seem all alike. How can the women tell them apart? They do tell them apart. It is as if each pair sings an intimate mantra to its owner, audible only to her. One day I too shall return to expectant slippers that stack up like the moon and the stars outside a marble building; one day I shall not have to wear child's shoes.

Vahni Capildeo

INVESTIGACIÓN DE ZAPATOS DEL PASADO

DENTRO DE LOS PORTONES: ZUECOS ROJOS DE LOS 70
CON HEBILLA LATERAL

El zapato para siempre, que apunta hacia casa, pertenece a mi madre.
Cuando se estaba construyendo nuestra casa, ella pisó el camino de
la entrada mientras el asfalto aún estaba blando, aún fraguándose.
Desde esa pisada, el camino de entrada, que está inclinado hacia
arriba, lleva el sello de su calzado de 1971. Su huella dice, *¡Trépate!*
Ven conmigo. Cualquiera que ponga el pie en ese molde se convierte,
por un momento, en una portadora de bonitas piernas de un zueco
color rojo fuego con una hebilla de plata piratesca en el costado.

FUERA DEL TEMPLO: SANDALIAS DORADAS Y PLATEADAS

Las sandalias que harán de mí un ser femenino pertenecen a muchas
mujeres. La fachada de la entrada del templo se esconde detrás de los
estantes de zapatos. Los visitantes entran descalzos, dejando atrás el
estiércol, los sapos secos, la gasolina derramada y los rastros de
kétchup de la calle. Cientos de pares de zapatos dorados y plateados
esperan aquí a las mujeres que reaparecerán de la vigilia con sabor de
albahaca y azúcar en la respiración profunda de sus bocas y con fibras
de alfombra entre los dedos de sus pies. Las sandalias, doradas y
plateadas, se parecen todas. ¿Cómo las pueden diferenciar las
mujeres? Ellas sí las diferencian. Es como si cada par cantara un
íntimo mantra a su dueña, audible sólo por ella. Un día yo también
volveré a expectantes zapatillas que se amontonan como la luna y las
estrellas fuera de un edificio de mármol; un día no tendré que llevar
zapatitos de niña.

SUNDAY BEFORE SCHOOL: WHITE SNEAKERS

Seven years of these shoes are a chemical memory. The Convent ruled that pupils' shoes must be white: absolutely white. Who can imagine a 1980s shoe that was absolutely white, without any logo, with no swoosh, not a single slogan? Sunday evenings, before the school week, I crouched down on the pink bathroom tiles and painted my shoes into the absolute of whiteness; like the Alice in Wonderland gardeners repainting roses. This task was performed with a toothbrush and with special paste that annihilated so many design features. Purity was attained by the application of a whitener that stank of scientific polysyllables. Convent-girl identity. Tabula rasa. Toxicity and intoxication: with good intentions, getting high on paste.

BAD MARRIAGE SHOES: SILVER BALLET SLIPPERS

When I met my ex, I was already committed to heels: black ankle boots with four-inch stacks for walking through snow; French cream curved suède stilettos for scaling fire-escape ladders on to rooftops to admire the winter sky; even after I left him, scarlet satin bedroom-only spiky mules to amuse myself. Early on, my ex said that the way women walk in heels looks ugly. And my nails made unnatural social appearances: emerald lacquer; cobalt; incarnadine. Sign of a bad marriage: I began to wear flats. The penitential mermaid shoes, worn once and once only, were a Gabor creation: distressed silver ballet slippers with netted and criss-cross side details which would make the material seem to swish with the changes of light on feet that go walking. Cool as moonlight on a tourist coastline. But the inner stitching hooked the softness of my skin, which has always been too soft; but I could not turn back, for we had tickets to an evening of Mozart; but the paper tissues that I stuffed into my shoes failed to act as a protective lining. Paper tissue snow-flecks teardropped with crimson blood created

DOMINGO ANTES DE LA ESCUELA: TENIS BLANCAS

Siete años de estos zapatos son un recuerdo químico. Convent exigía que los zapatos de las alumnas fueran blancos: completamente blancos. ¿Quién se imagina un zapato de los 1980 que fuera completamente blanco, sin ninguna marca, sin un *swoosh*, sin un solo eslogan? Los domingos por la tarde, antes de una semana de escuela, me ponía en cuclillas en las losetas rosas del baño y pintaba mis zapatos de la más absoluta de las blancuras; como los jardineros de Alicia en el País de las Maravillas repintando flores. Esta tarea era llevada a cabo con un cepillo y con una pasta especial que aniquilaba muchos de los aspectos del diseño. La pureza se alcanzaba con la aplicación de un blanqueador que apestaba a polisílabas científicas. Identidad de chica de Convent. Tabula Rasa. Toxicidad e intoxicación: con buenas intenciones, flotando extasiada de pasta.

ZAPATOS DE MAL MATRIMONIO: ZAPATILLAS DE BALLET PLATEADAS

Cuando conocí a mi ex, yo ya estaba comprometida con los tacones: botas negras hasta los tobillos con una plataforma de diez centímetros para caminar por la nieve; zapatos de ante crema con tacón francés de aguja curvado para trepar por escaleras de incendios hasta las azoteas para admirar el cielo de invierno; incluso después de dejarle, zapatillas altas de satén escarlata, solo para el dormitorio, para divertirme. Al principio, mi ex me había dicho que la manera de caminar de las mujeres con tacones se veía fea. Y mis uñas hicieron apariciones sociales poco naturales: laca esmeralda; cobalto; color encarnado. Señal de un mal matrimonio: empecé a llevar zapatos planos. Los zapatos penitenciales de sirena, puestos una vez y solo una, eran una creación de Gabor; zapatillas de ballet color plateado desgastado con detalles entrecruzados y de rejilla en los lados que hacían que el material pareciera undular con los cambios de luz sobre los pies que caminan. Fría como la luz de la luna en una línea costera turística. Pero el cosido interior se clavaba en la suavidad de mi piel;

a trail behind me as I ascended the many tiers of the wedding-cake concert hall.

BAREFOOT: PEARL PINK POLISH

Sitting next to someone can make my feet curl: shy, self-destructive and oyster-like, they want to shuck their cases, to present themselves, little undersea pinks; their skin still is too soft, their toes still too long, their ankles still too slender, for a modern fit. But he is not modern; he sits like stone, and my bare feet are cool, they will not have to bleed.

que ha sido siempre demasiado suave; pero no podía dar media vuelta, ya que teníamos boletos para una velada con Mozart; pero los pañuelos de papel con los que rellené mis zapatos fracasaron en su funcionar de forro protector. Copos de pañuelos de papel salpicados de sangre carmesí dejaban un rastro tras de mí mientras ascendía los muchos escalones del auditorio, como pisos del pastel nupcial.

DESCALZA: ESMALTE ROSA PERLA

Sentarme al lado de alguien puede hacer que mis pies se encojan: tímidos, autodestructivos y como ostras, quieren desbullar sus fundas, presentarse, pequeñas criaturas rosas bajo el mar; su piel aún es demasiado suave, sus dedos aún demasiado largos, sus tobillos aún demasiado estrechos, para un porte moderno. Pero él no es moderno; se sienta como una piedra, y mis pies descalzos están fríos, no tendrán que sangrar.

Vahni Capildeo

SLAUGHTERER

The tears curled from the cattle's eyes, their horns curled back, their coats curled like frost-ferns on windshields or the hair on the heads of Sikandar's soldiers. Two of my grandfather's sons, when he knew he was dying, took him from his bed. They supported him out the doorway so he could say goodbye to his favourite cattle. The cattle wept. They knew him. They are not like cattle here. They live among the household and on the hills, which are very green, and they eat good food, the same food as the household, cut-up pieces of leftover chapatti.

You do not get stories like that in books. I am telling you because you only have things to read. Whenever anybody tried to make me read a book or anything, I would fall asleep; my head would just drop.

What is the use of reading books? What can you do after that but get an office job? Do my friends who stayed at school earn as much as me? They all have office jobs; could they do a job like mine? Could they slaughter for seventy hours without getting tired or needing to sleep? It was hard at first. I used to dream the cattle. They would come to me with big eyes, like mothers and sisters. After a few weeks, they stopped coming to me in dreams. After about five years, I stopped feeling tired: I do not need to sleep. We do three or four thousand a day in Birmingham, only a thousand a night in Lancaster.

Tonight I am going to Lancaster. I will talk to you until Lancaster. Where are you from? You are lying on me. No, where are your parents from? Are you lying on me? I came here as a teenager, and at once they tried making me read. How old are you? Why do you only have things to read? I am sorry I am talking to you. You have brought things you want to read. Beautiful reader, what is your name?

You can feel the quality of the meat in the animal when it is alive: the way its skin fits on its flesh. You can feel the quality of life in the meat. The cattle here are not good. They inject them. Their flesh is ahhh.

Look, look how beautiful. I will show you pictures of the place. Look, it is very green.

Vahni Capildeo

MATARIFE

Las lágrimas rodaron de los ojos del ganado, sus cuernos curvados para atrás, su pelaje rizado como helecho de escarcha sobre el parabrisas o el pelo en las cabezas de los soldados de Sikandar. Dos de los hijos de mi abuelo, cuando él sabía que estaba muriendo, le sacaron de su cama. Le llevaron fuera de la casa, sosteniéndole, para que pudiera decir adiós a su ganado favorito. El ganado lloró. Le conocían. No son como el ganado aquí. Viven entre la gente de un hogar y en las colinas, que son muy verdes, y comen comida buena, la misma comida que la familia, pedacitos de restos de *chapatti*.

No encuentras historias como esta en los libros. Te lo digo porque tú solo tienes cosas para leer. Cuando alguien intentaba hacerme leer un libro o cualquier cosa, me dormía; se me caía la cabeza.

¿Para qué sirve leer libros? ¿Qué puedes hacer después aparte de conseguir un trabajo en una oficina? ¿Mis amigos que se quedaron en la escuela ganan tanto como yo? Todos tienen trabajos de oficina; ¿podrían hacer un trabajo como el mío? ¿Podrían matar durante setenta horas sin cansarse o necesitar dormir?

Al principio fue duro. Soñaba con el ganado. Venían hacia mí con ojos grandes, como madres y hermanas. Después de unas semanas, dejaron de aparecerse en mis sueños. Después de unos cinco años, dejé de sentirme cansado: no necesito dormir. Hacemos tres o cuatro mil cada día en Birmingham, solamente mil cada noche en Lancaster.

Esta noche voy a Lancaster. Te hablaré hasta Lancaster. ¿De dónde eres? Me estás mintiendo. No, ¿de dónde son tus padres? ¿Me estás mintiendo? Llegué cuando era un adolescente, y de golpe intentaron hacerme leer. ¿Cuántos años tienes? ¿Por qué solo tienes cosas para leer? Perdona que te hable. Trajiste cosas que querías leer. Bonita lectora, ¿cómo te llamas?

Puedes sentir la calidad de la carne en el animal cuando está vivo: la manera como la piel cubre la carne. Puedes sentir la calidad de vida en la carne. El ganado aquí no es bueno. Les inyectan. Su carne es aaajjj.

Mira, mira qué bonito. Te enseñaré fotos del lugar. Mira, es muy verde.

Vahni Capildeo

INTO DARKNESS / PLUS QUE NOIR

For Attillah Springer

*

Loupgarou

Speak to me though I cannot answer
These days I cannot think and speak when you are near

Dragging great chains of night in his audible walk round the houses
A candled coffin cleaving to his headless neck
Shining with the light of misunderstanding

The loupgarou is a lover
Perennial and never let in

*

Douens

Children you will have me though I never found you
Shades of growing swallowed by oversized sombreros

You go crying through the forest even where land has been cleared
Tearless and whooping hide-and-seek and your feet backwards on their stems
Trickling every cell of possibles that underwent expulsion

The douens dwell on the past
Allured by facelessness we follow

Vahni Capildeo

HACIA LA OSCURIDAD / PLUS QUE NOIR

Para Attillah Springer

*

Loupgarou

Háblame aunque no puedo responder
Estos días no puedo pensar ni hablar cuando estás cerca

Arrastrando grandes cadenas de noche en su audible ronda por las casas
Un ataúd con velas adherido a su cuello descabezado
Brillando con la luz del malentendido

El loupgarou es un amante,
Perenne y jamás se le deja entrar

*

Douens

Niños, ustedes me van a tener aunque nunca les encontré
Sombras de crecimiento tragadas por sombreros desmesurados

Ustedes andan llorando por el bosque, incluso por donde se ha despejado
el terreno
Sin lágrimas, ululando 'wuup wuup' y jugando al escondite, los pies
de ustedes del revés en sus tallos
Goteo tramposo de cada célula de los posibles que sufrieron la expulsión

Los douens se aferran al pasado
Cautivados por la falta de rostro les seguimos

*

Soucouyants

I need you inside me, inside my body as you are inside my mind
Knowledge of you moved me in firing myself, in taking flight

Fireball shedding her skin bloodkisses not just cattle
Her stored skin poisoned by raging neighbours with stamped thighs
She puts on a skin that smelts her, woman of no return

The soucouyant brings desire home
Earth and water make her tomb

*

Soucouyants

Te necesito dentro de mí, dentro de mi cuerpo como estás dentro mi mente
Saber de ti me movió a prenderme fuego, alzar el vuelo

Bola de fuego que muda su piel besos de sangre no solamente al ganado
Su guardada piel, envenenada por vecinos furiosos con caderas marcadas
Se pone una piel que la funde, mujer de no retorno

La soucouyant trae el deseo a casa
Su tumba está hecha de tierra y agua

Nicole Cecilia Delgado

ASESINATOS
        para I.L. y L.I.

a cuatro calles de mi calle:
contrabando de órganos humanos
narcomenudeo, prostitución infantil
un ingeniero se viste de mujer
para toquetear señoras en el metro
tacos de carne de perro
cucarachas monumentales merodean la basura
en esta esquina con frisos barrocos
se cometió un crimen de género
y un ave fénix resurge
entre montañas de colillas de cigarro

he perdido la inocencia en esta ciudad
llena de niños solos que hacen preguntas filosóficas
camino
reconozco las señales de la guerra en los semáforos
hay consignas de aerosol en todas partes

a cuatro calles, el espacio se bifurca bajo tierra
una ciudad más sanguinaria
se hunde debajo de mis pasos
otros niños rotos se disputan cloacas con ratones
el mercado vende hasta el luto de sus madres lejanas

a veces pienso
que la palabra sicario tiene demasiada melodía
y que el centro histórico oculta el terror más feroz

detrás de cada malabar baila un asesino
sólo hay que llegar a tiempo para ver la acción

Nicole Cecilia Delgado

MURDERS
for I.L. and L.I.

Four streets away from my street:
contraband of human organs
narco-trafficking, child prostitution
an engineer dresses like a woman
to grope women in the subway
dog-meat tacos
monumental cockroaches prowl the garbage
on this corner with baroque friezes
a gender-crime was committed
and a phoenix bird resurrects
between mountains of cigarette butts

I've lost my innocence in this city
full of abandoned children who ask philosophical questions
I walk
I recognize the signs of war in the stop lights
graffiti tags are everywhere

four streets away, the space divides underground
a bloodthirsty city
sinks below my steps
other broken children fight mice for sewers
the market sells even the mourning of their distant mothers

sometimes I think
that the word assassin is too melodic
and that the historic district hides a terror more fierce

behind every juggler a murderer dances
one only has to arrive in time to see the action

y todavía
aunque sé que matan, que asaltan
que los taxis de noche
son una ruleta inminentemente rusa

la ciudad me hace cosquillas

ayer colgamos del balcón un letrero que dice
bésame musho
para invitar a todos los vecinos al desarme

(mejor vivir entre paredes que tiemblan beso a beso
que contar cicatrices de plomo en las ventanas)

por eso, no puedo decirte *asesíname amor*
porque los muertos no besan y necesitamos
estar vivos
para empezar a hacer belleza con todos los escombros

and still
although I know that they kill, that they assault
that the night taxis
are an imminently Russian roulette

the city tickles me

yesterday we hung a sign from the balcony that says
bésame mucho
to encourage all our neighbours to disarm

(better to live between walls that tremble from kiss to kiss
than to count bullet scars on the windows)

that's why I can't tell you to *murder me love*
because the dead don't kiss and we need to
to be alive
to begin to make beauty out of all the debris

Nicole Cecilia Delgado

HOMBRE NUEVO

hombre con labios pintados
hombre que respinga y barba
hombre de látex o papel
niño no, hombre tampoco
con muertes y trucos de oficina sórdida
hombre corporación
hombre teléfono roto
hombre sofisticado y serio
hombre zapatos cerrados
muñeco de plástico
mordida de pájaro
hombre qué hago con tu sucio de mundo
con tu peste a gallinita ciega
con tu mordaza espantada
con tu ímpetu sagrado
con todos tus plomos
hombre tóxico
hombre máquina
mentira de vertedero digital
hombre tecnología
innovación magnética
hombre carrocería y tornillo
inteligencia matemática
obtusa penumbra química
hombre ciencia
hombre sobre ruedas
hombre con mochila o escopeta
hombre geométrico y enorme
hombre brujo
hombre mago
hombre, compárteme algo
siéntate conmigo un rato

Nicole Cecilia Delgado

NEW MAN

lipsticked man
nose-contouring and bearded man
latex or paper man
neither boy, nor man
with sordid office deaths and tricks
corporation man
broken phone man
sophisticated and serious man
closed-shoes man
plastic doll
bird peck
what do I do with your dirty world man
with your stink of blind man's bluff
with your terrified gagging jaw
with your sacred impulses
with all of your bullets
toxic man
machine man
digital dumpheap lie
technology man
magnetic innovation
bodywork and screw man
mathematic intelligence
obtuse chemical penumbra
science man
man on wheels
backpack or shotgun man
enormous and geometric man
witch man
magic man
man, share something with me
sit with me awhile

hombre descosido
fruto mordaz de un territorio raro
hombre escarcha
hombre lentejuela
hombre galaxia de poliéster y aserrín
fibra sintética
hombre que no existes
quedaron dos escamas tuyas
en mis manos rojas
hombre escurridizo
hombre piel de baba
hombre amazonas
hombre danubio
hombre mar muerto
hombre te extrañé
hombre tomemos café
hombre pervertido
poema hombre prostituta
hombre boca de albur
hombre duerme de día y suda de noche
(me enterré una espina en el jardín
de tu lengua venenosa
estoy escupiendo pelo)
hombre ábrete sésamo
pinta tus labios para darme besos
moja tus dedos en mi pila menstrual
hombre silencioso
hombre incomunicable y solo
hombre extinto
improbable melodía
tienes la hormona delirante y los ojos chinos
hombre mi vientre retorcido
hombre tu lado femenino
hombre hagamos de una vez el amor
hombre quién eres
hombre también soy yo

raggedy man
caustic fruit of a strange territory
glitter man
sequin man
galaxy of polyester and sawdust man
synthetic fibre
unreal man
two of your scales remained
in my red hands
slippery man
slimy-skin man
amazon man
danube man
dead sea man
I-missed-you man
let's have coffee man
pervert man
prostitute man poem
mouth of sexual word games man
sleep in the day and sweat in the night man
(in the garden
of your venomous tongue,
I got a splinter
I am spitting out hair)
open sesame man
paint your lips to give me kisses
drench your fingers in my menstrual font
silent man
lone and incommunicado man
extinct man
improbable melody
you have delirious hormones and weed-eyes
my gut-wrenching man
your feminine side man
hurry up let's make love man
who are you man

hombre luna llena hombre lobo
hombre sirena hombre medusa
monstruo de la laguna verde
abominable hombre periférico con la vagina blanca
hombre imposible
hombre orilla
hombre que sí
nohombre no
hombre no quiero tus hijos
mala leche
miedo ronco
hombre a media luz
hombre esta noche voy a dormir con otro hombre
insólito hombre anacrónico
abolido patriarca
hombre del futuro
magnífico hombre indefinido
sin precedente e indómito
mutante alucinógeno
hombre nuevo
por fin

I too am man
full moon man wolf man
mermaid man medusa man
monster of the green lagoon man
marginal abominable-man with a white vagina
impossible man
fringe man
man of course
don't man, don't
I don't want your kids man
bad-mind
hoarse fear
lights down low man
tonight I'm going to sleep with another man
out of sync and out of norm
patriarch abolished
man of the future
magnificent undefined man
without precedent and indomitable
hallucinogenic mutant
new man
finally

Nicole Cecilia Delgado

LECCIONES CHINAS

dice el tao:
sólo un cuenco vacío puede llenarse

por eso
no volví a visitar
al hombre rubio que vive junto al río
aunque juntara leña e hiciera sopa
y me abrazara de noche en otro idioma

por eso dejé de buscar el azar
que me llevara a encontrarme por azar
con mi vecino
aunque tuviera el pelo largo, un perro
y me regalara flores

por eso ya no sonreí a los músicos, los artesanos
aunque el pueblo se llenara de viajeros hermosos
cada jueves
y la noche estuviera abierta y alguno de ellos
quisiera después cocinar el desayuno

por eso no volví a levantar vagabundos en la calle
hombres-luz con los ojos
heridos de viento y los zapatos rotos
hombres que dibujaban transeúntes en una libretita
hombres vagabundos empuñando una gubia
silbando hojas muertas en el parque central
hombres vagabundos que me sedujeron tanto

por eso quemé mis diarios
y destruí el deseo inconcluso

Nicole Cecilia Delgado

CHINESE LESSONS

the tao says:
only an empty vessel can be filled

that's why
I didn't visit again
the blond man who lives next to the river
even though he might gather firewood and make soup
and hug me at night in another language

that's why I stopped looking for a chance
to just happen to meet
my neighbour by luck
even though he might have long hair, a dog
and give me flowers

that's why I no longer smiled at musicians, artisans
even though the town filled with handsome travellers
every Thursday
and the night was boundless and one of them
wanted to cook breakfast in the morning

that's why I didn't wake up vagrants in the streets anymore
men-of-light with eyes
wounded by wind and broken shoes
men who drew passers-by in a little notebook
vagrant men gripping a blade
swishing autumn leaves in central park
vagrant men who so seduced me

that's why I burnt my diaries
and destroyed the dubious desire

que me ataba a los hombres que no me hicieron caso
ellos también ocupaban demasiado aire dentro de mí

por eso dejé de atragantarme de culpa o desamparo
y dejé que se fueran por fin
los hombres que hace tiempo se habían ido
su fantasma con eco
su cola de cometa muerto
su viejísimo reclamo fermentado

ya no quise
ya no pude
piel de albergue
corazón de alcohólicos anónimos
filántropa aventando carne a los perros con sarna

cerré por remodelación el cántaro
los eché (dificultosamente) a todos de mi casa
crucé mis piernas transitadas
en forma de loto marchito
escuché por fin mi vulva silenciosa
reconstruí mis dientes y dormí
toda la noche

sólo entonces
mi cuerpo vacío
fue bello
nuevamente

that tied me to men who didn't bother with me
they also took up too much air inside of me

that's why I stopped choking on my guilt or helplessness
and let them finally walk away
the men who had already gone a long time ago
their echoing ghost
their dead comet's tail
their old fermented lure

I just didn't want
I just couldn't
shelter skin
alcoholic's anonymous heart
philanthropist tossing away meat to dogs with mange

I closed the water pot for remodelling
I threw them all (with difficulty) out of my house
I crossed my well-trafficked legs
into the form of a withered lotus
I finally listened to my silent vulva
fixed my teeth and slept
all night

only then
was my empty body
beautiful
once again

Thaís Espaillat

LA VIRGEN DE LA CUEVA SIEMPRE TIENE TRABAJO

A las tres comienza a llover aunque hace dos
segundos había un solazo.
La lluvia quiere ser buena ciudadana,
busca un zafacón
pero no encuentra,
así que llena la calle
de Tetrapacks
y fundas de plástico
y folletos color rosado que hablan del
Apocalipsis.

Busca a dónde irse porque no le gusta estar en el
medio,
pero no encuentra por donde colarse. Ahora
frente
a tu casa
hay
un
río
            (aunque para la gente
            que vive con un pie
            en el Ozama solo
            es otro día)

Los hoyos de las calles
se vuelven piscinas
de agua marrón.
Quizás para eso
siempre están ahí:
para ser
un parque acuático
para palomas.

Thaís Espaillat

LA VIRGEN DE LA CUEVA ALWAYS HAS WORK

At three it starts to rain even though two
seconds ago there was a complete sunfest.
The rain, wanting to be a good citizen,
looks for a garbage can
but it doesn't find one,
so it fills the street
with Tetra packs
and plastic bags
and pink leaflets that speak of the
Apocalypse.

It looks for where to go because it doesn't like to get in the
way,
but it doesn't find anywhere to trickle away to. Now
in front
of your house
there's
a
river
        (though for people
        who live with one foot
        in the Ozama,
        it's just another day)

The streets' potholes
turn into swimming pools
of brown water.
Maybe that's what
they're always there for:
to be
an aquatic park
for pigeons.

117

Estás tarde
porque la lluvia maravilla a los conductores
y hace que no puedan manejar
sin botar un poco de baba
en su nombre. Sales del tapón y le das a 180.
Moviste el río de la Churchill
y se lo echaste a la tipa de traje gris
y al pana en silla de ruedas que tiene un
hermano igualito a él.

La lluvia sabe por lluvia
no por vieja
        (como la doña
        de la casa de al lado)
Así que si te dice que todo está mal,
es para que te olvides de una vez,
porque ahorita a las cuatro sale el sol de las
doce.
Y ya casi es viernes,
así que viene romo
        (solo no lo pongas en
        Facebook porque
        la justicia no es ciega
        y le gustan tus fotos)

Mañana seguro vuelve a llover
y se refresca un poquito
la primera ciudad
de Hamerika.
Debería,
porque ya casi viene Navidad,
        (aunque según Plaza Lama
        llegó hace dos meses)

Qué linda se ve la ciudad cuando brillan las
calles

You're late
because rain astonishes drivers
and makes them unable to drive
without gobbing out some spit
in its name. You get out of the traffic jam and go 180.
You set the river on Churchill into motion
and splash it on the woman in the grey suit
and the guy in a wheelchair who has a
brother just like him.

Rain knows because it's rain
not because it's old
　　　　(like the lady
　　　　from the house next door)
So, if she tells you that everything's bad,
you can just forget that,
because now at four, a noon sun appears.
And it's almost Friday,
so here comes the rum.
　　　　(just don't put it on
　　　　Facebook because
　　　　justice isn't blind,
　　　　and it likes your photos)

For sure it'll rain again tomorrow
and freshen up
the first city
of Hamerica a little.
It should,
because Christmas is almost coming,
　　　　(though according to Plaza Lama
　　　　it arrived two months ago)

How beautiful the city looks
when the streets shine

y se ve lo que era lluvia bailando con el sol
(el problema es
que el que suda es uno)

and you see what was rain dancing with the sun
(the problem is
that you're the one who sweats)

Thaís Espaillat

INVADIRNOS SERÍA PERDER EL TIEMPO

No creo que los extraterrestres se parezcan a
mis vecinos
o a los tuyos,
que tengan cabeza gigante,
piel morada,
ojos en la nuca.

Seguro se parecen más
a las medusas invisibles,
al polvo que flota en la luz,
a las manchas de aceite.

Y no nos hablan porque somos aburridos.

Seguimos
caminando,
corriendo,
volando en círculos
y paralelogramos.
Y ellos existen en las grietas de los relojes,
las venas de los planetas que le huyen a los
telescopios.

O quizás sepan tanto que ya ni hablan,
y sólo mueren lento y sin sentirlo
o sintiéndolo tanto,
en camas que viajan entre nuestros satélites
y salen en algunas fotos
sacándonos sus mil lenguas,
con baba que despierta un volcán a los lejos.

Los extraterrestres seguro no escriben poesía,
ni hacen películas,

Thaís Espaillat

INVADING US WOULD BE A WASTE OF TIME

I don't think that extraterrestrials resemble
my neighbours
or yours,
that they have a giant head,
purple skin,
eyes on the napes of their necks.

I'm sure they look more
like invisible jellyfish,
dust motes that float in the light,
oil stains.

And they don't talk to us because we're boring.

We continue
walking,
running,
flying in circles
and parallelograms.
And they exist in the grooves of watches,
the veins of planets that escape from
telescopes.

Or maybe they know so much that they don't even talk anymore,
and only die slowly and without feeling it
or feeling it so much,
in beds travelling between our satellites
and they show up in some photos
sticking out their thousand tongues at us,
with slobber that awakens a distant volcano.

I'm sure that extraterrestrials don't write poetry,
nor do they make movies,

ni cocinan en televisión,
pero estoy casi segura de que tienen internet
y usan Tor para espiarnos.
Ahí es cuando se dan cuenta
de que no valemos la pena,
y nos dejan con nuestras drogas
y nuestro porno
y se alejan con sus tentáculos
o sus cosas sin nombre todavía,
temblando de lo estúpidos
que hemos sido siempre
mientras apagan la regleta
y de este lado todo se vuelve
color morgue,
fosa común,
suela de bota.

Los niños miran al cielo
y se dan cuenta
de que ya no hay más deseos.
Los astronautas se quitan sus cascos en
protesta,
no llegaron a la NASA mordiendo la capa de
ozono
para ser mineros.

La gente común en los supermercados y las
oficinas rodando y tecleando
con latas de garbanzo y plantas de plástico
como último paisaje,
gritan uno encima de otro, piden ayuda,
ayuda-por-favor-botella-vino-roto-jefe-
renuncio-mamá-te-odio

Y los extraterrestres cada vez más lejos
y más grandes

they don't cook on television,
but I'm pretty sure they have internet
and they use Tor to spy on us.
That's when they realize
that we're not worth it,
and they leave us with our drugs
and our porn,
and they move away on their tentacles
or their things that don't have a name yet,
trembling from how stupid
we have always been,
while they shut off the power strip,
and from this side everything becomes
the colour of a morgue,
a mass grave,
a boot sole.

Children look at the sky,
and they realize
that there are no more wishes.
Astronauts take off their helmets in
protest;
they didn't arrive at NASA eating through
the ozone layer
to be miners.

The common people in supermarkets and
offices rolling around and typing
with chickpea cans and plastic plants
as their final landscape,
they cry on top of each other,
they ask for help,
help-please-broken-wine-bottle-boss-
I-resign-mom-I-hate-you

And the extraterrestrials getting farther and farther away
and bigger

y más pequeños
y más con formas ajenas,
sus alas de fuego,
sus dientes de nitrógeno,
sus partes que no sé armar,
ahogándose
o respirando
o abriéndose
entre la basura
y la escarcha,
sonriéndole a los millones de bebés tragones
que han parido las estrellas muertas.

and smaller
and more alien in their forms,
their wings of fire,
their nitrogen teeth,
their parts that I don't know how to assemble,
drowning
or breathing
or making their way
between the trash
and the frost,
smiling at the millions of hoggish babies
that dead stars have given birth to.

Thaís Espaillat

RESIDENCIAL BOLÍVAR

Brinquemos desnudos
por los techos
de tu residencial
con las manos
pintadas de escaleras

Que nos vea la luna,
y el ángel de los mormones,
y la gente del edificio de en frente;
brillando como los botones
de un pantalón que se cae.

Quizás sea cierto
eso que oí un día,
que debajo de la iglesia
hay un búnker para
el fin de mundo
y tengamos que brincar
hasta allá
cuando salga el sol
y el mundo tenga
que hacerse de nuevo.

No sé qué pasará
cuando ya no haya
más azoteas
que llenar
de cenizas,
ni techos que saltar

Pero no me sueltes,
por favor.
Que yo no sé
volar
como tú.

Thaís Espaillat

BOLÍVAR RESIDENTIAL COMPLEX

Let's skip naked
on the roofs
of your complex,
our hands
painted from staircases.

Let the moon see us,
and the angel of the Mormons,
and the people of the building out front;
shining like the buttons
of trousers that fall down.

Maybe it's true
what I heard one day,
that under the church
there's a bunker for
the end of the world,
and we'll have to leap
over there
when the sun comes up
and the world has
to remake itself.

I don't know what will happen
when there are no longer
more rooftops
to fill
with ashes,
no roofs to jump over.

But don't let go of me,
please.
For I don't know
how to fly
like you do.

Sonia Farmer

SIRENOMELIA

There's never a happy ending to this chapter. No records of Anne's child exist. In one version, Anne leaves it. In another version, it is stillborn.

In this version, Anne must have played house with Jack for months only to wake from the dream with childbirth.

She clutches a stained bundle of sheets and wails. A large wave breaking onto the sand can be heard in a roar just outside the window: *Are you ready to return to me?*

She opens the door and lets the sea take the sheets, and then the child with a fused tail, and then herself. She hopes what they say about the sea and grief is true: that bathing in a leaving tide will wash the sadness straight out of your soul.

She lights a candle every night in the window of the house on the shore. It is a lighthouse, she decides. That is to say, it is a tombstone. Nothing returns to shore as whole as it left.

Sonia Farmer

SIRENOMELIA

Jamás tiene un final feliz este capítulo. No existen registros de la criatura de Anne. En una versión, Anne la deja. En otra versión, es mortinata.

En esta versión, Anne debe haber jugado a la casita con Jack durante meses hasta que el parto la despertó del sueño.

Ella se agarra a un brazado de sábanas manchadas y gime. Se puede oír el rugir de una gran ola rompiendo en la arena justo fuera de la ventana: *¿Estás lista para volver a mí?*

Abre la puerta y deja que el mar se lleve las sábanas, y luego la criatura con la cola fusionada, y luego ella. Espera que lo que dicen del mar y el duelo sea verdad: que bañarse en marea menguante limpia por completo la tristeza de tu alma.

Prende una vela todas las noches en la ventana de la casa en la orilla. Es un faro, decide. Es decir, es una lápida. Nada vuelve a la orilla tan entero como cuando se fue.

Sonia Farmer

THE TRIAL

I can always tell us apart
in airport lines.
It is best if we not
let ourselves be known;
those tied to an island
don't know how to
see it the right way.

I plead guilty – I do not see it
a bright flashy poster way,
a scattered cartoon logo way,
an endless sandy beach way.

I plead guilty to hating
the tourist girl there
with perfect teeth
in love after a five-day-four-night
honeymoon – saying
love as if she were versed
in the many shapes
of it, the many weights of it.

How smooth her words are,
how sharp mine – how much
they cut my mouth, get stuck
in my throat.

Little girl, have you ever
bitten down on a conch pearl?
Love here is like that: sometimes
you lose things –
or else the ugly slug of your tongue

Sonia Farmer

EL JUICIO

Siempre puedo distinguirnos
en las filas de aeropuerto.
Es mejor que no nos demos
a conocer;
los que estamos atados a una isla
no sabemos cómo
verla de la forma correcta.

Me declaro culpable – no la veo
como un poster brilloso y llamativo,
como un logo con un batiburrillo de caricaturas,
como una interminable playa de arena.

Me declaro culpable de odiar
la niña turista esa
con dientes perfectos
enamorada después de una luna de miel
de cinco días y cuatro noches – diciendo
amor como si estuviera versada
en sus muchas formas,
en sus muchas cargas.

Qué suaves son sus palabras,
que agudas las mías – cuánto
cortan mi boca, se atrancan
en mi garganta.

Muchachita, alguna vez
has mordido una perla de concha?
El amor aquí es así: a veces
pierdes cosas –
o más bien la fea babosa de tu lengua

makes from all the sharp
little words an unexpectedly
perfect globe of desire,
and then another and another,
until you wear this longing
around your neck.

The island is not your lover
until it has broken your teeth
then asked you to stay a while longer
while you hang yourself with
its gifts.

I plead guilty to conspire:
once, a lover pressed his mouth
to the phone and said
come back, but I could not hear him.
I heard only the ocean in my ears
and felt only these salty sighs
breaking on my teeth.

I plead guilty to placing the sand
in his shoes one grain at a time,
day by day; I plead guilty
to knowing it would only end
with our underwater words:
I never meant to flood your house,
I only meant to drown it.

hace de todas las
palabritas punzantes un inesperado
globo perfecto de deseo,
y luego otro y otro,
hasta que llevas este anhelo
alrededor de tu cuello.

La isla no es tu amante
hasta que ha roto tus dientes
para luego pedirte que te quedes un poquito más
mientras te ahorcas con
sus regalos.

Me declaro culpable de conspirar:
una vez, un amante pegó su boca
al teléfono y dijo
vuelve, pero no le pude oír.
Oí solo el océano en mis orejas
y solo sentí estos suspiros salados
rompiendo en mis dientes.

Me declaro culpable de haber puesto arena
en sus zapatos grano a grano,
día tras día; me declaro culpable
de saber que solamente terminaría
con nuestras palabras submarinas:
Jamás quise inundar tu casa,
solamente la quise ahogar.

Sonia Farmer

THE OTHER WOMAN

We are not sure when exactly Anne met fellow disguised female pirate Mary Read. They may have met on Nassau, or they may have met when Jack's crew intercepted a Dutch merchant ship.

In one version, they have an affair. This is a limited understanding of what would become a relationship so complex, even Calico Jack could not crack it.

Anne stares at the young man signing the ship records. She is remembering her dream, the one where she is another who is part of her. Is she in love with Mark Read? Is Mark Read in love with her?

They decipher each other's faces. Anne thinks of a diver's feet burned by fire coral. A bird tucked under the arm of a wave. The struggle of seaweed. She touches Mark's face and Mark tries to say he is Mary but nothing comes out because they both know what they see in the lines of their faces and it needs no words. The others they may call it sun damage but these two they know well the consequences of desire.

Sonia Farmer

LA OTRA MUJER

No sabemos con seguridad exactamente cuándo Anne conoció a la otra pirata vestida de hombre, Mary Read. Puede que se conocieran en Nassau, o puede que se conocieran cuando la tripulación de Jack interceptó un buque mercante holandés.

En una versión, tienen un affaire. Esta es una visión limitada de lo que se convertiría en una relación tan compleja, ni siquiera Calicó Jack la pudo adivinar.

Anne mira intensamente al joven que firma los artículos del barco. Recuerda su sueño, ese en el que ella es otra que es parte de ella. ¿Está ella enamorada de Mark Read? ¿Está Mark Read enamorado de ella?

Se descifran la cara, la una a la otra. Anne piensa en los pies de un buceador quemados por coral de fuego. Un pájaro metido bajo el brazo de una ola. La riña de las algas. Le toca la cara a Mark y Mark intenta decir que él es Mary pero no le sale nada porque ambos entienden lo que ven en las líneas de sus caras y no necesita palabras. Los otros pueden llamarlos efectos del sol, pero estas dos las conocen bien las consecuencias del deseo.

Gelsys García Lorenzo

ESPERA

En el sueño hay una casa de techo a dos aguas. Tengo el presentimiento de que algo comenzará a caer de súbito. ¿Anfibios? ¿Sangre? ¿Cuerpos desmembrados? ¿Muñecas de plástico? ¿Carne enlatada? ¿Envoltorios de nailon? ¿Periódicos sobre los que alguien ha dormido? Todo el sueño estoy allí mirando. La casa es la Revolución: inmensa, con un falso portón, con cariátides, con bombillos fluorescentes. Y espero todo el tiempo que algo caiga lentamente: como un bautizo o como una profanación, no sé bien. Nunca cae nada, pero sé que en algún momento pasará.

Gelsys García Lorenzo

WAITING

In the dream there is a house with a gable roof. I have a premonition that something will suddenly start to fall. Amphibians? Blood? Dismembered bodies? Plastic dolls? Canned meat? Plastic wraps? Newspapers someone has slept on top of? All the dream, I'm there watching. The house is the Revolution: immense, with a fake gate, with caryatids, with fluorescent bulbs. And all the time, I'm waiting for something to slowly fall: like a baptism or a desecration, I don't really know. Nothing ever falls, but I know that at some point it will happen.

Gelsys García Lorenzo

PEREGRINO

Un país que peregrina el año entero. Un camino interminable. Velas, girasoles, rodillas sangrantes, cruces improvisadas, escapularios rústicos, fotos, mechones de pelo, pies descalzos. Nomadismo de la superstición. Un pueblo que cruza de un extremo a otro la isla. Casi 1000 km en dirección Occidente para ver una escultura de yeso de un hombre tullido en una pequeña capilla al lado del leprosorio. Casi 1000 km hacia el Oriente para acceder a otro santuario donde hay una pequeña muñequita ataviada en oro. Un país que va de la lepra y la carne supurante a la joyería, a la corona de diamantes y oro que un Papa mandó ponerle a una dudosa imagen hallada en altamar, una imagen escapada de un naufragio.

No importa en qué dirección se recorran esos 1000 km: en un sitio u otro están los mismos rostros, las mismas velas, continuando esa marcha indetenible que es la Revolución.

Gelsys García Lorenzo

PILGRIM

A country that goes on pilgrimage the entire year. An endless road. Candles, sunflowers, bleeding knees, improvised crosses, rustic scapulars, photos, strands of hair, bare feet. Superstitious nomadism. A people that crosses the island from one end to the other. Nearly 1000 km westward to see a plaster sculpture of a crippled man in a small chapel next to the leprosarium. Almost 1000 km to the East to access another sanctuary where there is a small doll attired in gold. A country that goes from leprosy and suppurating flesh to jewellery, to the crown of diamonds and gold that a Pope ordered to be put on a dubious image found on the high seas, an image that escaped from a shipwreck.

It doesn't matter in which direction these 1000 km are travelled: in one place or another, there are the same faces, the same candles, continuing that unstoppable march that is the Revolution.

Gelsys García Lorenzo

LOS TRES AUTÓMATAS

Los tres célebres autómatas del siglo XVIII nos parecen burdos hoy, sus mecanismos simplistas. Sin embargo, continúan hablando de condiciones inalterables. El acto de la escritura queda inmortalizado. Nadie duda de que sempiternamente continuaremos escribiendo, no importa sobre cuál superficie ni qué caracteres, ni qué código empleemos: en esencia, el acto de escribir será el mismo. Luego está el dibujante: el visionario, la sublimación del sentido visual: alegato de que habrá que seguir mirando en busca de lo que hay debajo. Y finalmente, la figura femenina del conjunto de la que han afirmado los más generalistas que toca el piano y otros con un poco más especificidad que toca el órgano. En verdad es una clavecinista: ejecutora de un instrumento del que muy poco ya conocemos. Figura que nos fuerza a redefinir el mundo una y otra vez cada vez que escuchamos sus notas.

Gelsys García Lorenzo

THE THREE AUTOMATONS

The three celebrated automatons of the eighteenth-century seem crude to us today, their mechanisms simplistic. However, they still speak to unalterable conditions. The act of writing is immortalized. No one doubts that we will continue to write eternally, no matter on which surface or what characters, or what code we use: in essence, the act of writing will be the same. Then there's the drawing one: the visionary, the sublimation of the visual sense: an affirmation that we have to continue looking in search of what is here below. And finally, the feminine figure in the ensemble, who, most generalists have affirmed, plays the piano, or others, with a little more specificity, the organ. In truth, she is a harpsichordist: she is the performer of an instrument that very few of us now know. A figure that forces us to redefine the world again and again each time we listen to her notes.

Gelsys García Lorenzo

EL DICTADOR

El dictador como un invento decimonónico.
Un invento bello,
magnífico,
atractivo,
pero inútil.
Un invento más allá de las leyes del mercado,
para admirar en un museo de maravillas,
en una exposición de curiosidades,
para verlo unos segundos
y dejarlo atrás
y olvidarlo para siempre.

El dictador como un reloj de viento o un piano de vapor.

Gelsys García Lorenzo

THE DICTATOR

The dictator as a nineteenth-century invention.
A beautiful invention,
magnificent,
attractive,
but useless.
An invention that's beyond the laws of the marketplace,
to be admired in a museum of wonders,
in an exhibition of curiosities,
to be seen for a few seconds,
and be left behind
and forgotten forever.

The dictator as a wind-clock or a steam piano.

Gelsys García Lorenzo

DON'T STOP IT

El imperialismo es una máquina
expendedora de chicles.
Cigarrillos apagados
luego de tres bocanadas de humo.
72 estrellitas de plástico.
Paranoia.
Franjas azules y rojas para jugar a la rayuela.
Ancianitas que cruzan la calle
con una escopeta como bastón.
El imperialismo es una máquina de sentido.
Indetenible.

Gelsys García Lorenzo

DON'T STOP IT

Imperialism is a gum
vending machine.
Cigarettes stubbed out
after three puffs of smoke.
72 small plastic stars.
Paranoia.
Blue and red rows for playing hopscotch.
Little old ladies crossing the street
with a shotgun for a cane.
Imperialism is a meaning-making machine.
Unstoppable.

Millicent A. A. Graham

THE GATHERING

For nine nights we gather
coffee mugs and white rum, with round bread
to feed our dead and those that have travelled

from far. We come when the cusp
of day reddens heaven, and there is
no famine of tears, when the families wring out

their hearts like wet rags and hang them
on old cedar slabs. We come
with our heads dressed, with candles,

each face a twisted wick;
to raise a song, to chant,
flailing like shaken leaves

Millicent A. A. Graham

EL JUNTE

Durante nueve noches recogemos
tazas de café y ron blanco, con pan redondo
para alimentar a nuestros muertos y aquellos que viajaron

desde lejos. Llegamos cuando la cúspide
del día enrojece el cielo, y no hay
hambruna de lágrimas, cuando las familias escurren

sus corazones como trapos húmedos y los cuelgan
en una plancha de cedro. Llegamos
con la cabeza cubierta, con velas,

cada cara una mecha retorcida;
nos levantamos a cantar, un canto,
moviéndonos con arrebato, como
hojas temblorosas.

Millicent A. A. Graham

CATADUPA

It's tourist time in Catadupa. Yesterday's air
is sealed in a kindergarten desk. No hand comes
to lift the lid to screw face at cheese-trix crumbs
alive in webs and planets of chewed out bubblegum.
Nothing trickles from the tarnished gold
lip of the standpipe in the raked yard where
the earth has forgotten the hash of soles.
No one is sick today. The chainey root
and raw-moon bush have caused the pot-
water to rise. River cataracts spew as well,
tossing an occasional rosebud-apple.
Here, everyone is gathering wooden birds to sell.
Behind the black huffs of the steamer,
and the charge of that one-eyed bull,
is the pelting song of a Singer
sewing machine, spitting out tracks of new clothes
to barter for a few pound notes.
That was before the '90s, when we measured out
too small a cloth for ourselves, before we sought
new routes, eastward, through the
mountain way.
Funny how the school is empty, still;
machines derail and birds decay.

Millicent A. A. Graham

CATADUPA

Es temporada turística en Catadupa. El aire de ayer
está sellado en un pupitre de kínder. No llega ninguna mano
a levantar la tapa para mirar con cara de desdén las migas
de cheese-trix vivas en telarañas y los planetas de chicle mascado.
Nada gotea del deslustrado labio dorado
de la toma de agua en el patio rastrillado donde
la tierra ha olvidado las pisadas entrecruzadas de suelas.
Nadie está enfermo hoy. La *chainey root*
y el *raw-moon bush* han hecho que las aguas
potables subieran. Las cataratas de río también salpican,
soltando una pomarrosa de vez en cuando.
Aquí, todos recogen pájaros de madera para vender.
Detrás de los negros resoplidos del tren de vapor
y la carga de este buey de un solo ojo,
está la canción martilleante de la máquina
Singer, escupiendo vías de prendas nuevas
que canjear por unos pocos billetes de libra.
Esto fue antes de los noventa, cuando mediamos una tela
demasiado pequeña para nosotros, antes de que buscáramos
nuevas rutas, por la montaña, hacia el este.
Qué raro que la escuela esté vacía, silente;
las maquinas descarrilan y los pájaros se pudren.

Millicent A. A. Graham

THE ROAD

Take the country road, press on till you reach
the corner where the shops are burnt
orange, with the doors pealed open
and a stoop; coloured by the Maroon mud

'til a stranger waves back in un-expectation,
and you can't help but smile, naked
as those dangling boys

Keep to the broken rind
that holds the serrated tracks
of a people who have pressed on

Millicent A. A. Graham

EL CAMINO

Coge la carretera del campo, persevera hasta que llegues
a la esquina donde los kioscos son naranja
quemado, con las puertas peladas de par en par
y un escalón pintado por el barro de Cimarrones

hasta que un extraño te devuelve el saludo
sin esperar algo de ti, y tienes que sonreír, desnudo
como esos chicos sentados en el muro con las piernas colgando

Mantente dentro de la peladura rota
del camino donde hay las huellas rugosas dejadas
por una gente que ha perseverado.

Zulema Gutiérrez Lozano

TODOS LOS DÍAS A LA MISMA HORA

/ se alargan los edificios hasta el cielo / tú me besas y te retuerces encima de mis tetas / tú y los otros están sobre mis tetas / y mis espejuelos de sol / y el sol también sobre mis tetas pero todos creen que es una pelota de playa / no son de goma pero soportan el peso del mundo calladitas / tómate el agua sucia de la calle / el odio de los vecinos / los partidos de fútbol repletos de inocentes y asesinos / el ajedrez con sus movimientos inteligentes / bébete el vino de la viña podrida de tus padres / y la musiquita depresiva de los adolescentes de tu vida / bonita mierda tu vida / no vayas a gritar/ espera pasar los cuarenta y busca la mejor posición para tu edad / lee a los clásicos y finge entenderlo todo / no hagas preguntas y critica a las que no entienden a los clásicos/ llámalas putas sucias / pobrecitas chicas de verano / míralas desde tu altura porque tus tetas aguantan como diosas griegas / ¿cómo vas a desmayarte en medio de la calle? / un algodoncito perfumado entre las tetas / un blister de redondelitos azules entre las tetas / el secreto del éxito ¿también entre las tetas? / el cielo luce lejano y pequeño como un grano de azúcar / lejano / pequeño y da vueltas / damos vueltas con los ojos entrecerrados y los edificios se adormecen con el sonido de mi bastón contra las rocas de un camino de fin de semana / el bastón de ciega criatura inocente contra el odio de los días / te siento llegar desde el vientre / desde la cima de los edificios que me crecen en el vientre / soy Alicia adormecida y lúdica / ¿qué quieres insecto azul? / ¿qué más podrías quitarme? / cuál es el idioma para traducir el humo de tu narguile / ¿llegaré intacta? / o me perderé en el descampado / cerca de un tren que pasa todos los días a la misma hora /

Zulema Gutiérrez Lozano

EVERY DAY AT THE SAME TIME

/ the buildings stretch up to the sky / you kiss me and squirm on top
of my breasts / you and the others are above my breasts / and my
sunglasses / and the sun is also over my breasts but everyone thinks
it's a beach ball/ they're not made of rubber, but they quietly support
the weight of the world / drink in the dirty street water/ the hatred
of the neighbours / the football matches crowded with innocents and
murderers / the chess games' intelligent moves / drink up the wine
of your parents' putrid vineyard / and the depressing music of the
teenagers in your life / your life's lovely shit / don't go around
screaming / wait until you pass forty, and look around for the best
situation at your age / read the classics and pretend to understand
everything / don't ask questions and criticize those who don't
understand the classics / call them dirty whores / poor little summer
girls / look at them from your elevated height because your breasts
poke up like Greek goddesses / how are you going to faint in the
middle of the street? / a perfumed cotton ball between your breasts
/ a blister pack of little round blues between your breasts / is the secret
of success between your breasts, too? / the sky looks distant and as
small as a grain of sugar / distant / small and turning / we spin with
our eyes half-closed, and the buildings are lulled by the sound of my
cane against the rocks of a weekend walk / the cane of a blind,
innocent being against the hatred of days / from my belly, I feel you
arriving/ from the top of the buildings growing in my belly/ I'm Alice,
sleepy and playful / what do you want blue insect? / what else could
you take away from me? / what is the language to translate the smoke
from your hookah / will I arrive intact? / or will I get lost in the open
lot / near a train which passes every day at the same time? /

Zulema Gutiérrez Lozano

METRALLA

/ hay algo que destroza más que el miedo / martilla el vientre y me
retuerce las vísceras pujando por salirse de mi carne / jaula insípida/
aguanto porque soy una mujer con dos hombres dentro / algunos
claman por el ángel / solo Dios podría detener la sombra / pero Dios
se está merendando un par de niños en la mesa del fondo de un bar
de carretera / mientras el blues es el único baño de luz sobre las
sombras / es temible la guerra / pero la metralla no es nada / hay algo
que destroza más que el miedo / alguna vez fui inocente / fui dos niños
cogidos de la mano / dos futuros monstruos tendidos sobre la hierba
para contar los pétalos de su flor preferida / dos niños que son uno
/ dos niños que son yo misma / la mujer con ojos de noche / la que
toma paciente su trago en la barra del mismo bar de carretera donde
Dios vierte pimienta sobre vísceras y dedos infantiles / del otro lado
de la puerta / ángel contra demonio / demonio contra demonio /
ángel contra ángel / y todos contra Dios que engulle dedos
salpimentados con placer / yo y mis dos hombres sangramos en
correspondencia a nuestra altura mientras diamantes rojos salen por
mi naríz / acertaron contra el pecho y el vientre de los jugadores de
billar / su sangre atrae a las ratas del sótano / Dios las mira con codicia
/ podría engullirlas de un solo bocado / ¿qué es eso de disparar
diamantes por orificios tan pequeños? / comentan a mis espaldas /
algunos consultan enciclopedias médicas para hallar la causa de tal
desajuste / otros bajan la mirada y aprietan el paso / tal es el miedo
a los disparos / a las piedras preciosas / a las narices ajenas / pero hay
cosas que se mueven entre la gente y destrozan más que el miedo /

Zulema Gutiérrez Lozano

SHRAPNEL

/ there is something that destroys more than fear does / it hammers my belly and twists my viscera, pushing to come out of my flesh / insipid cage / I hold it in because I am a woman with two men inside / some cry for the angel / only God would be able to stop the shadow / but God is snacking on a couple of children at the table at the back of a roadside bar / meanwhile the blues is the only light bathing the shadows / war is dreadful / but shrapnel is nothing / there is something that destroys more than fear / I once was innocent / I was two children holding hands / two future monsters lying on the grass, counting the petals of their favourite flower / two children who are one / two children who are myself / the woman with night eyes / the one who patiently sips her drink at the counter of the same roadside bar where God pours pepper on children's guts and fingers / from the other side of the door / angel against demon / demon against demon / angel against angel / and all against God, who pleasurably gulps down seasoned fingers / my two men and I bleed in proportion to our height while red diamonds come out of my nose, / striking against the chest and belly of the pool players / their blood attracts basement rats / God looks at the rats greedily / he could gobble them up in a single bite / what is this firing of diamonds out through such small orifices? / they comment behind my back / some of them consult medical encyclopedias to find the cause of such a disorder / others lower their gaze and hurry away / such is the fear of the shots / of the precious stones / of the noses of others / but there are things that pass between people and destroy more than fear does /

157

Zulema Gutiérrez Lozano

DEL OTRO LADO DE LA NOCHE

/ antes de la balacera el maletero estaba cargado y era el centro de nuestra alegría / debajo del puente haremos la parada / ¿has visto morir a alguien? / pregunta Sofía / he visto a Dios masturbarse frente a la foto de una pelirroja / he visto tus muslos y tus tetas morirse de la pena porque no son del agrado de Dios / aunque seas pelirroja / le pellizco el pezón izquierdo / ella se ríe y comienza a quitarse la ropa en el asiento delantero del Mustang / ¿a Dios le gustará la humedad entre mis piernas? / salto sobre ella / olvido que Dios no tiene puntos débiles / eso pasó antes de la balacera / Sofía es una mancha roja que la carretera incorpora como un tatuaje / Sofía lo dio todo por Dios que siempre tenía el maletero cargado y era feliz / Sofía se apagó como los truenos que rompen la alegría / la alegría que aguarda por un puente para volar al otro lado de la noche / después de la balacera Dios grita que está listo para irse / pero es mentira / Dios no puede morir / Dios folla pelirrojas en el asiento trasero de un Mustang / y estar listo es una mentira / siempre supe cómo ser Dios / pero Dios no está en ninguna parte / nadie me sostiene mientras me desangro / y la lluvia comienza a derramarse / después de la balacera /

Zulema Gutiérrez Lozano

FROM THE OTHER SIDE OF NIGHT

/ before the shower of bullets the trunk was loaded and was the centre
of our happiness / under the bridge we'll make a stop / have you seen
someone die? / Sofia asks / I've seen God masturbate in front of the
photo of a redhead / I've seen your thighs and breasts die of shame
because they're not to God's liking / even though you're a redhead
/ I pinch her left nipple/ she laughs and starts to take off her clothes
in the front seat of the Mustang/would God like the wetness between
my legs? / I jump on her / I forget that God doesn't have weak spots
/ this happened before the shooting/ Sofia is a red stain the highway
absorbs like a tattoo / Sofia, who always had a full trunk and was
happy, gave God everything / Sofia went out like lightning that
shatters happiness / the happiness awaiting a bridge for flying to the
other side of night / after the shooting God shouts that he's ready to
go / but it's a lie / God can't die / God fucks redheads in the back seat
of a Mustang/ and being ready is a lie / I always knew how to be God
/ but God isn't anywhere/ no one holds me up while I bleed out/ and
the rain starts to pour / after the shootout /

Khadijah Ibrahiim

THE ATTIC IS A SILENT PLACE

"We speak to you by parables, but would willingly bring you to the
right, simple, easy, and ingenuous exposition, understanding, decla-
ration, and knowledge of all secrets."

Each room at Grandma's house
had its own story with secrets
concealed in sky-high ceilings,
covings and walls,
like the attic room on the 2nd floor
where the door was rarely opened,
if at all.

Steps snaked up to the attic
where cobwebs hung, and nobody
ever talked about going there —
unlike the three-room basement,
another dark place of damp and cold
with a kitchen range aged with time
and an old pine door, repaired
with bent-up nails, that creaked.

The basement led to the back yard where
washing was hung and soil dug hard
like back home in Jamaica,
a sprawling gooseberry bush hugged the wall
and berries were picked for wine 'n jam treats.
But way up in the attic, darkness stood still —
and dusty rails and door handles
were a sign not to enter.

It took a curious mind, an adventurous
soul — or a fass child whose ears

Khadijah Ibrahiim

EL DESVÁN ES UN LUGAR SILENCIOSO

"Les hablamos con parábolas, pero de buena gana les traería la correcta, simple, fácil, e ingenua exposición, comprensión, declaración, y conocimiento de todos los secretos."

Cada cuarto en la casa de abuela
tenía su propia historia con secretos
ocultos en techos altísimos,
molduras y paredes,
como el desván en el segundo piso
donde la puerta rara vez estaba abierta,
por no decir nunca.

Los pasos serpenteaban hasta el desván
donde colgaban telarañas, y nadie
hablaba nunca de ir allí –
a diferencia del sótano de tres espacios,
otro sitio oscuro, húmedo y frío
con un fogón de cocina envejecido con los años
y una puerta vieja de pino, reparada
con clavos doblados, que chirriaba.

El sótano llevaba al patio trasero donde
se tendía la colada y el suelo era duro de cavar
como en nuestra Jamaica,
un arbusto trepador de grosellas abrazaba el muro
y se recogían las grosellas para hacer meriendas de vino y mermelada.
Pero en lo alto del desván, la oscuridad se detenía –
y los pasamanos y los tiradores de puerta polvorientos
eran señal de no entrar.

Hacía falta una mente curiosa, un alma
aventurera – o una niña precoz, dura

too hard – who couldn't resist discovering
another den for Samantha, Wayne and I
to play in during school holidays.

The attic was a silent place, with a single
dim bulb that added to the mystery.
A flick of the switch and an Aladdin's
cave was found, four rooms filled with junk,
all kinds of things: used chemistry sets –
from Uncle Douglas –
old boxes with family names,
and other things not quite belonging,
things you couldn't place –
like the room next to the stairs.

It smelled earthy, musty, a place
that invited no questions, just acceptance.
In it stood a table covered with a white cloth
clean as the day, a red one too.
Candles dressed the table as if an altar
in St Augustine's church where I gave out hymnbooks,
and next to it was a robe or apron,
its use mysterious, for at the age of seven –
too shy to ask questions,
since I would have to admit to being nosey –
I had to keep the secret of what I'd seen.

Thirty years and more, with 56 Cowper St
demolished a time ago by
Chapeltown's cries for modernisation,
(re-gentrification from beneath our feet),
and with Grandma's ashes scattered and
Grandad then living at Roxholme Grove,
these childhood adventures
were a sepia thought at the back of my mind,
until I met an elder,

de oído – que no pudiera resistirse a descubrir
otro escondrijo donde Samantha, Wayne y yo
pudiéramos jugar durante las vacaciones escolares.

El desván era un lugar silencioso, con una sola
bombilla tenue que añadía misterio.
Al encender la luz aparecía una cueva de
Aladino, cuatro cuartitos llenos de porquería,
todo tipo de cosas: kits de química usados –
del tío Douglas –
cajas viejas con nombres de familiares,
y otras cosas que no tenían lugar,
cosas sin categoría –
como el cuartito al lado de las escaleras.

Olía a tierra, a cerrado, un sitio
que no contemplaba preguntas, solo aceptación.
Ahí, había una mesa cubierta con un paño blanco
limpio como la primera luz del día, uno de rojo también.
Unas velas adornaban la mesa como si fuera un altar
en la iglesia de St. Augustine donde yo repartía himnarios,
y al lado había una bata o un delantal,
su uso un misterio, porque a la edad de siete años –
demasiado tímida para hacer preguntas,
ya que tendría que admitir que era entrometida –
tuve que guardar el secreto de lo que había visto.

Treinta años y más, con el 56 de la calle Cowper
demolido hacía un tiempo por
los gritos de Chapeltown para la modernización,
(re-gentrificación desde debajo de nuestros pies)
y con las cenizas de abuela esparcidas y
abuelo viviendo en Roxholme Grove,
estas aventuras de niñez
eran un pensamiento en sepia perdido en mi cabeza,
hasta que conocí a una anciana,

a Jamaican-born woman,
who, after introductions and smiles
and a kind exchange of words,
revealed her links to my grandparents,
mentioned her Rosicrucian faith,
and at that moment the attic room
at Cowper Street came back and
I began to imagine its purpose –
to seek self-knowing –
as a secret to be kept, better not revealed.

In big people talk the mystery of things
never leaves you, until they are made clear.

nacida en Jamaica,
que, después de presentaciones y sonrisas
y un intercambio amable de palabras,
reveló sus vínculos con mis abuelos,
mencionó su fe rosacruz,
y en ese momento recordé el cuartito del desván
en la calle Cowper y
empecé a imaginar su propósito —
lograr conocerse a sí mismo
un secreto que es mejor que sea guardado, en lugar de revelado.

En palabras de mayores el misterio de las cosas
nunca te abandona, hasta que se aclara.

Khadijah Ibrahiim

ROCK AGAINST RACISM

In our back-to-back and through-terraced houses,
working-class black and white
youth played Snap!
Sex Pistols latched onto this white heat,
graffitied Elizabeth's head,
stuck two fingers up, wore safety-pins
and spat on the Union Jack.
We watched them pogo dancing up and down
to The Clash's *white riot* of reggae-snatched rhythms,
while Maggie snatched milk,
brought recession and the poll tax.
And when The Specials rocked against racism,
they marched right past my street
up to Potternewton Park
'til it was *like a zebra crossing, black and white,*
black and white as far as you can see.

Khadijah Ibrahiim

ROCK CONTRA EL RACISMO

En nuestras casitas adosadas, viviendas sociales en hilera,
jóvenes negros y blancos de clase obrera
jugaban a Snap!
Los Sex Pistols se agarraban a este calor blanco,
grafiteaban la cabeza de Isabel,
levantaban dos dedos malos, llevaban imperdibles
y escupían en la Union Jack.
Los mirábamos bailar pogo brincando arriba y abajo
al son de *white riot* de The Clash,
ritmos robados del reggae,
mientras Maggie robaba la leche,
traía la recesión y el impuesto a la comunidad.
Y cuando The Specials tocaban rock en contra del racismo,
marchaban justo en frente de mi calle
hacia el parque Potternewton, hasta que era
como *un paso de cebra, negro y blanco,*
negro y blanco hasta donde alcanza la vista.

Khadijah Ibrahiim

WHEN MY TIME COME

"The lord is my shepherd I shall not want,
He maketh me to lie down in green pastures"
     — Psalm 23

Mi dear chile,
we are livin' in our last days,
so when mi time come,
I waant to be buried in mi red suit,
the one I just buy.

I buy a new one every five years
just for de occasion,
I like to keep with the fashion
and dis suit favour de roses in my garden –
you know how I love dem so.

So look here, child,
when mi time come I waant you
to remember
dis is de suit I waant to be buried in,
de red one right here,
trailing from neck to hem
wid beads and silk embroidery
just like royalty,
a colour of importance.
I saw de queen wearing one just like it pon TV.

So remember wat mi show you;
see how it tailor stitched in and out
with good threads,
like mi granny use to do.
She bury in red too.

168

Khadijah Ibrahiim

CUANDO LLEGUE MI HORA

"El Señor es mi pastor; nada me falta.
En verdes praderas me hace descansar"
— Salmo 23

M'ija querida,
vivimos nuestros últimos días
pues, cuando llegue mi hora,
quiero que me entierren en mi traje rojo,
el que compré hace poquito.

Me compro uno nuevo cada cinco años
solo para la ocasión,
me gusta estar al día con la moda
y este traje se parece a las rosas de mi jardín –
ya tú sabes cómo me gustan.

Entonces, mira, m'ija,
cuando llegue mi hora quiero
que recuerdes
que este es el traje en el que quiero ser enterrada
el rojo este de aquí,
que fluye desde el cuello hasta el dobladillo
con bordado de seda y pedrería
igualito a la realeza,
un color de importancia.
Vi que la Reina llevaba uno
exactamente igual en la TV.

Entonces, recuerda qué te enseñé,
ves el entalle perfecto dentro y fuera
con buenos hilos,
como hacía mi abuelita.
A ella también la enterraron de rojo.

169

And when de Lord calls
I want to be wearing a red suit,
de one I handpick especially –
I walk de whole day till carn bun mi toes.

I like to look good at all times,
no-one is going to say
I never dress away till de end of my days.
Mi buy mi suit from Marks and Spencer,
all mi underwear too,
put dem in de trunk
with all mi fine nightwear and tings,
fold in camphor balls.
Mi a ole woman, 75 years just gone,
but mi a no fool,
mi make all mi plans;
put down insurance
fe horse-drawn carriage,
gospel singers, saxophone player,
and a red rose for each and every one.

Mi no waant bury a England,
mi waant mi ashes spread cross de River
Thames, make de waves teck
mi back to which part mi did come from.

And when all and sundries come to the house,
start dig, stake claim to what dem waant,
to wat dem no waant,
when tears flare and tongues clash difference,
I want my daughter to remember
dis is the red suit I waant to be buried in,

the red one, right here.

Y cuando el Señor me llame
quiero llevar puesto un traje rojo
el que escogí especialmente –
caminé todo el día hasta que me ardieron los callos de los dedos.

Me gusta verme bien en todo momento,
nadie dirá que
no me vestía nunca bien hasta el fin de mis días.
Me compré el traje en Marks and Spencer,
toda la ropa interior también,
la puse en el baúl
con todos los camisones finos y cositas,
doblados con bolas de alcanfor.
Soy una viejita, 75 años se fueron, así como así,
pero no soy una pendeja
lo tengo todo planeado;
pagué en plazos el seguro
para el coche fúnebre tirado por caballos,
cantantes de góspel, un saxofonista,
y una rosa roja para todos y cada uno.

No quiero ser enterrada en Inglaterra,
quiero que mis cenizas sean esparcidas
en el río Támesis, para que las olas me lleven
de vuelta al lugar de donde yo vengo.

Y cuando toda clase de gente venga a casa,
y ellos empiecen a escarbar, reclamen – como buscadores de oro –
lo que quieren y lo que no quieren,
cuando se enciendan las lágrimas y se desate el duelo de lenguas,
quiero que mi hija recuerde que
ese es el traje en el que
quiero que me entierren,

el rojo, ese mismo.

Yaissa Jiménez

PUERTO DE LA MUERTE

Puerto de la muerte,
así bautizarán a Sansoucí a partir del día cero.
Cuando el tiempo se paralice,
de las lágrimas de Yemayá
nacerá un hechizo aterrador.
Del fondo de la mar
saldrán flotando los cuerpos,
todas las hijas de la luna
volverán a reclamar justicia,
flotarán en las aguas
y encallarán directo en el ferry
y en los pesqueros.
Que la cúpula de turistas sea testigo,
que se espanten, que vomiten,
que se les encoja el alma.
Que este mar de cuerpos muertos
avise que en la isla encantada
la inquisición no ha terminado,
que aquí las brujas aún son asesinadas.

Yaissa Jiménez

PUERTO DE LA MUERTE

Puerto de la Muerte,
from day zero, that's how Sansouci will be baptised.
When time is paralysed,
a horrifying spell will be born
from Yemayá's tears.
From the bottom of the sea,
corpses will float up.
All the daughters of the moon
will come back to demand justice.
They will drift in the waters,
washing up against the ferry
and the fishing boats.
So that the tourists from their domed lookout will bear witness,
panic and vomit,
their souls shrinking.
So that this sea of dead bodies
announces that the inquisition hasn't ended
in the enchanted island,
that here, witches are still being murdered.

Yaissa Jiménez

TE LA VUELVO A TRAER

A Chavela Vargas

El regreso, Chavela hoy regresa.
Refutas y le dices a su lengua
que no te hable, que duele.
A su boca que no te bese, que pica.
A sus dedos que no te toquen,
Chavela, que te pintan.
Soy de las que te alientan a sentirla,
y es con su ropa puesta, mi bella,
que te beso el alma,
que te sobo las tetas, Chavela,
que te beso la espalda.
Es sin temor, Chavela, que te la recuerdo,
para eso uso flores en mi cabello,
para eso te pinto su firma con mi saliva.
No soy yo, Chavela, son sus ojos que te miran.
No soy yo, Chavela, nunca lo he sido,
soy ella, ha vuelto Chavela
para decirte que te quiere besar.
Entrégame el trago y bébelo en mi boca,
hazte mil mundos en tu cabeza, hermosa,
que no tengo más palabras para evocarla.
Entre tus piernas, Chavela, ni siquiera respiro.
Porque te quiere morder el alma Frida,
porque te quiero morder el alma yo.
Cuando la noche se acabe,
guardarás el rifle escondido en tu boca,
cuando el día vuelva, me vestiré
y tú me buscarás de nuevo llorando,
pa'ver si gritar su nombre
la despierta y te vuelve a ver.

Yaissa Jiménez

I BRING HER BACK TO YOU AGAIN

To Chavela Vargas

The return, today Chavela comes back.
You deny it and tell her tongue
not to talk to you, that it hurts.
You tell her mouth not to kiss you, it itches.
You tell her fingers not to touch you,
Chavela, they paint you.
I'm one of those women who entreat you to feel her,
and it's with her clothes on, *mi bella,*
that I kiss your soul,
I caress your titties, Chavela,
I kiss your back.
It's without fear, Chavela, that I remind you of her,
that's why I use flowers in my hair,
that's why I paint her signature on you with my saliva.
It's not me, Chavela, it's her eyes that look at you.
It's not me, Chavela, it never has been,
I'm her, she's come back Chavela
to tell you that she wants to kiss you.
Hand me the drink and taste it in my mouth,
imagine a thousand worlds in your mind, *hermosa,*
since I have no more words to evoke her.
Between your legs, Chavela, I don't even breathe.
Because Frida wants to bite into your soul,
because I want to bite into your soul.
When the night is over,
you'll put away the rifle hidden in your mouth,
when the day comes again, I'll dress myself
and you'll look for me again crying,
to see if shouting her name
wakes her up and she sees you again.
To see if with my borrowed face

Pa'ver si con mi rostro prestado
te acoge en mi abrazo
y te mato el frío con copias de su calor.

she welcomes you with my embrace
and I warm you from the killing cold
with copies of her heat.

Yaissa Jiménez

CAPERUZA NO LE TEME A NADA

Caperuza no le teme a nada.
Ni al puñal, ni al deseo, ni a las alas.
No le teme a su risa
ni a la risa burlona
de los que persiguen su desdén.

No le teme ni siquiera al silencio,
ni a que llene la nada
con su incómoda presencia.
Caperuza no les teme a los recuerdos,
menos al que dejó su padre en su pelvis desnuda.

No le teme al frío literal,
No le teme a frío poético,
ni al banal y menos al metafórico.
Tiene tiempo sin temerle al fuego,
ni a las dagas ardientes.
No le teme al temor,
la muy valiente no le teme al olvido.
Caperuza no le teme al mar,
ni a las bestias, ni al clima.
Se mete en la tierra herida
y deja que las alimañas coman de su carne viva.
No le teme al viento,
se deja en la brisa
y permite que la azote contra las montañas.

Desde hace mucho
Caperuza busca miedos nuevos.
Se come las espinas
buscando sentir el ardor
del aviso previo del peligro.

Yaissa Jiménez

RIDING HOOD FEARS NOTHING

Riding Hood doesn't fear anything.
Not the dagger, desire, or the wings.
She doesn't fear her own laughter
or the giggling mocking
of those showing their disdain.

She isn't even afraid of the silence,
or that it fills the nothingness
with its uncomfortable presence.
Riding Hood doesn't fear reminiscence,
except memories her father left in her naked pelvis.

She isn't afraid of cold that's literal.
She doesn't fear the cold that's poetic
banal, or, much less, metaphorical.
It's been a while since she feared fire
or burning blade.
She doesn't fear fear,
so brave, she's not afraid of oblivion.
Riding Hood doesn't fear the sea,
or beasts, or the weather.
She moves over the wounded earth
and lets vermin feed on her living flesh.
She doesn't fear the wind,
she gives herself to the breeze
and allows it to whip her against the mountains.

For a long time,
Riding Hood has been looking for new terrors.
She eats thorns
wanting to feel the ardour
of a danger warning.

Busca en los frascos de su bruja favorita
alguna yerba obsesiva
que amenace con quitarle la vida.
Pero cuando lo intenta,
Caperuza se ve sin emociones a la vista
y bebe el contenido
sin siquiera ver temblar la mano.

Caperuza busca ser esclava.
Procura tal locura
para acudir a un regazo cálido
que le quite lo sola
y sentirse al fin susceptible
a la inclemencia del miedo puro.

She searches in the flasks of her favourite witch
for some herbal obsession
that threatens to take away her life.
But when she tries it,
Riding Hood finds herself emotionless
and drinks the contents
her hand not even quivering.

Riding Hood seeks to be a slave.
She procures such madness,
to turn to a warm lap
so that she won't be alone,
finally feeling susceptible
to the mercilessness of pure fear.

Cindy Jiménez-Vera

STILL LIFE

Escoge un objeto fácil,
como las uñas de tu madre muerta.

Cuando hayas escogido el objeto,
colócalo en una mesa o en el piso.
A veces, el objeto está colocado en un ataúd.
En esos casos ya no hay opción.

Asegúrate de que haya una fuente directa de luz.
Las lámparas de la funeraria pueden funcionar.
Si no hay energía eléctrica disponible,
lleva una vela y una caja de fósforos para encenderla.

Mira el objeto detenidamente.
Tómate seis minutos.
Es el tiempo suficiente para que te lo creas.
Esa que yace en el féretro
te dio la vida hace unos años.
Muy pocos. Quizá menos de los que te quedan.

Comienza a dibujar el objeto
por cualquier parte
con la que te sientas cómodo:
la placa, la cutícula, la lúnula,
o el pliegue lateral de la uña.
Evita dibujar la matriz.
Es la parte viva y la más importante.
La matriz de la uña produce células sanas
— por eso las uñas de los muertos siguen creciendo en la tumba —,
y el objeto que hemos de dibujar
debe ser completamente inanimado.

182

Cindy Jiménez-Vera

STILL LIFE

Select a simple object,
like the fingernails of your dead mother.

When you have chosen the object,
place it on a table or on the floor.
Sometimes, the object is located in a casket.
In such cases, there isn't an option.

Make sure there is a source of direct light.
Funeral parlour lamps can work.
If no electric power is available,
bring a candle and a box of matches to light it.

Gaze closely at the object.
Take six minutes.
That's enough time for you to believe it.
The one who lies in the coffin
gave you life a few years ago.
Very few. Maybe less than what you have left.

Begin to draw the object,
starting with any part
that makes you feel comfortable:
the plate, cuticle, lunula,
or side walls of the nail.
Avoid drawing the matrix.
It's the living and most important part.
The nail matrix produces healthy cells
– that's why nails of the dead keep growing in the grave – ,
and the object that we have to draw
must be completely inanimate.

Luego de trabajar las sombras de las uñas
con el grafito o con la técnica de tu preferencia, añade detalles:
manchas, quebraduras, rasgos de esmalte, sucio.

Toma descansos cuando sea necesario,
es un proceso que conlleva tiempo.
Piensa en los árboles que sembró con esas uñas.
¿Acaso crecieron de un día para otro?

Cuando termines el dibujo, obsérvalo detenidamente.
Sigue practicando.

After shading the nails with graphite
or with the technique of your preference, add details:
stains, chips, flecks of polish, grime.

Rest when needed,
it's a process that takes time.
Think about the trees she planted with these nails.
Did they just grow from one day to the next?

When you finish the drawing, observe it closely.
Keep practicing.

Cindy Jiménez-Vera

DISNEY ON ICE

El metro va atestado de niñas vestidas con tules rosados, amarillos, azules y blancos. Algunas llevan tiaras sobre sus cabezas. Un ejército de madres y algún padre que no tuvo más remedio que cambiar el partido de béisbol televisado por una función dominical de princesas de Disney sobre hielo les acompañan. Al llegar frente al Coliseo, donde en pocos minutos empezará la función que tanto había soñado ver su hija, el ruido de la multitud parece silenciarse con la mirada de terror de esta joven madre.

Hace algunos años, en lugar del Coliseo que yace frente a sus ojos, había una comunidad llamada Tokío. De niña creció feliz junto a su abuelo. Luego llegaron ellos con su idea de erigir una estructura colosal para eventos de todo tipo y promesas de brindarles ayudas para mudarlos a una vivienda mejor. Estarían tan bien amparados que podrían tener una casa propia. El abuelo quien lucía sus canas por astucia, más que por sus años, se negó rotundamente a mudarse de Tokío. Ante la inminencia de la destrucción de su casa, envío a la niña con un tío en la ciudad. Los demoledores entraron a desalojar al único habitante testarudo que se negó a salir.

El cadáver colgó del techo. Pegado al vientre llevó un papel que leía: *sáquenme ustedes a mí y al peso de mi mierda, hijos de puta.*

Inmóvil, entre el tren y el andén, la joven madre sostiene con gran fuerza la mano de su pequeña, quien tiene una varita mágica en la otra. ¿O es un cetro de princesa de Disney?

Cindy Jiménez-Vera

DISNEY ON ICE

The subway is crowded with girls dressed in pink, yellow, blue, and white tulles. Some wear tiaras on their heads. Accompanying them is an army of mothers, and some father who didn't have any choice but give up his televised baseball game for a Sunday showing of Disney princesses on ice. Upon arriving in front of the Colosseum, where in a few minutes the show that her daughter has dreamed of so much will start, the noise of the multitude is seemingly silenced by this young mother's look of terror.

Some years ago, instead of the Colosseum that looms before their eyes, there had been a community called Tokío. As a child, she grew up happy with her grandfather. Then they came with their idea to erect a colossal structure, for events of all kinds, and promises to provide her grandfather with help to move them to better housing. They would be so well looked after that they would be able to have their own house. The grandfather, who had grey hair more for his wisdom than for his years, flatly refused to move from Tokío. Given the imminent threat of destruction of his home, he sent the girl to an uncle in the city. The demolition crew entered to evict the only stubborn inhabitant who refused to get out.

The corpse was hanging from the ceiling. A piece of paper stuck to his stomach read: *you take me out, me and the weight of my shit, you sons of bitches.*

Motionless, between the train and the platform, the young mother tightly holds the hand of her little girl, who has a magic wand in her other one. Or is it the sceptre of a Disney princess?

Cindy Jiménez-Vera

FRENTE A LA XILOGRAFÍA SIN TÍTULO (2000) DE MARTA PÉREZ GARCÍA

Las mujeres rurales
somos más de un tercio
de la población mundial,
y el 43 por ciento
de la mano de obra agrícola.
Labramos la tierra,
y plantamos las semillas
que alimentan naciones enteras.
Pero, el hombre
nos condena a la pobreza,
nos priva del mismo acceso a la tierra,
créditos, materiales agrícolas,
mercados y cadenas de productos
cultivados de alto valor.
En su lugar, nos convida
al trabajo invisible y no remunerado
llamado amor incondicional,
sacrificio de madre,
abnegación de abuela,
ejemplo de esposa.
Y, así callamos esta violencia
de vivir en peores condiciones
que los campesinos
y las mujeres urbanas.
Por eso, nuestros actos políticos
son producto del afecto.

Ayer, fui una mujer de Lares
con trenzas largas.
Enseñé a muchos hombres
a organizarse y luchar

Cindy Jiménez-Vera

STANDING BEFORE THE UNTITLED WOODCUT (2000) BY MARTA PÉREZ GARCÍA

We rural women
are more than one-third
of the world population,
and 43 percent
of the agricultural labour force.
We work the land
and plant the seeds
that feed entire nations.
But men
condemn us to poverty,
deprive us of the same access to land,
credit, agricultural supplies,
markets, and high-end
produce networks.
Instead, they bid us to do
invisible, uncompensated work,
called unconditional love,
maternal sacrifice,
disavowal of grandmother,
exemplary wife.
And, that's why we keep quiet
about this violence
of living in worse conditions
than the peasant farmers
and city women.
That is why our political actions
are products of affection.

Yesterday, I was a woman of Lares
with long braids.
I taught many men

contra los colonizadores españoles.
Pero, la historia me recuerda
porque cosí una bandera
para que un hombre diera la misa
y otros hombres declararan la República.

También fui una mujer
que criaba gallinas ponedoras
en Arecibo, Puerto Rico.
Mis hijos
se alimentaron de sus huevos
de un amarillo feroz
como el hambre.
Y con la mantequilla y la leche
de las vacas que ordeñé
todos fueron a la universidad.
Algunos dejaron la isla
para abrirse una esperanza
de otro color
el de la migración.
Su producción intelectual
es materia de estudio
en varios países.
Nadie habla de mí.

Hoy soy una de las patronas de Veracruz.
Cocino para cientos de migrantes
centroamericanos que viajan
encima de un tren
hacia los Estados Unidos.
Almaceno la comida,
la reviso, la preparo y la sirvo.
Espero a la orilla de las vías.
Cargo bolsas de comida caliente
y agua fresca
porque algunos no han comido

to organize themselves and fight
against Spanish colonizers.
But, history remembers me
because I sewed a flag
so that a man would give mass
and other men declare the Republic.

I was also a woman
who raised laying hens
in Arecibo, Puerto Rico.
My children
were fed on their eggs,
as fierce a yellow
as hunger.
And with the milk and butter
of the cows I milked,
all of them went to the university.
Some left the island
to expose themselves to hope
of another colour,
that of migration.
Their intellectual output
is material for study
in various countries.
No one speaks about me.

Today, I am one of the *patronas* of Veracruz.
I cook for hundreds of
Central American migrants
who travel towards the United States
atop a train.
I store the food,
check it, prepare it, and serve it.
I wait at the edge of the tracks.
I carry bags of hot food
and fresh water

desde hace más de una semana.
Corro para estar lista
para el paso de La Bestia.
Y les lanzo los alimentos.
Con esta obra de afecto
desde mi cuerpo agreste
y mis manos rurales
no solucionaré el mundo.
Solucionaré la vida.
Y eso es algo.
Porque querer a la gente no cuesta,
son hermanos de la humanidad.
Graciasmadregracias,
quédiostebendiga
me gritan hondureños, salvadoreños,
guatemaltecos, y nicaragüenses,
desde La Bestia en movimiento.
Me toco el pecho desde lejos.
Este amor me pinta el vientre
de colores alucinantes.
Mira mis espigas
de un barroco antillano,
naturaleza salvaje.
Mi piel queda al relieve
tras la plancha perdida
de la versificación
que irrumpe con violencia
esta madera de donde brotan
ojos, bocas, lenguas, torsos,
animalia, destrozo
creador de la vida.
Fíjate bien,
hombre,
ahora mismo
todos los animales
se alargan como el trigo

because some haven't eaten
for more than a week.
I run to be ready for when
La Bestia passes.
And I throw the food to them.
With this affectionate act
by my undomesticated body
and my rural hands,
I won't fix the world.
I will solve *life*.
And that's something.
Because loving people doesn't cost anything,
they're our brothers in humanity.
Thankyoumotherthankyou,
maygodblessyou,
Hondurans, Salvadorans, Guatemalans,
and Nicaraguans shout
from La Bestia in motion.
I am touched, from afar.
This love paints my belly
in stunning colours.
Look at my stalks of wheat,
their baroque,
wild Antillean nature.
My skin remains, put into relief,
by the poetry of
reduction cuts
that burst with violence
across this wood,
where eyes, mouths, tongues, torsos,
animalia, devastation,
creator of life
all sprout.
Take note,
men,
now all the animals

en saludo glorioso
a las mujeres rurales
como esperanza de futuro
y entre todos ellos
hay un espacio para ti.

rise up tall like wheat
in glorious greeting
to rural women,
a hope for the future,
and amongst them all,
there is a space for you.

Ann-Margaret Lim

AT THE KARAOKE BAR, 21ST CENTURY HOTEL

I sit at the bar in the 21st Century Hotel
Beijing, drinking cheap Chinese liquor.
The room is dark, full of smoke, with a song
scrolling on the screen I crane my neck to follow.
There's a man. Girls look into his eyes
as he caresses the mic and sings.

His song stops and a girl takes the mic
and he floats over to me and says:
You're very pretty, orders me American whisky.
And I remember you, Daddy,
telling me how your parents shipped you off at six
to Canton, to know your culture.

I remember you playing the harmonica,
the banjo, singing Chinese opera,
telling me stories of being brown in China,
being loved by a Chinese stepmother;
of girls intrigued by an oval face,
long brown limbs and massive waves of hair;
of being the village basketball star.

I remember how we talked
and think: tomorrow I'll pack
the Mao cap, Chinese cigarettes,
Fung Fung Yen, Fa Chung for my daddy.

Ann-Margaret Lim

EN EL BAR DE KARAOKE, HOTEL 21st CENTURY

Sentada en el bar del Hotel 21st Century
Beijín, bebo licor chino barato.
La habitación está oscura, llena de humo, con una canción,
corriendo por la pantalla, que estiro mi cuello para poder seguir.
Hay un hombre. Las chicas le miran a los ojos
mientras él acaricia el micrófono y canta.

Su canción se detiene y una chica coge el micrófono
y él se me acerca suavecito y me dice:
Eres muy bonita, me pide un whisky americano.
Y me acuerdo de ti, papi,
contándome como tus padres te enviaron a los seis años
a Cantón, para que conocieras tu cultura.

Te recuerdo tocando la harmónica,
el banjo, cantando ópera china,
contándome historias sobre ser moreno en China,
ser querido por una madrastra china;
de chicas intrigadas por una cara ovalada,
extremidades morenas largas y pelo ondulado en abundancia;
sobre ser la estrella de baloncesto del pueblo.

Recuerdo cómo hablábamos
y pienso: mañana empacaré
la gorra de Mao, cigarrillos chinos
Fung Fung Yen, Fa Chung para mi papi.

Ann-Margaret Lim

ON READING THISTLEWOOD'S DIARY

*The songs of the slave represent the sorrows of his heart; and he is relieved by
them, only as an aching heart is relieved by its tears.*

— Frederick Douglass

III

Dear Phibbah,

Your name half-rhymes with Syvah —
the dance move that's in.
So when I think of you, I say,
Syvah, syvah, syvah, like in the song,
and you know, Phibbah, it's not a bad comparison,
for when women syvah, they squat for takeoff,
spread wings and fly.

When they syvah, Phibbah,
their feet remember
the wheels and turns you did
at fellow slaves' wakes,
singing, *When I die hallelujah bye, bye
I'll fly away.*

And the takeoff,
when the body comes fully into play,
is the throwing off of shackles,
and I sing: *Syvah, syvah, syvah,*
and think of you, Phibbah,
in miserable slavery.

How you suffered through each infection
Thistlewood gave you

Ann-Margaret Lim

AL LEER EL DIARIO DE THISLEWOOD

Las canciones del esclavo representan los pesares de su corazón; y
le alivian, solo como las lágrimas alivian a un corazón dolorido.
— Frederick Douglass

III

Estimada Phibbah,

Tu nombre casi rima con Syvah —
el paso de baile que está de moda.
Así que cuando pienso en ti, digo,
Syvah, syvah, syvah, como en la canción
y tú sabes, Phibbah, no es una mala comparación
porque cuando las mujeres hacen syvah, se agachan para lanzarse,
despliegan las alas y vuelan.

Cuando ellas hacen syvah, Phibbah,
sus pies recuerdan
las vueltas y giros que hacías
en los velatorios de compañeros esclavos,
cantando, *Cuando yo muera, aleluya, adiós, adiós*
echaré a volar.

Y el levantamiento,
cuando el cuerpo entra completamente en acción,
es para romper y liberarse de los grilletes,
y yo canto: *Syvah, syvah, syvah*,
y pienso en ti, Phibbah,
en la miserable esclavitud.

Cuánto sufriste por culpa de cada infección que
Thistlewood te pasó,

as he cummed every skirt it crossed his mind to fuck;
how you must have wailed when his son –
your mulatto child died.
This wasn't in the diary. He kept it 'dignified'.
And as the women release in
syvah, syvah, syvah,
their hands like albatross' wings,
I think: *Phibbah, in what moment*
did you hatch your freedom plan
on this confounded man?

al llenar de su esperma cada falda con que le apetecía joder;
cuánto debes haber sollozado cuando el hijo de él —
tu niño mulato, murió.
Esto no estaba en el diario. Él lo mantuvo "digno".
Y en la descarga de
syvah, syvah, syvah,
cuando las mujeres levantan las manos
como alas de albatros,
pienso: *Phibbah*, ¿*en qué momento*
tramaste tu plan para ser liberada
de este hombre condenado?

Ann-Margaret Lim

STAR INTERVIEWS ANDRE BROWN

She wear dem black shoes to work every day
to play modda to two girls I never meet.

I wait for 'ar to come home to mi
an' de zinc room where wi sleep

with the snake in wi bellies,
till mawning bring one more empty day

an' I walk to school,
sell de rubber bands ah fin'

fo' de sling shot de boys play shooting wit';
fo' de rope de girls twist and skip.

At fourteen, ah look fi mine on de street.
She go church,

come home from work wit' stories
of two sistas inna exam;

in college;
at home, waiting.

An' I carry home mutton,
hook up cable,

an' she pray fi' mi
on 'ar knees.

Last year ah move 'ar up,
out a de zinc room.

An' last year de bwoy
dem hol' I.

Ann-Margaret Lim

STAR ENTREVISTA A ANDRE BROWN

Ella lleva esos zapatitos negros para trabajar cada día
para hacer de mamá a dos niñas que jamás he visto.

La espero a que vuelva a casa, a mí
y al cuartito de zinc donde dormimos

con una culebra en nuestras barrigas,
hasta que la mañana trae un nuevo día vacío

y camino a la escuela,
vendo gomitas que encuentro

para los tirachinas con los que los niños disparan;
para la cuerda con la que las niñas saltan y esquivan.

A los catorce, me las busco en la calle.
Ella va a la iglesia,

vuelve a casa del trabajo con cuentos
de las dos hermanas en un examen;

en la universidad y entonces
se quedan esperando en casa.

Y llevo cordero a casa,
conecto el cable,

y ella reza por mi
de rodillas.

El año pasado la saqué
del cuartito de zinc.

Y el año pasado Babylon
me encerró.

Hannah Lowe

DANCE CLASS

The best girls posed like poodles at a show
and Betty Finch, in lemon gauze and wrinkles,
swept her wooden cane along the rows
to lock our knees in place and turn our ankles.
I was a scandal in that class, big-footed
giant in lycra, joker in my tap shoes,
slapping on the off-beat while a hundred
tappers hit the wood. I missed the cues
each time. After, in the foyer, Dad,
a black man, stood among the Essex mothers
clad in leopard skin. He'd shake the keys
and scan the bloom of dancers where I hid
and whispered to another ballerina
he's the cab my mother sends for me.

Hannah Lowe

CLASE DE BAILE

Las mejores niñas posaban como caniches en un campeonato
y Betty Finch, de gasa amarillo limón y arrugas,
pasaba su bastón de madera por las filas para
ponernos las rodillas bien estiradas en posición y girarnos los tobillos.
Yo era una calamidad en esa clase, gigante vestida de lycra
de enormes pies, bufona con mis zapatos de claqué,
golpeando a contratiempo mientras cien
bailarines zapateaban la madera. Entraba cada vez
a destiempo. Después, en el vestíbulo, papá,
un hombre negro, estaba de pie entre las madres de Essex
vestido de piel de leopardo. Sacudía las llaves
y buscaba entre la floración de bailarinas dónde me escondía
y yo le susurraba a otra compañera
es el taxista que mi madre manda para mí.

Hannah Lowe

THREE TREASURES

Jamaica in the attic in a dark blue trunk,
sea-salt in the hinges. What must it look like
all that wide blue sea?

England downstairs in a rocking chair.
Nanna rocking with her playing cards,
cigs and toffee, tepid tea

Jamaica frying chicken in the kitchen,
pig-snout in the stew-pot,
breakfast pan of salt-fish, akee

China in the won-ton skin,
gold songbird on the brittle porcelain,
pink pagoda silk settee

Jamaica in the statues, lignum vitae heads
of dreadlocks; Anansi, rebel spider
in the storybooks, the poetry

England eating peaches on the patio,
hopscotching, Mum in wellies, secateurs
around the rosebush and the raspberries

England painting midnight with a sparkler,
cousins throwing Guy Fawkes on the bonfire,
orange ash confetti

England for the English in graffiti
on the roundabouts and bus-shelters,
Please Sir! on TV

Hannah Lowe

TRES TESOROS

Jamaica en el desván en un baúl azul oscuro,
sal de mar en las bisagras. ¿Cómo debe verse
todo ese ancho mar azul?

Inglaterra en el piso de abajo en una mecedera.
Abuelita meciéndose con su baraja de cartas,
cigarrillos y toffees, té tibio

Jamaica friendo pollo en la cocina,
morro de cerdo en el caldero,
sartén de pescado salado, *akee*

China en la pasta de won-ton,
pájaro cantor dorado en frágil porcelana,
diván de seda rosa pagoda

Jamaica en las figuras talladas, cabezas con rastas
hechas de *lignum vitae*. Anansi, araña rebelde
en los libros de cuentos, la poesía

Inglaterra comiendo melocotones en el patio,
jugando a la rayuela, Mamá con botas de agua, tijeras de podar
alrededor del rosal y las frambuesas

Inlgaterra pintando la medianoche con una bengala,
primos lanzando Guy Fawkes a la hoguera,
ceniza de confeti naranja

Inglaterra para los ingleses en grafitis
en los redondeles y paradas de autobús,
Please Sir! en la tele

Jamaica on the phone at 3 a.m.,
my father's back-home voice through fuzz
and crack: *My friend, long time no see*

China in the Cantonese he knew
but wouldn't speak, in letters stuffed
in shoe-boxes, ink-stick calligraphy

China in his slender bones,
in coral birds of stitched bamboo,
China in an origami butterfly, that flew

Jamaica en el teléfono a las 3 de la madrugada,
la voz jamaicana de mi padre atravesando la estática y
la crepitación: *Amigo mío, cuánto tiempo sin verte*

China en el cantonés que sabía
pero no hablaba, en cartas puestas
en cajas de zapatos, caligrafía de tinta de barra

China en su fina osamenta,
en el bordado de pájaros color coral y bambú,
China en una mariposa de origami, que voló

Hannah Lowe

FISHES

The doorbell rings all week while you are lying
          in the single bed downstairs, the curtains holding back
the winter light. Someone laughs in the kitchen.
          Everybody's smoking. *Your daddy dying, girl.* Barbara
with her Tupperware of rice and peas. Last week
          you called for this. Now we trickle water on your lips
and like a child, you lick, some instinct deep within you
          craves this small relief. Tuesday, Auntie Dy
is on the doorstep, saying *Hello Han* as though a decade
          hasn't passed and suddenly I'm in her arms, my aunt
who disappeared, returned. The doctor, shiny headed, African,
          calls you Mr Lowe, shouts *Please Sir, can you hear me?*
We speak in whispers at the door. He tells us what the night
          will bring. I see your brain cells then,
a thousand small fishes, crossing the ocean.

Hannah Lowe

PECES

El timbre suena toda la semana mientras estás acostado
        en la cama pequeña del piso de abajo, las cortinas atrapando
la luz invernal. Alguien ríe en la cocina.
        Todo el mundo está fumando. *Tu papi se está muriendo, chica.*
        Barbara
con su Tupperware de arroz con gandules. La semana pasada
        se lo pedías. Ahora te rociamos los labios con agua
y como un niño, te los relames, algún instinto en lo más profundo de tu ser
        tiene antojo de este pequeño alivio. El martes, la tití Dy
está en el umbral de la puerta, diciendo *Hola Han* como si una década
        no hubiera pasado y de golpe estoy en sus brazos, mi tía
que desapareció, regresó. El médico, cabeza lustrosa, africano,
        te llama Sr. Lowe, grita *¿Por favor, señor, me oye?*
Hablamos a susurros en la puerta. Él nos cuenta qué traerá
        la noche. En ese momento, veo tus células cerebrales,
mil pececitos, cruzando el océano.

Canisia Lubrin

GIVE BACK OUR CHILDREN

Born
with mouthfuls of ocean
give back our looted brains
our boys with shackles
at the scrotum, that manhood
famed for, sentient for DNA,
unaided. Earthquake models
of pissing whips. We need
no deep-cut postures
to support the weight
of plotted shadows, drifting
the wild quadrupeds
in our girl's starlit tears
still, fractured, refusing
to water our own
pillaged times

Our children are born
with mouthfuls of cotton
hands full of plantation
dirt. We need no deep
conversations about them,
dead, still hanging
like dried cassava, aplomb
free inside our quarky throats
while we're still walking
long, long miles charged
and singing, or morphed,
in immigrant schemata.
To be heard is, to exist is,
to exit virtual news-
worthiness. The voice, second

Canisia Lubrin

DEVUELVAN A NUESTROS NIÑOS

Nacidos
con bocas llenas de océano
devuelvan nuestros cerebros saqueados
nuestros niños con grilletes
en el escroto, esa hombría
celebrada, reconocidos por ese ADN,
desamparados. Modelos de terremotos
de látigos y meado. No necesitamos
posturas profundamente laceradas
para sostener el peso
de sombras trazadas,
los cuadrúpedos salvajes flotando
en las lágrimas de nuestras niñas, iluminadas por estrellas
inmóviles, fracturadas, negándose a
regar nuestras propia
época de pillaje

Nuestros niños nacen
con bocas llenas de algodón
manos llenas de tierra de la hacienda.
No necesitamos conversaciones profundas
sobre ellos, muertos,
todavía colgando
como yucas secas, con aplomo libres
dentro de nuestras gargantas compuestas de *quarks*
mientras todavía caminamos
tantas y tantas millas cargados
y cantando, o mutados,
en esquemas de inmigrantes.
Ser oído es, existir es,
dejar atrás noticias virtuales –
meritorio. La voz, segunda

213

class turning heavy
at some remount of numbered
warrantees. Give back
our children, still
born indigo

with mouthfuls
with mouthfuls of blood
with mouthfuls of arc
with mouthfuls of dreams
with mouths full of cotton
with mouths full
with mouths
thank all the deities
for their
root-thick hearts
for the cosmic bulk
of their lips

clase volviéndose pesada
en alguna reposición de garantías
numeradas. Devuelvan a
nuestros niños, aún
nacidos índigos

con bocas llenas
con bocas llenas de sangre
con bocas llenas de arco
con bocas llenas de sueños
con bocas llenas de algodón
con bocas llenas
con bocas
agradece a todas las deidades
por sus
corazones gruesos como raíces
por sus llenos
labios cósmicos

Canisia Lubrin

VILLAGE CRESCENDOS

Just because we're magic, doesn't mean we're not real.
        — Jesse Williams, BET Awards

The long reach of this Massav Tree into the square is yours,

still in sight of the savannah. But even that is untrue:
we still scraping for bread in the after-bond of our flesh and age.
Not the way we both lived in a valley by the bay, penniless
as the spider looks. Not according to the Christ's coming. I don't yet

know what to mean besides looking out for better days,
besides rags for women named after terrain so hot
volcano bow in shame. But don't forget we laughed: how we learned
to boil the morning

sun from the woods of this mabouya, the intimate heat
bursting rum barrels all over town. How to remove our self
from the mirror – how just leaving here
with our blood unboiling was no way to pay our passage
into that cold Victorian country,
to no longer have to stand before that god of grief in thanksgiving
for food you wouldn't want to feed a fly. How toward everything
we're owed, we offer our reconstituted spine.
Who knows why the long reach of our canoes roll and return
that old Rasta drum to its cut cattle, the thing we can afford to ignore.

Repeat after me: give them a bad time.
That rapid-like vapour of the dry season turning
stone to bread, that still-Bob rocking steady its herbed gospel,
even now, as bookie bucktooth a will as I can tie to the boundary
of your chaffed lips. Still as you hold up that passion vine
your little son used to tame unruly goats, to bind me to

Canisia Lubrin

CRESCENDOS DE ALDEA

Solo porque somos mágicos, no significa que no seamos reales.
  — Jesse Williams, Premios BET

El largo alcance de este árbol *Massav* hasta la plaza es tuyo,

todavía a la vista desde la sabana. Pero hasta eso no es verdadero:
escarbamos todavía para conseguir el pan en los pos-lazos de esclavitud
y fraternidad, en nuestra carne y época.
No de la manera en la que ambos vivíamos en un valle al lado de la bahía,
sin un centavo tal como se ve una araña.
No de acuerdo con la llegada de Cristo. Aún no sé

qué quiera decir además de buscar tiempos mejores,
además de trapos para mujeres que llevan el nombre de terrenos tan calientes
que el volcán se arrodilla avergonzado. Pero no olvides que nos reímos:
como aprendimos del bosque de este *mabouya*

a hervir el sol matutino, el calor íntimo
astillando barriles de ron por toda la ciudad. Como extirparnos
del espejo — como solamente saliendo de aquí
con nuestra sangre sin hervir no era forma de pagar nuestro pasaje
a este frío país victoriano,
para ya no tener que pararse en frente de ese dios de la tristeza dando las gracias
por comida con la que no querrías alimentar a una mosca. Como a todo
nos debemos, ofrecemos nuestras columnas vertebrales reconstituidas.
Quién sabe por qué el largo recorrido de nuestras canoas mece y devuelve
ese viejo tambor Rasta a su ganado despellejado, aquello
que podemos permitirnos ignorar.

Repite después de mí: haz que lo pasen malísimo.
Ese vapor rápido de la estación seca convierte la piedra
en pan, ese Bob todavía rocksteadyando su evangelio herbáceo,
incluso ahora, con toda la voluntad *bookie bucktooth* con la que puedo atar al borde

217

the unsettling of time in your gut, to make the years shadow
me like wheat transmutes grain: to be like rain,
wet with a decent happiness
to buff the scars that will not change me with your mouth
with river rock thrown mad on brown grass warning all
who think to enter and make ruse. What is today?
What calm period make them stories drift
in spite like the whole flow of mad rivers in this cropped island?

What collection of mothers we praise as they dip
their thumbs in the basin of each other's clavicles,
dab their foreheads with an oil as holy as their sweat
and nettle. You, gift my short heart some way to break –
Reach for me and let me feel myself be born
in that malady of troubles where bees still mark your throat.

So you sling back every letter on this half-burning page,
run its ash through time like metre through the line,
where shadows buss-up between
life and what short sound death make when it 'fraid.

Never there more desperate than anything
in a noose.

The impulse to drag your wretched arm out
from under that dome of burning bush and hallowed ground,
to spit out bittersweet root teas brewed for washing down
this life without sin,
this work of open windows,
splintered beds heat-bleached into practical jokes:

and you levy your anonymous coda against giving up,
against birth and plans for keeping alive –
by the heave of that same Massav branch.

de tus labios agrietados. Aún así, mientras tú sostienes la vid del maracuyá,
tu hijo pequeño amansaba cabras revoltosas para atarme
a la agitación del tiempo en tu tripa, para hacer que los años me acechen
como el trigo transmuta granos: para ser como lluvia,
mojada con una alegría decente
para dar brillo con tu boca a las cicatrices que no me cambiarán
con piedras del río tiradas con furia encima de la grama marrón
advirtiendo a todos quienes piensan entrar y hacer artimañas. ¿Hoy qué día es?
¿En qué plácido periodo están estos cuentos a flote
a pesar de todo el flujo de ríos furiosos en esta isla cultivada?

Qué colectiva de madres alabamos mientras se hunden
los pulgares la una a la otra en la pileta de sus clavículas,
untan ligeramente sus frentes con un aceite tan sagrado como su sudor
y ortiga. Tú, regálale a mi corto corazón alguna manera de romperse –
Tómame en brazos y déjame sentirme nacer
en esa dolencia de pesares, donde las abejas todavía marcan tu garganta.

Pues, tú retiras cada letra en esta página a medio quemar,
haces correr su ceniza a través del tiempo como la métrica a través del verso,
donde las sombras irrumpen entre
la vida y el sonido breve que hace la muerte cuando está asustada.

Nunca hay nada más desesperado que cualquier cosa
en un nudo corredizo.

El impulso de arrastrar tu brazo miserable
desde abajo de esa cúpula de arbusto ardiente y tierra sagrada,
para escupir agridulces infusiones de raíces hechas para limpiar y regar
esta vida sin pecado,
esta labor de ventanas abiertas,
astilladas camas blanqueadas por el calor
hasta convertirse en bromas pesadas:

y tú impones tu coda anónima en contra de rendirse,
en contra del nacimiento y los planes para mantenerse con vida –
por el vaivén de la misma rama de *Massav*.

Canisia Lubrin

TURN RIGHT AT THE DARKNESS

after Afua Cooper

Not a single cloud at summer's centre,
So vapours rise having run out of country,
of pavement to disappear in. Here,
this beginning season of straw hats: the basic bronze
of semi-nude tourists was like the dead, awaken

to walk through the wooden city blocks.
Montreal – what have you begun here?
Are these your Nouvelle-France remains
of an aboriginal dark? The place of here
that had died unfolding in creek, wood, totem?

But me. I am here for Marie-Joseph Angélique,
whose story pains still the boundaries of Old Montreal.
Not yet canonized with folk songs, with metonymy
of air tornado'd in the throat: hear me full of the tragedy of her life,
the black rubber keeping silent the exploding atoms in the power lines

that here still bespeaks the province. What still forms
the northern edge of the St. Lawrence? Holy Notre-Dame
singled in the high-priced art. Rue Berri burning what axis
levels through Saint-Laurent. Saint-Paul, how you bow
even lower at the parallel run of Notre-Dame.
None of you
ever touching.

But what brave cold scars the maker of repair I seek,
whether witness or destroyer in the tested language
of sunlight forming in the permalink of the savage child,
the shaman's shaman yet, the brass of forgetting still here speaks:

Canisia Lubrin

A LA OSCURIDAD, DOBLA A LA DERECHA

siguiendo a Afua Cooper

Ni una nube en medio del verano,
por eso los vapores se levantan al quedarse sin campo,
sin pavimento en el que desaparecer. Aquí,
este comienzo de la estación de sombreros de paja: el bronce básico
de turistas semidesnudos era como si los muertos despertaran

para caminar por las manzanas de una ciudad de madera.
¿Montreal—qué has empezado aquí?
¿Son estos tus restos de Nouvelle-France
de una oscuridad aborigen? ¿Aquí, el lugar
que había muerto en su recorrido a través de arroyo, bosque, tótem?

Pero yo, estoy aquí para Marie-Joseph Angélique,
cuya historia aún causa dolor a las fronteras del Viejo Montreal.
Todavía no canonizada en canciones populares, con metonimia
de aire girando como un tornado en la garganta: óyeme
llena de la tragedia de su vida,
mientras el caucho negro mantiene en silencio
los átomos que explotan en las líneas eléctricas

que aquí todavía señalan la provincia. ¿Qué forma todavía
el borde norte del San Lorenzo? La Sagrada Notre-Dame
singular en el arte de alto precio. Rue Berri enciende
el axis que cruza Boulevard Saint-Laurent. Más abajo
en el curso paralelo de Rue Notre-Dame,
como te arqueas, Rue Saint-Paul.
Ninguno de ustedes
se toca jamás.

Busco – pero qué frías cicatrices valientes – quién hace reparación,
ya sea testigo o destructor en el lenguaje inmemorial

unbury your vex, oh, glossed maple flame
in the amphetamine glass, the jaded plane,
mimic of Oort clouds, still an interstellar show
of how radical the water under pressure.

Like I seek Angélique, amorphous, disguised,
quantum of that dead man's cool,
in the rogue geometries of a dumb gallows
talking plain the danger as though it were a simple dip
on a map. A place to turn right
at the darkness
between here and the master's room.

de la luz solar que se forma en el enlace permanente del niño salvaje,
el chamán del chamán, sin embargo el latón del olvido aquí todavía habla:
    desentierra tus agravios, oh, lustrosa llama de arce
    en vidrio de anfetamina, el desencantado llano verde,
    imitación de la nube de Oort, todavía un espectáculo interestelar
de cuán radical es el agua bajo presión.

Como busco a Angélique, amorfa, disfrazada,
quantum de esa placidez de hombre muerto
en las geometrías rebeldes de una horca muda
hablando llanamente del peligro como si fuera una leve depresión
en un mapa. Un sitio donde doblar a la derecha
a la oscuridad
entre aquí y el cuarto del amo.

Shara McCallum

RACE

You are the original incognito.
Transparent, all things shine through you.
She's the whitest black girl you ever saw,
lighter than "flesh" in the Crayola box.
But, man, look at that ass and look at her shake it
were just words, not sticks or stones, flung
when dresses were the proof that clung like skin,
when lipstick stained brighter than any blood.
Girl, who is it now you'd want to see you?
And what would that mean: *to be seen?*
Why not make a blessing of what
all these years you've thought a curse?
You are so everywhere, so nowhere;
in plain sight you walk through walls.

Shara McCallum

RAZA

Eres la incógnita original.
Transparente, todo brilla a través de ti.
Es la chica negra más blanca que hayas visto jamás,
más clara que el "carne" de la caja de Crayolas.
Pero, chico, mira ese culo y mírala sacudirlo
solo eran palabras, no palos ni piedras, lanzadas
cuando los vestidos eran la prueba que se te agarraba como la piel,
cuando el pintalabios manchaba más brillante que cualquier sangre.
Chica, ¿quién tú quisieras que te viera ahora?
Y qué significaría eso: ¿*ser vista*?
¿Por qué no conviertes en bendición lo que
todos estos años has creído una maldición?
Estás tan en todos lados, tan en ningún lado;
a la vista de todos tú atraviesas paredes.

Shara McCallum

HISTORY AND MYTH

This was the most beautiful land that eye could behold...
                    —Christopher Columbus

The way mist shrouds mountains
                              Long ago I learned a lesson
salt roils inland from sea
                              in etymology
Nanny roams Cockpit Country
                              Xaymaca Arawak land of wood and water
Nanny leader of the Maroons
                              Santiago Spanish patron saint
mystifying the British
                              Jamaica brined in English
bouncing bullets off her backside
                              Long ago
refusing a treaty that would
                              I was made to understand
barter one's freedom for another's
                              history
Nanny like the goat so-named
                              is a word

          that will not cease bleating

Shara McCallum

HISTORIA Y MITO

Es la tierra más hermosa que ojos humanos hayan visto...
—Cristóbal Colón

La manera en que la niebla envuelve las montañas
                   Hace tiempo aprendí una lección
desde el mar, la sal se revuelve hacia tierra firme
               en etimología
Nanny ronda por Cockpit Country
               Xaymaca tierra arahuaca de madera y agua
Nanny líder de los Cimarrones
               Santiago santo patrón español
desconcertando a los británicos
               Jamaica puesta en salmuera en inglés
rebotando balas con su trasero
               Hace tiempo
rechazando un tratado que canjearía
               me hicieron comprender que
la libertad de unos por la de otros
               historia
Nanny, como la cabra así llamada
               es una palabra

               que no cesará de balar

Shara McCallum

WHAT I'M TELLING YOU

My father played music. He played a guitar and sang. My father recorded his songs in the same studio where Bob Marley played with his band. And if you know who Bob is and are thinking "One Love", dreadlocks, ganja, *hey mon*, then you are straying from the centre of this poem, which is the recording studio where I slept on the floor while my father sang and strummed his guitar. And where Bob, who was only a brother in *Twelve Tribes* to me at four or five, said to the man who called me *whitey gal* that I was not, that I was a daughter of Israel, that I was Stair's child. That same Bob who you've seen shaking his natty dreads and jumping up and down; that same man with the voice of liquid black gold became a legend in my mind too at four or five as a record somewhere in a studio in Jamaica started to spin.

Shara McCallum

LO QUE TE CUENTO

Mi padre tocaba música. Tocaba una guitarra y cantaba. Mi padre grababa sus canciones en el mismo estudio donde Bob Marley tocaba con su banda. Y si saben quién es Bob y están pensando "One Love", rastas, ganja, *hey mon*, entonces se están desviando del centro de este poema, que es el estudio de grabación donde yo dormía en el piso mientras mi padre cantaba y rasgaba su guitarra. Y donde Bob que para mí, a los cuatro o cinco años, solo era un hermano en Twelve Tribes, le dijo al hombre que me llamó *whitey gal* que no lo era, que era una hija de Israel, que era la niña de Stair. Ese mismo Bob al que han visto sacudiendo sus rastas y dando saltos; ese mismo hombre con la voz de oro negro líquido también se convirtió en una leyenda en mi mente a los cuatro o cinco años mientras un disco en algún lugar en un estudio de Jamaica empezaba a girar.

Jamila Medina Ríos

HUERTO

El útero
— con toda su carga simbólica —
pinzado
por patas agrulladas
de tijera:
incomparable con un brazo
con un pellizco en un brazo
incluso incomparable con la boca
una mordida en la boca.
El útero
abierto a recibir la sombrilla-medusa
el paraván tentacular
como la espina dorsal de algún pez frío.

Para qué abre una mujer las piernas
frente a la lengua dura del espéculo
y hace poner ahí una cortina de hierro.
Acompañada por la música del amolador de cuchillos
la mujer afila la filigrana de su locura
sexar sexar sexar
cerrar abrir serrar
el pasadizo de la respiración
tensar los límites del gozo
llegar al borde negro.
La madre extraída de la puta
con la extirpación del huerto
la mujer-la ye(r)ma
abierta-diluida
a recibir sin peligro la babaza
como un hoyo en la arena.

Por la tarde — en la tarde desmayada —
cuando el útero va regresando a su matriz

Jamila Medina Ríos

WOMB GARDEN

The uterus
– with all its symbolic load –
pinched
by crane legs
of scissors:
incomparable with an arm
with a pinch on an arm
even incomparable with the mouth
a bite inside the mouth.
The uterus
open to receive the jellyfish-umbrella
the tentacular torpedo
like the dorsal spine of some cold fish.

Why does a woman open her legs
in front of the hard tongue of the speculum
and have an iron curtain put up there.
Accompanied by the music of the knife grinder,
the woman sharpens the filigree of her madness
sex her sex her sex her
close open saw
the respiratory passageway
tighten up the limits of bliss
get to the black border.
The mother extracted from the whore
through excision of the garden plot
the woman-egg yolk or barren land
open-diluted
to receive with no danger the slick ooze
like a hole in the sand.

In the afternoon – in the weary afternoon –
when the uterus is returning to its matrix

231

como un cesto tejido de moluscos
aun sabiendo que no puede ejercitar los miembros
la mujer se abre provocando a entrar.

Qué desacompasado el pulso del amante
cuando penetra y cede
la seda roja del himen.
Qué despreocupado ahora
— el cuello torcido del útero
sellada la boca fría —
seguro
de que no habrá brazos que lo jalen.

Cuando la lengua de la medusa empieza
su cosquilleo indefenso
el amante todavía sonríe con la cabeza erguida
y pega dentro — amordazando —
con el pez martillo / con el pez serrucho / con la mano abierta.

¿A las puertas del huerto
quién se atreve a llamar
con ese golpeteo sordo?
Tanteando
        s o n r o j a d a
    alrededor del bálano brilloso
            — c o m o   e l   h í g a d o   c r u d o
                c o m o   e l   h í g a d o   r o j o —
                r e t r a y é n d o s e
como una anémona asustada
la sombrilla
acompasada
clava y enseña las varillas
lame
y desangra
se apoltrona
y muerde.

232

like a woven basket of molluscs
though knowing she can't exercise her privy members,
the woman opens up, provoking one to enter.

How the lover's pulse races
when he penetrates and yields
the red silk of the hymen.
How carefree now
— the torqued neck of the uterus
the cold mouth sealed —
sure
that arms won't be pulling on it.

When the language of the jellyfish begins
its helpless tingling
the lover still smiles with head erect
and slips it inside — love dance of squeezing in —
the hammerfish / the sawfish / and the open hand.

At the doors of the womb garden
who dares to call
with that dull thumping?
Groping
        flushed
    around the shiny tip
            — like raw liver
                like red liver —
        retracting
like a scared anemone
the rhythmic
umbrella
shoves in, showing its ribs
licks
and gushes blood out
snuggles in
and bites.

Jamila Medina Ríos

EN LOS APRISCOS

Siempre he envidiado la soledad de la celda, la sombra del corredor del fondo, la humedad de aquel útero, la daga que se clava en mitad del alma de los locos cuando gritan vencidos en los apriscos. La paz de la descarga eléctrica.

Paso en carros lentos por Mazorra, paso en carros rápidos, descarrilada en la montaña rusa, por la prisión de Guanajay. Tuerzo el cuello, imagino el paredón, la lava que se derrama del panóptico a los ventanales, taladrando la pared de las prisiones, el dedo fisgón de ojo del guardia hurgando en las camisas de fuerza y en las sayas de las legradas. ¿O es que se puede parir en prisión? Envidio habitar pues ese útero sin claro de bosque promisorio, encerrado en su celda, soñando un lecho de río como lodo.

De dónde este placer por la locura, la violencia, la teatralidad del travestido. Curiosidad malsana de voyeur. Simpatía por los masturbadores solitarios, por los psicoanalistas y sus histéricas, los pedófilos, los transexuales, los asesinos en serie, los drogadictos, los fetichistas, los evisceradores y las putas; empatía por absolutamente todos los que alimentan algún morbo o excentricidad. Coleccionistas de sellos y de carne.

Cuando me vuelva loca voy a gritar mancha de plátano, cuello de botella, blúmer de señora, mano de golpes, molleja. Cuando me lleven al manicomio, maniatada, transida, no voy a transmutarme en pez o rodaja fresca de pepino; voy a sentarme en una esquina a pensar cómo volverme una nada de corcho, un espejismo, un humo sobre el té, un molusco en la arena.

Jamila Medina Ríos

IN THE PENS

I have always envied the solitude of the cell, the shadow of the long-
distance runner, the moistness of that uterus, the dagger that sticks
in the middle of the soul of the insane when they scream defeated in
the pens. The peace of the electric discharge.

I pass by Mazorra in slow cars, I pass by in fast cars, derailed on the
roller coaster, by the prison of Guanajay. I crane my neck, imagine
the walled yard, the lava that flows from the panopticon to the
windows, drilling into the wall of the prisons, the prying finger of the
guard's eye poking at the straitjackets and skirts of those whose
uteruses have been scraped. Or is it possible to give birth in prison?
Well, then I envy inhabiting that uterus without the clearing of a
promising forest, locked in its cell, dreaming a river bed like mud.

Where did it come from? This pleasure for madness, violence, the
theatricality of the transvestite. Unhealthy voyeur curiosity. Sympa-
thy for solitary masturbators, for psychoanalysts and their hysteric
women, paedophiles, transsexuals, serial killers, drug addicts, fetish-
ists, eviscerators and whores; empathy for absolutely everyone who
feeds some morbidness or eccentricity. Collectors of stamps and
flesh.

When I go crazy, I'm going to shout plantain stain, bottleneck traffic,
lady's britches, ass-kicking beat-down, gizzards and sweetbreads.
When they take me to the insane asylum, handcuffed, in anguish, I
will not transmute myself into fish or a fresh slice of cucumber; I'm
going to sit in a corner and think about how to become the nothing
of cork, a mirage, steam over tea, a mollusc in the sand.

Jamila Medina Ríos

FUR(N)IA

El ejercicio de la escritura apostado fuera de la escritura y escindiéndola con el rabo del ojo. Una cisura practicada en una escritura que se insiste furnia.

Huecos de araña, huecos de nariz, boca, cuencas de ojos, oídos, vulva, vagina, bahía de bolsa, ombligo, ano. E incluso el descubrimiento de intersticios bajo la lengua, entre los dientes y la encía, debajo de la rodilla, encima del codo, en la jabonera de las clavículas, en los 16 arcos entre dedo y dedo de los pies, en las axilas, en el vacío de las manos juntas y de las manos echadas hacia atrás, en las comisuras, en las arrugas de la frente, en los labios agrietados, en el hedor de las patas de gallina, en la hendidura de la entrepierna, bajo el peso de las trenzas y los senos, en la nuca rendida, en la blandura del tobillo, en los valles y altozanos del vientre, en la morada debajo de las uñas, en los pliegues ilegibles de las palmas de las manos, en las furnias rajadas del nudillo. Mujer agujereada, mujer (alfombra) arrollada, mujer (paracaídas) plegadura.

Mujer ubre y odre y útero. Mujer embocadura de río. Máter. Materia. Madreperla sobre madrépora. Madre-del-verbo. Ave María. Damajuana.

Un cuerpo que desea a otro que soba y horada. Lecho de arena y concha, para ser (des)hollado. Playa, puerto, embarcadero, varadero, abrevadero, aliviadero, bebedero de yeguas y de patos.

Huevo. Ovario. Canasto.

Mujer de mimbre, caña flexible, cáñamo, flauta dulce, espiga, lirio desmadejado. Mujer de estambre. Punta bordada de mujer.
El ejercicio de la escritura como un latigazo en la carne para abrir zanjas y liberar fluidos. Mujer orines, mujer sangre, mujer fécula, mujer leche. Avalancha riada. Arrollo murmullo. Espumarajo arcada. Balanceo de columpio mujer. Nanadora. Acunadora. Sanadora. Vaina.

El ejercicio no como la erección de un panóptico sino como una obturación, ensanchamiento de la dilatación del ser habitada, explorada, cavada, perforada, aserrada, rajada, acribillada, trepanada, traspasada, desabrochada, desvirgada, defenestrada, abierta. La mujer

Jamila Medina Ríos

FUR(N)IA

The exercise of writing that is positioned outside of writing and split apart with cut-eye. A fissuring practised in writing that demands fury/sinkhole.

Spider holes, nose holes, mouth, eye sockets, ears, vulva, vagina, pocket bay, navel, anus. And even the discovery of interstices under the tongue, between the teeth and the gums, below the knee, on the elbow, in the soap dish of the clavicles, in the 16 arches between fingers and toes, in the armpits, in the emptiness of cupped hands and hands reaching backwards, in the corners of the lips, in forehead wrinkles, in chapped lips, in the stench of crow's feet, in the cleft of the crotch, under the weight of braids and breasts, on the furrowed nape, in the soft spot of the ankle, in the valleys and hillocks of the belly, in the abode under the finger nails, in the unreadable creases of the palms of the hands, in the sunken lines of the knuckles. Woman full of holes, rolled-up (rug) woman, furled (parachute) woman. Udder and wineskin and uterus woman. Rivermouth woman. Mater. Matter. Mother-of-pearl over mother-of-stony-coral. Mother-of-the-Word. Ave Maria. *Damajuana* seed.

A body that desires another which caresses and pierces. Sand bed and conch, to be footprinted / flayed. Beach, harbour, jetty, dry dock, watering trough, overflow channel, watering hole for mares and ducks. Egg. Ovary. Woven basket.

Wicker woman, flexible cane, hemp, wooden flute, stalk, wilted lily. Woven woman. Embroidered trim of a woman.
The exercise of writing like a whiplash in the flesh to open up trenches and release fluids. Urine woman, blood woman, starch woman, milk woman. Avalanche torrent. Murmur of creek flash-flooding. Foaming spit archway. Balancing of the swing woman. Lullaby woman. Cradle-rocker woman. Healer woman. Seedpod.

The exercise unlike the erection of a panopticon but rather like an obstruction, a widening of the dilatation of being inhabited, ex-plored, excavated, perforated, sawn, shredded, riddled, skull-drilled, breached, undone, cherry-popped, ousted, opened. The porous-

la porosa. La leporina, la li(e)bre, la leprada. Y el ejercicio como una amputación de lo que no tiene y sobra. Matadura del padre al excavar la raja. Matadura de la madre al ejercitar el equilibrio con las manos extendidas sobre el cordón umbilical, y saltar la cuerda, hacer pulsos, tobilleras y argollas de narigón, y jugar al ahorcado. Clava y clavadura. Encaje: con un ejercicio haciadentro y haciafuera de inserción y deserción. Furia y furnia.

Una escritura que se insiste ensenada tiene una rabia, una península confesa, oracular. El armadillo que se encueva, que se acoquina, que se aova, que se empolla, puede empezar a vomitar garras lenguas tentáculos pezuñas. Extremidades. Palpos, pulpos. Vecindades. Mano en la oscuridad. Arañazos hilos. Lengua anhelante. Imán. Hambrunas. La escritura vaso constrictor, la escritura contenida, la escritura conteniendo ser la escritura abrazo.

La voz de sirena corporizada perfume, pañuelito al viento, valla de publicidad. Mujer brazo gitano. Mujer brazo, duro, de la ley. Magnolia de acero. Magdalena desleída en el té, que atrae poderosamente... recuerdos. Lágrimas de cocodrilo. Estalactitas. Casimbas ojo del invierno. Mujer tijera, cuchillada, estaca, pica hielos, dientes de peineta, de sierra y de león. Mujer pasamontañas. Armadillo en chino: como el animal engalanado para cruzar la cordillera. Mujer muralla. Mujer fusta de cobra. Aviborada.

Mujer pócima. Una escritura que mata a la mujer alargando su veneno, si se deja crecer la lengua y se autosacia o penetra, como un ouroboros infernal. Hermafroditismo en el tacto. Una sensibilidad que se empoza y se amordaza con su propia tentación. Saca tu lengua, mujer, de la carnada. Cierra la boca. Los negros no se ríen alto, las mujeres no se abren tanto para comer o bostezar. Tápate eso, cochina. Una escritura que se mira y cuyo clítoris crece de excitación verbal es de temer. La furia en furnia. Silenciada. No la furnia en furia. Llamamiento. Llamarada. Esa mujer anémona. Hágase una p/ hiel líquida que apague a la ninfómana. Ábrase mujer linfa. Apurar el trago amargo, probar con la lengua una escritura sin muerte ni grito ni dolor. Sin hincar las rodillas... sobre granos de trigo. La letra con sangre entra. Déjate hacer. Dejarse hacer. Dejarse ser...

one woman. The harelip woman, the free / hare, the leper. And the exercise like an amputation of that which one doesn't have and has in excess. Friction burn of the father from excavating the slit. Friction burn of the mother from balancing with her hands extended over the umbilical cord, jumping rope, arm-wrestling, ankle-cuffs and nose rings and playing hangman. Nail and nail puncture wound. Lace-making/encasing: with an exercise inwards and outwards of insertion and desertion. Fury and sinkhole.

A writing that demands an inlet of rage, a confessed, oracular peninsula. The armadillo that burrows, that cringes, that lays eggs, that incubates, can start to vomit claws tongues tentacles hooves. Extremities. Palps, octopi. Vicinities. Hand in the dark. Scratches threads. Longing tongue. Magnet. Famines. The vein-constricting writing, the contained writing, the containing writing that is the writing embrace.

The voice of the siren embodying perfume, handkerchief in the wind, publicity billboard. Jellyroll woman, gypsy-arm-woman. Hard arm of the law woman. Steel magnolia. Madeleine dissolved in the tea that powerfully brings back… memories. Crocodile tears. Stalactites. Water well, the eye of winter. Scissor-woman, slash, stake, ice pick, teeth of the Spanish haircomb, of the saw and of the dandelion. Balaclava woman. Armadillo in Chinese: like an animal adorned to cross the mountain ridge. Fortified-wall-woman. Whip-of-the-team-of-mares-woman. Vipered woman.

Potion woman. A writing that kills a woman enlarging her venom, if she lets her tongue grow and satiates or penetrates herself, like an infernal ouroboros. Hermaphroditism in the touch. A sensibility of throwing oneself down the well and muzzling oneself with one's own temptation. Woman, take your tongue out of the bait. Close your mouth. Black people don't laugh loudly, women don't open up so wide to eat or yawn. Cover that up, pig. A writing that looks at itself and whose clitoris swells from verbal excitation is fearsome. Fury/ furia is in sinkhole/ furnia. Silenced. Sinkhole/ furnia isn't in fury/ furia. A calling. A sudden blazing. That anemone woman. Let there be liquid bile to extinguish the nymphomania. Open up lymph woman. Finishing to the last bitter sip, testing with the tongue a writing without death or scream or pain. Without sinking to the knees… onto grains of wheat. Words enter only with blood. Allow yourself to let it happen. To let it happen. To let it be…

239

Monica Minott

LYCHEE GUARD

As a little girl I avoided death notices.
It was as if by looking I would cause
someone close to be pulled.
Funny how things change.
Thirty years ago, girls walked
unmolested on the streets,
houses needed no steel bars,
laden lychee trees no guard.

Monica Minott

EL GUARDA DE LICHIS

De niña evitaba las esquelas mortuorias.
Era como si al mirarlas, yo causara que
se llevaran a alguien cercano.
Qué raro cómo cambian las cosas.
Hace treinta años, las niñas caminaban
sin que les molestaran en la calle,
las casas no necesitaban rejas,
los árboles cargados de lichis, tampoco un guarda.

Monica Minott

SISTER BERNICE

(Passing the Kumina Baton, 2014)

Sister Bernice was a cousin, so we get it.
Giftings pass from mother to daughter, father to son.
Where there's no direct descendant, it pass to cousin,
like the throne of England.

Bernice Henry of Port Morant was the reigning
Kumina Queen. Not her fault she get it after Papa John
tek way himself before we born; he follow the river down
from Spring Hill to turn teacher, closing chapter.

But it was a haunting, this compulsion – I had to dance.
No surprise when the track John set before us,
book and bag schooling, take us back to great great granny
Mama Minott, the original Kumina queen.

Duty-bound I went to the send-off for Bernice, her feet
no longer responding to drum beats. I was spectator
till Jim raised *Roll Jordan Roll*. It was then the weeping
and jumping seize me. I joined the circle moving to Bandu

around the coffin: the wailing, the jumping, the twirling
was tribute to her tireless feet; as the spirit moved upon us,
Kumina baton was passing, as we sang *Roll Jordan Roll*,
as we roll on the ground. I wanted to claim it, wanted

to assure her that Kumina was safe, for Rex
who journeyed to Portland and baptize,
had in turn baptize many, not knowing that
one of the many was a rightful inheritor.

Monica Minott

SISTER BERNICE

(*Toma de testigo Kumina, 2014*)

Sister Bernice era una prima, por eso lo recibimos.
El don pasa de madre a hija, de padre a hijo.
Donde no hay descendiente directo, pasa a primo,
como el trono de Inglaterra.

Bernice Henry de Port Morant era la Reina Kumina
regente. No era su culpa que lo recibiera cuando Papa John
partió antes de que naciéramos; él siguió río abajo
desde Spring Hill para hacerse maestro, cerrando un capítulo.

Pero era un ímpetu ancestral, esta compulsión – yo tenía que bailar.
No es de sorprender que el camino que John empezó para nosotras,
una educación de libros y mochila, nos llevara de vuelta a nuestra
        tatarabuela
Mama Minott, la reina Kumina original.

El deber me obligó a ir a la despedida de Bernice, sus pies
ya no respondían al sonido de los tambores. Fui espectadora
hasta que Jim lanzó *Roll Jordan Roll*. Fue entonces que el llanto
y los saltos me apresaron. Me uní al círculo moviéndose al ritmo de Bandu

alrededor del ataúd: los sollozos, los saltos, los giros
eran un tributo a sus pies incansables; a medida que el espíritu se movía en
        nosotros,
el testigo Kumina pasaba, mientras cantábamos "*Roll Jordan Roll*",
mientras rodábamos en el piso. Quería hacerlo mío, quería

asegurarle a ella que la Kumina estaba segura, por Rex
que viajó a Portland y se bautizó,
a su vez bautizó a muchos, sin saber que
una de los muchos era una heredera legítima.

I touch her face in the coffin; it put on a shine,
same time they pick up on the chorus:
Roll Jordan, roll. My soul arise in heaven Lord
Roll Jordan, roll.

Le toqué la cara en el ataúd; se le puso resplendente
al mismo tiempo que retomaban el estribillo:
Roll Jordan, roll. My soul arise in heaven Lord
Roll Jordan, roll.

Monica Minott

SILENCING THE STONES

Nine-year-old girl pulled from the rubble
fifteen days after the earthquake,
hope for survivors gone.
Funeral fires lit, she stirred
among ghoulish companions,
her hair dressed in dust.
But when she opened her eyes
she rivalled the sun.

Monica Minott

SILENCIANDO LAS PIEDRAS

Niña de nueve años sacada de entre los escombros
quince días después del terremoto,
la esperanza de encontrar sobrevivientes perdida.
Fuegos funerarios prendidos, ella despertó
entre aterradores compañeros fallecidos,
su pelo vestido de polvo.
Pero cuando abrió los ojos,
compitió con el sol.

Monica Minott

DUPPY RUN

Early morning. Sunshine bounce back
off bottles dangling from the almond tree
in Mr Pink's yard, like spirit that won't rest.
"I swear to you, throwing salt on doorstep
not enough for today's advancements.
Tek more than that these days," Pink said.
"Left Jamaica as a boy." Now seventy-five,
his childhood worries linger. Looming
high in the almond tree, he set
protection fi ketch any bounce-back.
People say he returned home to get rid
of the cold clipping his bones,
or to better understand his need
to decorate almond tree like Christmas
all year round. Twenty-nine recycled plastic
bottles full of water, dangling. I guess
he discovered plastic progress in the First World,
moved ahead of us. Now, when he scream at night,
cowering in his bed, shaking like leaf,
is plastic he see, and not duppy.

Monica Minott

AHUYENTAR DUPPIES

Temprano en la mañana. Los rayos de sol rebotan
en botellas que cuelgan del almendro
del patio de Mister Pink, como un espíritu que no descansa.
"Te juro, lanzar sal en el umbral de la puerta
no basta para los avances de hoy en día.
Ahora hace falta más," dijo Pink.
"Dejé Jamaica de niño." Ahora a los setenta y cinco,
sus preocupaciones de niño perduran. Las botellas
pendiendo en lo alto del almendro, las puso como protección
para atrapar cualquier rebote sobrenatural.
La gente dice que regresó a casa para quitarse
de encima el frío pegado a sus huesos,
o para entender mejor su necesidad
de decorar el almendro como si todo el año
fuera Navidad. Veintinueve botellas de plástico
recicladas llenas de agua, colgando. Supongo que
descubrió el progreso del plástico en el primer mundo,
nos pasó por delante. Ahora, cuando grita por la noche,
escondido en su cama, temblando como una hoja,
es plástico lo que ve, y no *duppies*.

Mara Pastor

MOHO

Los carros de mi casa
tenían los retrovisores pegados con silicona
porque no había dinero para repararlos.
Los espejos fragmentados
como en un rompecabezas mal hecho.
Cuando mirabas por ellos
veías a conductores ebrios, mujeres golpeadas,
adolescentes maquillándose,
niños olvidados en los asientos traseros,
parejas camino a los moteles o a la iglesia,
asesinos vestidos de empresarios,
monjas serias que miraban hacia el frente,
al vecino evangélico gritándole a la esposa,
yerberos capsuleando, novios recién casados,
ambulancias,
músicos camino a los conciertos en el anfiteatro,
transacciones de droga, de armas, de huesos,
plátanos verdes traídos de Dominicana
y piñas gigantes más dulces que la miel,
volkys de colores,
los contabas y poco a poco desaparecieron,
cañas de pescar, tablas de surfear,
las varetas de madera con las que enmarcaba el padre
y que los amiguitos de la escuela
llamaban escopetas,
veías a los policías
que querían multarnos por ir rápido, por ir lento,
por ir con los retrovisores rotos pegados con silicona,
a la heroinómana en el semáforo
que se quedaba pidiendo monedas
cuando los carros mohosos aceleraban
para llegar a la casa,

Mara Pastor

RUST

The cars at my house
had rearview mirrors glued on with silicone
because there wasn't money to repair them.
The mirrors fragmented
like a badly-worked jigsaw puzzle.
When you looked into them,
you'd see inebriated drivers, beaten women,
teenagers putting on make-up,
children forgotten in back seats,
couples on the way to motels or church,
murderers dressed like businessmen,
serious nuns staring straight ahead,
the evangelical neighbour shouting at his wife,
herb smokers with rolled up car windows, newlyweds,
ambulances,
musicians on their way to concerts in the amphitheatre,
dealings for drugs, arms, bones,
green plantains brought in from the Dominican Republic
and giant pineapples sweeter than honey,
colourful volkys
you'd count them, and then, little by little, they disappeared,
fishing poles, surf boards,
the wood trim that father used for framing
and school friends
called shotguns,
you'd see the police
who wanted to ticket us for going fast, for going slowly,
for driving with broken rearview mirrors glued on with silicone,
the woman heroin addict at the stop light
left asking for coins
when rusty cars sped up to get home,
to school, to the university, to work.

a la escuela, a la universidad, al trabajo.
Retrovisores rotos,
movilidad enmohecida por el salitre
mar por todas partes, reflejo de fractal en aguacero,
posibilidad de Yunque, ave costeña, *yagrumo*,
flamboyán como hemorragia del camino.
En los carros mohosos de mi casa
se hicieron pequeñas revoluciones
amorosas y escolares,
pronuncié correctamente la palabra *periódico*,
conduje rápido por las autopistas y la ruta panorámica,
me escapé al grito de Lares y a veces vi fantasmas:
los ferrocarriles dándole la vuelta a la isla
y los rostros de la gente
asomados por las ventanas de los vagones
sin que nadie se quejara de no tener aire acondicionado,
a mis tíos sin cinturón yendo por la número uno
antes del accidente que hizo llorar tanto a mi madre
y a mi abuelo subiendo la ventana automática
como si fuera un gran adelanto para la familia.
Porque el pasado de esta isla sólo puede verse
en un retrovisor roto con espejos mal pegados:
recuerdos enmohecidos
que están más cerca de lo que parece.

Busted rearview mirrors,
mobility rusted away by salt,
sea everywhere, rain storm's fractal reflection,
possibility of Yunque, coastal bird, *yagrumo,*
flamboyant tree like a haemorrhage along the road.
In the rusty cars at my house
little romantic and schooltime
revolutions were carried out,
I correctly pronounced the word newspaper, *periódico,*
I drove rapidly along the highway and panoramic route,
I got away to the Grito de Lares, and sometimes I saw phantoms:
railroad trains making a loop around the island
and the faces of people
hanging out of the carriage windows,
with nobody complaining about the lack of air conditioning,
my uncles without seatbelts driving on Number 1
before the accident that made my mother cry so much,
and my grandfather raising the automatic window
as if it were a grand advancement for the family.
Because this island's past can only be seen
in a badly-glued broken rearview mirror:
rusted out memories
that are closer than they appear.

Mara Pastor

ATRÓN

Se acabaron las promesas,
decían nuestros carteles.
Emmanuel quiso saber si eran
carteles en contra del suicidio.
Preguntó mirándome a los ojos.
Su papá me advierte
que Emmanuel habla mucho.
«No le hagas caso si no quieres».
Emmanuel lee sílaba a sílaba el cartel que pinto.
A-ca-da-bu-i-tre-le-lle-ga-su-pi-ti-rre.
Emmanuel sabe que un pitirre es un pájaro bravo.
Lo ha visto en el campo cuando su papá lo lleva al río.
Y un buitre es un pájaro que come carne muerta
como las tiñosas que sobrevuelan la autopista.
Emmanuel me dijo que las tiñosas son como Atrón.
«¿Quién es Atrón?» le pregunté.
«Un hombre rubio que hará un muro en el mar
para que no podamos llegar a Estados Unidos».
Emmanuel sabe eso porque lo ha visto
en la televisión. Emmanuel me pregunta
si los buitres son como Atrón.
El papá de Emmanuel lo llama desde el tablado.
«Nos vamos» le grita. «Despídete».
Él se va corriendo.
Habla con el papá y regresa.
«Dice mi papá que me llames a su teléfono
si vuelven a juntarse aquí para hacer carteles.
Quiero pintar con ustedes en contra de Atrón».

Mara Pastor

ATRÓN

Se acabaron las promesas –
All out of promises,
said our posters.
Emmanuel wanted to know if they were
posters against suicide.
He asked, looking me in the eyes.
His dad warned me
that Emmanuel talks a lot.
"Don't pay any attention to him if you don't want to."
Emmanuel read syllable by syllable the poster I was painting:
A-ca-da-bu-i-tre-le-lle-ga-su-pi-ti-rre.
Ev-er-y-vul-ture-has-its-petch-ary.
Emmanuel knew that the *pitirre* is a fiercely determined bird.
He saw one in the countryside when his dad had taken him to the river.
And a vulture is a bird that eats dead meat
like the turkey buzzards that fly over the highway.
Emmanuel told me that those red-head buzzards are like Atrón.
"Who is Atrón?" I asked.
"A blond guy who is going to make a wall in the sea
so that we can't reach the United States."
Emmanuel knew that because he had seen it
on television. Emmanuel asked me
if the vultures are like Atrón.
 Emmanuel's dad called to him from the boardwalk.
"Let's go," he shouted. "Say goodbye."
He went running.
He talked to his dad and came back.
"My dad said to call me on his telephone
if you're going to get together again here to make posters.
I want to paint with you guys against Atrón."

Mara Pastor

JEEP CHEROKEE

Desde que regresé,
entre mi padre y yo,
hay una Jeep Cherokee.
Es la guagua vieja
que dejó mi hermano
cuando se fue al ejército.
Vuelvo a tener el carro
de cuando iba al colegio.
Como ahora gano lo mismo
que cuando era estudiante,
la Jeep es una limosina.
Hace 20 años también lo era.
A mi padre, que tiene 76 años,
le gusta que yo tengo algo suyo,
algo que solo él sabe reparar.
«Le cambié el aceite».
«No confíes en ningún mecánico».
«No es el radiador».
«Arreglé el parabrisas».

Cada vez que lo veo hablamos de la Jeep
como si fuera una pequeña niña
a la que tiene que cuidar.

Mara Pastor

JEEP CHEROKEE

Since I returned,
between my father and me,
there has been a Jeep Cherokee.
It's an old 4 x 4 jalopy
that my brother left behind
when he joined the Army.
I ended up with the car that I had
in high school.
Since I now earn as much
as I did when I was a student,
the Jeep is a limousine.
Twenty years ago, it was, too.
My father, who is 76 years old,
likes that I have something of his,
something that only he knows how to repair.
"I changed the oil."
"Don't trust any mechanic."
"It's not the radiator."
"I fixed the windshield."

Every time I see him, we talk about the Jeep
as if it were a small girl
he has to take care of.

Mara Pastor

POETA NACIONAL

Si todo sigue así,
Si todos se van ahora
que no hay agua,
dinero ni coquíes,
la isla será tomada
por iguanas
y leones marinos.
Me harán un busto.
Será facíl ser poeta nacional
entre gallinas de palo.

Mara Pastor

POET OF THE NATION

If everything continues like this,
If everyone leaves now
that there's no water,
money, or *coquí* frogs,
the island will be taken over
by iguanas
and lion fish.
They will make a bust of me.
It will be easy to be the national poet
among bush-chicken iguanas.

Esther Phillips

BIRTHDAY VISIT TO CUBA

How the skies spoke on your birthday!
the same reverberation I've heard
in your voice – only this morning
there's an ellipsis in the echo.

For these ten days you're harvest-
ing memories I cannot share.
You are bone-gathering:
a fist once folded in defiance,
the feet that spurned an empire
hobbled now among gravestones;
a headband red as Rodney's blood
bleached by the years' indifference.

They fete you, as they rightly should.
While the young and bright pay tribute
to title and tenure, you sit, half-listening,
honing your reluctant peace.

You see how the *Beast* may win after all:
its subterranean smell invades the city
in the half smirk on the cashier's face;
the branding of appetite with cell phones
and DVD players; the brag of steel
and chrome over iron, cracked but enduring,
a barter of nation for illusion of capital.

When you return, I'll have a meal,
a change of clothing, a space for luggage
ready for you. But there's not room enough
to house the ashes your eyes may speak of.

Esther Phillips

VISITA DE CUMPLEAÑOS A CUBA

¡Cómo hablaron los cielos en tu cumpleaños!
La misma reverberación que he escuchado
en tu voz — solo que esta mañana
hay una elipsis en el eco.

Durante estos diez días cosechas
recuerdos que no puedo compartir.
Estás recolectando huesos:
un puño en su día cerrado de manera desafiante,
los pies que repudiaban un imperio
trabados ahora entre lápidas;
una cinta roja en la cabeza como la sangre de Rodney
descolorida por la indiferencia de los años.

Te festejan, como debe ser.
Mientras los jóvenes y brillantes rinden homenaje
al título y al rango, tú estás sentado, escuchando a medias,
puliendo tu paz reacia.

Ves cómo después de todo la *Bestia* puede ganar:
su olor subterráneo invade la ciudad
en la media sonrisa sardónica de la cara del cajero;
el mercadeo de un apetito con celulares
y reproductores de DVD; el alarde del acero
y el cromo en lugar del hierro, resquebrajado pero duradero,
el trueque de nación por ilusión de capital.

Cuando regreses, tendré una comida,
una muda de ropa, un espacio para el equipaje
listos para ti. Pero no hay suficiente espacio
para albergar las cenizas de las que hablen tus ojos.

Esther Phillips

MEETING-POINT

(for George & my grand-daughter, Zoe)

She had shed the "Uncle" at his bidding,
no doubt. "George," she calls,
sure of her place at the summit of the world,
"may I come in?" The door opens, a glimpse
of white hair, and she runs into the room.

We watch her transition from outright refusal
to, "My George". First the array of balloons
he bought and blew up himself, her three-year
old laughter artless, bursting free.
This playmate makes the funniest faces,
becomes her willing audience as she reads the stories
she contrives; she sings for him, she dances.

We watch him reading silently. She, eyeing him
all the while, waits with the rarest patience.
Perhaps this book will teach him how to answer
all the "Whys?" she's heaping up,
or prompt him to another round of games.

Time, too, is playing its peculiar game:
old age recedes, philosophy declines, all titles bow.
Inside this room he is a child again, and she,
unwise as yet to his burden of years, lifts
it as lightly as the ball they toss between them,
or the yellow balloon floating outside the room.

Esther Phillips

PUNTO DE ENCUENTRO

(para George y mi nieta, Zoe)

Ella había dejado el "Tío" a petición suya,
sin duda. "George" le llama,
segura de su lugar en la cumbre del mundo,
"¿puedo entrar?" La puerta se abre, una primera ojeada
al pelo blanco, y entra corriendo a la habitación.

La vemos pasar de un rechazo categórico
a, "Mi George". Primero, la gama de globos
que compró e infló él mismo; libre, su risa ingenua
de niña de tres años estallaba.
Este amiguito de juegos hace las muecas más divertidas,
está dispuesto a ser su público mientras ella lee los cuentos
que se ingenia; ella le canta, le baila.

Lo vemos leer en silencio. Ella, lo mira con atención
todo el tiempo, espera con una paciencia rarísima.
Tal vez este libro le enseñará cómo responder
todos los "¿Porqués?" que ella hacina,
o le incite a otra ronda de juegos.

El tiempo, también, está jugando su particular juego:
la vejez retrocede, la filosofía disminuye, todos los títulos se despiden.
Dentro de esta habitación él es de nuevo un niño, y ella,
ajena todavía a la carga de los años de él, la levanta
con la misma ligereza con la que se pasan la pelota,
o el globo amarillo que flota fuera de la habitación.

Esther Phillips

REVOLUTION

How to revolve harmoniously
around a fixed point has always
been our question.
You, with your Marxist stance. ·
Me, with my love of Christ.

You waged a patient war against
my "closed" mind. Book after book
informed me how a Marxist looked
at Jesus; symbolism, not the literal,
was the enlightened approach;
the Word was mired in politics and fable.

Again, how to resolve the question
of the body? For you, the seat of pleasure.
For me, however sweet its plunder,
still the temple.

Product of history and social formation —
the sum total, in your view, of the human.
I hold man is his dual nature:
God-shaped though flawed and prone to error.

*   *   *

How are we now, years on
from earlier tensions when we thought it
worth our while to strive for common ground?

I've opened the door much wider
to your deity, Reason, but find him shy
of going beyond my mind.

264

Esther Phillips

REVOLUCIÓN

Cómo dar vueltas harmoniosamente
alrededor de un punto fijo siempre ha
sido nuestra cuestión.
Tú, con tu postura marxista.
Yo, con mi amor a Cristo.

Tú libraste una paciente guerra en contra de
mi mente "cerrada". Libro tras libro
me informé de cómo un marxista ve
a Jesús; el simbolismo, no lo literal,
era el enfoque iluminado;
la Escritura estaba sumida en política y fábula.

Entonces, ¿cómo resolver la cuestión
del cuerpo? Para ti, la sede del placer.
Para mí, sin importar cuán dulce el botín,
aún el templo.

Producto de la historia y la formación social –
la suma total, a tu juicio, del humano.
Yo considero al hombre en su doble naturaleza:
moldeado a imagen de Dios, pero imperfecto y propenso al error.

*   *   *

¿Ahora, cómo nos encontramos, a años
de tensiones anteriores cuando creíamos que
merecía la pena esmerarse para encontrar puntos en común?

Le he abierto mucho más la puerta
a tu deidad, la Razón, pero veo que le falta
ir más allá de mi mente.

I've asked him what is this essential
loneliness? Why seek purpose and
meaning? Why long for certainty
and what is the source of that longing?

Why poetry? From what abyss
does poetry spring – distilled, clearer
than thought, multi-hued, each sense held
in abeyance to its wonder?

How does Faith cast her upward beam
and reconfigure stars?

But more than all, Reason remains
dumbfounded when I ask him this:
what is that greater Love
that makes me love you still?

Le he preguntado ¿qué es esta
soledad esencial? ¿Por qué buscar propósito y
sentido? ¿Por qué anhelar certeza
y cuál es el origen de este anhelo?

¿Por qué poesía? ¿Desde qué abismo
emana la poesía? – destilada, más clara
que el pensamiento, con multitud de tonos, cada sentido dejado
en suspenso a la luz del asombro?

¿Cómo consigue la Fe lanzar su haz ascendente
y realinear las estrellas?

Pero más que nada, la Razón se queda
boquiabierta cuando a él le pregunto:
¿cuál es ese mayor Amor
que me hace aún amarte?

Jennifer Rahim

ON QUITTING COLUMBUS

just when I decide to quit
Columbus

write his name off my list
of complaints

shake the dust from my feet
like the saved

that story end-up like a cliché
on my page

only this time the players
switch sides

ups and declare the state a jail
for a salvation mission

to hook criminals while Crime
living free

behind gated communities
tight security,

watching the movie, safe
from *them*

that drag-out, handcuff
parade of black

with back broad enough
to carry fault for everybody

Jennifer Rahim

AL DEJAR ATRÁS A COLÓN

justo cuando decido dejar atrás
a Colón

sacar su nombre de mi lista
de quejas

sacudirme el polvo de los pies
como los salvados

esa historia acaba como un cliché
en mi página

solo que esta vez los jugadores
cambian de bando

van y declaran el estado una cárcel
para una misión de salvamento

para atrapar criminales mientras el Crimen
anda suelto

detrás de comunidades de acceso controlado
con fuertes medidas de seguridad

donde miran la película, a salvo
de *ellos*

ese rotundo palizón, esposados,
desfile de negros

con las espaldas lo bastante anchas
para cargar con la culpa de todos

make it hard to let History sail,
bury the hatchet

when the track look the same –
a rerun from another age

or a language playing dead only
to ambush change

hace difícil dejar zarpar la Historia,
enterrar el hacha de guerra

cuando parece la misma pista –
una reposición de otra época

o una lengua haciéndose la muerta solo
para tender una emboscada al cambio

Jennifer Rahim

FOUR MEDITATIONS ON SMALL

(*the practice of precise diction*)

i

Small in my language
began not as an adjective
but a noun. Adjectives,
you see, were the luxury
of a spanish *discoverer*
who came upon a land
he described as smaller
than his own, greener
than his own, warmer
than his own, and thought,
Paradise, meaning
(in his language)
a place of easy times,
and better, easy profits.
In my language, you see,
I first learnt *small*
as a proper (meaning suitable)
noun for plunder.

ii

Once the *discoverer* landed,
small became less idyllic
as some of the owners
resisted being claimed,
insisted on their culture,
their language, their faith.
Vexed by such self-possession,

Jennifer Rahim

CUATRO MEDITACIONES SOBRE PEQUEÑO

(la prática de la dicción precisa)

i

Pequeño en mi lengua
no empezó como un adjetivo
sino como un nombre. Los adjetivos,
sabes, eran el lujo
de un *descubridor* español
que se encontró con una tierra
que describió como más pequeña
que la suya, más verde
que la suya, más calurosa
que la suya, y pensó
Paraíso, es decir
(en su lengua)
un lugar de vida fácil,
y aún mejor, ganancias fáciles.
En mi lengua, sabes,
primero aprendí *pequeño*
como un nombre propio
(es decir, adecuado) para saqueo.

ii

Una vez el *descubridor* desembarcó,
pequeño se volvió menos idílico
cuando algunos de los propietarios
se resistieron a ser declarados súbditos,
insistieron en mantener su cultura,
su lengua, su fe.
Enojado por su insistencia en ser dueños de sí mismos,

273

he fired his diction like a gun
and named each *native*,
(in his language) *other*.
You see, in my language,
small was first a common
(meaning nuisance) noun
that had to be annihilated.

iii

The *discoverer* dreamed
the fierce economy of sugar
which required making *small*
a continent, a people
he named *niggers* meaning
(in his language), nothing.
Small was the dark theology
preached in the holds
of slave ships, the cargo lost
by drowning, the middle passage,
narrow gate without promise,
the further lie of Indentureship
that used a people "pure and
simple," (synonym for *small)*
and gave almost nothing
at the end of it all.
In my language, you see,
small was first a collective
(meaning race) noun
sentenced to loss.

iv

String of islands,
we first learnt you as *small*
(meaning nouns) colonies

274

él disparó su dicción como una pistola
y denominó cada *nativo*
(en su lengua) *otro*.
Sabes, en mi lengua,
pequeño primero era un nombre
común (es decir, estorbo)
que tenía que ser erradicado.

iii

El *descubridor* soñó
la feroz economía del azúcar
que requeriría hacer *pequeño*
un continente, una gente que
él llamó *niggers* es decir
(en su lengua), nada.
Pequeña era la oscura teología
predicada en las bodegas
de los barcos de esclavos, el cargamento perdido,
ahogado, la travesía transatlántica,
estrecho portón sin promesa,
y una mentira más,
la de la servidumbre por contrato
que utilizó una gente "pura y
simple" (sinónimo de *pequeña*),
y no dio casi nada
al final de todo.
En mi lengua, sabes,
pequeño era primero un nombre
colectivo (es decir, raza)
sentenciado a sufrir pérdidas.

iv

Cordón de islas,
primero te aprendimos como *pequeñas*

of nothingness, at best
imitations of greater places;
Antilles lesser or greater,
chain of the *discoverer's* passage,
his language present
in politician's tyrannies,
cable t.v. cultures, foreign-
used economies and policies,
in dreams of cooler climates,
and the pull of their currency.
In my language, you see,
small may yet be an abstract
(meaning mentality) noun
that threatens sovereignty.

colonias (es decir, nombres)
de nada, a lo sumo
imitaciones de sitios de mayor grandeza;
Antillas Menores o Mayores,
cadena de la travesía del *descubridor*,
su lengua presente
en las tiranías de los políticos,
las culturas de la TV por cable,
las economías y políticas extranjeras
de segunda mano,
en sueños de climas más fríos,
y el poder atrayente de su moneda.
En mi lengua, sabes,
pequeña aún puede ser un nombre
abstracto (es decir, mentalidad)
que amenaza la soberanía.

Jennifer Rahim

DEAR POETRY

Don't get me wrong,
but today
I have a bone to pick
with you.
I not ungrateful
how you choose me
outta everybody,
how you decide to come
and live with me,
give me your company.
I not ungrateful how
yuh take me, bring me
to a life so sweet
not even ripe mango
could beat.

So I not complaining
that is under my roof
you choose to stay,
three times by plenty
call my name.
Truth be told,
I was never so happy
to know how
is so long you holding
candle for me,
that yuh never change
your mind about me.

And is with my two eye
wide open I say yes –
this is my life, no more

Jennifer Rahim

ESTIMADA POESÍA

No me malinterpretes,
pero hoy
te voy a cantar
la cartilla.
No soy una desagradecida
por cómo me escogiste a mí
entre toda la gente,
decidieras venir
a vivir conmigo,
regalarme tu compañía.
No soy una desagradecida
por cómo me acogiste, me llevaste
a una vida tan dulce
que ni siquiera un mango maduro
podría superar.

Por eso no me quejo
de que sea bajo mi techo
donde escogiste quedarte,
de que llamaras mi nombre
tres veces un montón.
La verdad sea dicha,
no había sido nunca tan feliz
como al saber cuánto
hace que iluminas mi camino,
que nunca cambiaste
de parecer sobre mí.

Y es con mis dos ojos
abiertos de par en par que digo sí –
esta es mi vida, ya no más
huir,

running away,
no more making circles,
dizzying mihself,
chasing after mih own tail
only to end-up right,
back with you
again.

And now I so full
I caring more poem-
pickney than I know how,
and these days
I so forget mihself
mirror can't see me –
so-and-so want to know
if I take up and 'migrate
and dem malicious mouth
spreading rumour
that is dead
I come and dead.

What they don't know
is my days busy –
picking up after you,
serving at your table,
gathering every crumb
that hit ground, sweeping
out every corner
so nothing lose –
not one bit of you –
making this life
into a singing
that could shine stars,
warm the sun, cool
breeze, even heal
that two-timing lisp

ya no más caminar en círculos,
mareándome a mí misma,
persiguiéndome la cola
para acabar
volviendo otra vez
a ti.

Y ahora me siento tan llena
cuido de más poemas-
hijos de los que sé cómo,
y últimamente
me olvido tanto de mí misma
ni el espejo me ve –
ese y el otro quieren saber
si me dio por emigrar
y las malas lenguas
van rumoreando
que estoy muerta
que me he muerto.

Lo que no saben
es que ando bien ocupada –
recogiendo detrás de ti,
sirviendo tu mesa,
recogiendo cada miga
que se da contra el piso, pasando
la escoba por cada esquinita
para que nada pierda –
ni un poquitito de ti –
haciendo de esta vida
un cantar
que podría alumbrar estrellas,
calentar el sol, enfriar
la brisa, hasta sanar
el traicionero ceceo
de Anansi – de verdad –

on Anansi — true-
true, all-day-
all-night spinning
your light.

I not complaining
though I must let you know
it not always easy
to grow the words
we make together,
and sometimes lines
raise eyes, shake worlds —
cause me and all to turn.
And though people think
I stupidy to stay with you,
I know better:
is carry I have to carry
with you the weight of us
being here together.

So this time,
I not saying I not staying;
but tonight, I feel
I want to kick off my shoes,
put up my feet and sip
soothing lime laced
with a heavy-han' pour
of good island rum —
and a dash of Angostura
for the bitter. I want
to close my eyes
and feel the Atlantic
wash over me.
And I want to listen
to Etta belting out
one and a thousand times

de verdad, todo el día –
toda la noche hilando
tu luz.

No me quejo,
aunque debo decirte
que no es siempre fácil
hacer crecer las palabras
que hacemos juntas,
y a veces los versos
arquean cejas, estremecen mundos –
hacen que yo y todos nos demos la vuelta.
Y aunque la gente crea que
soy una estúpida por quedarme contigo,
yo sé que no es así:
debo llevar contigo
la carga de que
estemos aquí juntas.

Por eso esta vez,
no digo que no me voy a quedar;
sino que esta noche, siento
que quiero descalzarme,
poner mis pies en alto y tomar
reconfortante lima verde mezclada
con un generoso trago de
buen ron isleño –
y una pizca de Angostura
por lo amargo. Quiero
cerrar los ojos
y sentir el Atlántico
anegarme.
Y quiero escuchar
a Etta cantar a viva voz
una y mil veces
ese verso desamparado – *At last*

that unsheltered line – *At last*
my love has come along.
Tonight Love, I want you
to write me
a poem.

my love has come along.
Esta noche, Amor, quiero que
me escribas
un poema.

Shivanee Ramlochan

THE RED THREAD CYCLE
i. ON THE THIRD ANNIVERSARY OF THE RAPE

Don't say Tunapuna Police Station.
Say you found yourself in the cave of a minotaur, not
knowing how you got there, with a lap of red thread.
Don't say forced anal entry.
Say you learned that some flowers bloom and die
at night. Say you remember stamen, filament,
cross-pollination, say that hummingbirds are

vital to the process.

Give the minotaur time to write in the police ledger. Lap
the red thread
around the hummingbird vase.

Don't say I took out the garbage alone and he grabbed me by the waist
and he was handsome.
                    Say Shakespeare. Recite Macbeth for the tropics.
Lady Macbeth was the Queen of Carnival
and she stabbed Banquo with a vagrant's shiv during J'ouvert.
She danced a blood dingolay and gave her husband a Dimanche Gras
upbraiding.

I am in mud and glitter so far steeped that going back is not an option.
Don't say rapist.

Say engineer of aerosol deodorant because pepper spray is illegal,
anything is illegal
Fight back too hard, and it's illegal,
>your nails are illegal

286

Shivanee Ramlochan

EL CICLO DEL HILO ROJO
i. EN EL TERCER ANIVERSARIO DE LA VIOLACIÓN

No digas el cuartel de policía de Tunapuna.
Di que te encontraste en la cueva del minotauro, sin
saber cómo llegaste ahí, con un regazo de hilo rojo.
No digas entrada anal forzada.
Di que aprendiste que algunas flores florecen y mueren
de noche. Di que recuerdas estambre, filamento,
polinización cruzada, di que los colibrís son

vitales para el proceso.

Dale tiempo al minotauro para escribir en el registro policial. Rodea
con el hilo rojo
la vasija para colibrí.

No digas saqué la basura sola y me agarró por la cintura
y él era hermoso.
          Di Shakepeare. Recita Macbeth para los trópicos.
Lady Macbeth era la Reina del Carnaval
y apuñaló a Banquo con la navaja de un vagabundo durante J'ouvert.
Ella bailó un *dingolay* de sangre y dio a su marido un regaño de Dimanche Gras.

Estoy tan hundida en barro y escarcha que retroceder no es una opción.
No digas violador.

Di ingeniero de desodorante de aerosol porque el espray de pimienta es ilegal,
cualquier cosa es ilegal.
Defiéndete demasiado duro, y es ilegal,
>tus uñas son ilegales

Don't say you have a vagina, say
he stole your insurance policy/ your bank boxes/ your first car
downpayment
Say
he took something he'll be punished for taking,
not something you're punished for holding
like red thread between your thighs.

No digas que tienes una vagina, di que
te robó tu póliza de seguro/tu caja fuerte/ la paga y señal de tu primer carro
Di
que él se hizo con algo que se le castigará por coger
no algo que te castigan por tener
cogido como hilo rojo entre tus muslos.

Shivanee Ramlochan

CLINK CLINK

When you were young, you learned to keep out of the bar.
This kept you decent.
You had scrubbed knees, a moon face, two hairplaits like black rope,
thick as pregnant pit vipers with red ribbon tongues.

At nine, you bled.

At twelve, you listened to your nani when she said –
Stand by the Carib fridge and stay still.
Don't look into the bar. Don't smile. Don't move.
Prashant uncle want to see how big you get.

You counted sixteen cold Carib.
A Green Shandy.
Eleven Stag.
The icepick forgotten from the last defrost.
A basin of scotch bonnet, waiting to be pepper sauce.

You drew a smiley face on the condensation.
You were grinding dhal, and there was yellow dust on your legs.
You never forget the shortpants you had on.

In truth, you still don't know any man named Prashant.

All you recall
is a bar fridge reflection, a haze of chest hair, a flash of platinum bera.
A clink, to say you wasn't ugly.
A clink clink, to say you was real nice.

After that day,
you stood outside the bar window, counting everything in sight.

Shivanee Ramlochan

CLING CLING

Cuando eras pequeña, aprendiste a mantenerte lejos del bar.
Esto te mantuvo decente.
Tenías las rodillas frotadas, cara como una luna llena, dos trenzas como
    soga negra,
gruesas como víboras embarazadas con lazos rojos por lengua.

A los nueve, sangraste.

A los doce, escuchaste cuando tu abuela te dijo –
Párate delante de la nevera de Caribs y quédate quieta.
No mires al bar. No sonrías. No te muevas.
Tío Prashant quiere ver cuán grande estás.

Contaste dieciséis Caribs frías.
Una Green Shandy.
Once Stags.
El picahielos olvidado de la última vez que se descongeló.
Un cuenco de *scotch bonnet*, esperando ser salsa picante.

Dibujaste una cara sonriente en la condensación.
Estabas moliendo *dhal*, y había polvo amarillo en tus piernas.
Nunca olvidarás los pantalones cortos que llevabas.

En verdad, aún no conoces ningún hombre llamado Prashant.

Todo lo que recuerdas
es el reflejo en una nevera de bar, una neblina de vello pectoral, un destello de
    bera de platino.
Un cling, para decir que no eras fea.
Un cling cling, para decir que eras lindísima.

Después de ese día
te quedaste fuera de la ventana del bar, contando todo lo que estaba
    a la vista.

Shivanee Ramlochan

VIVEK CHOOSES HIS HUSBANDS

Your father said not to take faggots to your bed, so you called
        them festivals.

Corpus Christi gave his body up between bites of bread,
leavened a Sunday on your tongue so hot
that you chased the burn with olive oil,
sprung from some garden where other men
have fallen to their knees.
You knifed the best sounds of him clean
with eucharist-butter, blessed the back and the sides of his body,
going over catechism scars with tonguepoint,
cock heavy and poised for betrayal.

You splinter the colours of Phagwa in your bed. You let him
        abeer-bleed
your sheets, consummation morning a slitthroat red,
powder on your lashes, red powder on your nosebridge, joy soft
        as if you
were sucking that nectar from the cunt of an improbable other.
Small suitors of red
lining the backs of his knees. You cling to the backs of his knees
and let the temple peal bells of bright orgasm over you.

Samhain you found in an Aberystwyth dive bar, and when he
        asked you
What island does your voice come from, handsome?
You showed him mouth-first, worked glottals over his girth,
        tasted his
grandfather's name in your soft palate for weeks after,
the ancestry of him roving in your spit,
routing you for fire,
cleaning you for the virgin-kill.

Shivanee Ramlochan

VIVEK ESCOGE SUS MARIDOS

Tu padre dijo que no trajeras maricones a tu cama, así que les llamaste
    festivales.

Corpus Christi se rindió al cuerpo de él entre mordiscos de pan,
hizo fermentar un domingo en tu lengua tan caliente
que consagraste la quemadura con aceite de oliva,
germinada en algún huerto donde otros hombres
    han caído de rodillas.
A cuchillo, sacaste los mejores sonidos de él, limpiándolos
con mantequilla-eucaristía, bendijiste el detrás y los lados de su
    cuerpo,
repasando sus cicatrices de catecismo a punta de lengua,
la pinga pesada y lista para la traición.

Desparramaste astillas de colores de Phagwa en tu cama. Dejaste que
    manchara
tus sabanas con la sangre de *abeer*, la mañana de consumación un rojo
    garganta degollada,
polvo en tus pestañas, polvo rojo en el puente de tu nariz, alegría
suave como si estuvieras chupando el néctar del coño de una
    improbable otra.
Pequeños pretendientes de rojo
forrados detrás de sus rodillas. Te agarras detrás de sus rodillas
y dejas que el templo repique campanas de orgasmo brillante encima
    de ti.

Encontraste a Samhain en un bar de mala muerte de Aberystwyth, y
    cuando te preguntó
¿De qué isla es tu voz, guapo?
Le enseñaste la boca primero, ejercitaste las glotales sobre su
    amplitud, saboreaste
el nombre de su abuelo en el velo de tu paladar semanas después,

The day you marry Hanukkah is a glock pointed to your father's
    face.

You tell him
I am the queen
the comeuppance
the hard heretic that nature intended.

su ascendencia errante en tu saliva,
dirigiéndote hacia el fuego,
limpiándote para la caza virginal.

El día que te cases con Hanukkah será una *glock* apuntando a la cara
de tu padre.

Le dirás a él
Yo soy la reina
lo merecido
el terco hereje que la naturaleza engendró.

Legna Rodríguez Iglesias

CUALQUIER PORQUERÍA

Las patas de una escritora
merecen unos lindos All Star
las manos de una escritora
merecen alcohol
para manos
un producto que elimina
el 99.9 porciento
de los gérmenes
los ojos de una escritora
merecen espejuelos
negros y traidores
que no den espacio al sol
ni a la guasasa
que nadie me vea llorar
por el camino
la nariz de una escritora
merece un poco de Kleenex
para llorar si hay que llorar
y echar afuera los mocos
que hay que echar
el clítoris de una escritora
merece una presión
mi alma merece una fiesta
música
y cualquier porquería
que la haga reír.

Legna Rodríguez Iglesias

WHATEVER NONSENSE

The feet of a woman writer
deserve some pretty All Stars
the hands of a woman writer
deserve alcohol
a product that eliminates
99.9 percent
of germs
the eyes of a woman writer
deserve deceptive,
black glasses
that let neither the sun in
nor gnats
so that nobody sees me cry
on the way
the nose of a woman writer
deserves a bit of Kleenex
for crying if one has to cry
and blowing out the snot
that one has to get rid of
the clitoris of a woman writer
deserves pressure
my soul deserves
a party, music
and whatever nonsense
that makes it laugh.

Legna Rodríguez Iglesias

SERÍA RARO, MUY RARO, QUE OLVIDARA

Sería raro, muy raro, que olvidara
La imagen luminosa en el laboratorio.

Aquellos flamboyanes viniéndoseme encima
Y yo tan acostada desnuda para abajo.

Estaban en el techo. La imagen, en el techo.
Flamboyanes enormes, de fuego. Flamboyanes.

Abrí mis dos piernitas y dejé que se hundiera
Dentro de mí aquel bate de béisbol con un nylon.

Es preciso, so sorry, es preciso y exacto.
¿Pero los flamboyanes también eran precisos?

¿Para un ultrasonido de solo seis semanas
Es preciso un paisaje de árboles de fuego?

En el techo los árboles parecían más falsos
De lo que son los árboles que no tienen raíces.

Ni raíz, ni semilla, ni fundas de semillas,
Ni tronco, ni follaje, ni pétalos, ni ramas.

A pesar de que el bate de béisbol era largo
La sangre salió igual.

En el laboratorio, flamboyanes de sangre.
No recuerdo la música: Beyoncé o Rihanna.

Legna Rodríguez Iglesias

IT WOULD BE STRANGE, SO STRANGE, FOR ME TO FORGET

It would be strange, so strange, to forget
The luminous image in the lab clinic,

Those flamboyant trees looming over me
And me lying flat with my lower half nude.

They were on the ceiling. The image, on the ceiling.
Enormous flamboyant trees, on fire. Flamboyants.

I opened my two legs and allowed that baseball bat
Covered with a plastic baggie to sink into me.

It's necessary, *so sorry*, it's necessary and it's precise,
But were the flamboyants also necessary?

For an ultrasound at only six weeks,
Is the landscape of flame trees necessary?

On the ceiling the trees looked more fake
Than those trees that don't have roots do.

No root, no seed, no seed pods,
No trunk, no foliage, no petals, no branches.

Though the baseball bat was long,
Blood still flowed out.

In the lab clinic, bloody flamboyant trees.
I don't remember the music: Beyoncé or Rihanna.

Legna Rodríguez Iglesias

LA BARRIGA

Frente al Mississippi
No se me notaba la barriga.

En el Motel de 75 dólares la noche
no se me notaba la barriga.

Junto a la estatua de José Martí
Con la que chocamos por casualidad
No se me notaba la barriga.

En la casa de William Faulkner
Donde me quedé fría y tiesa
Mi barriga era nada.

Con 7 grados centígrados
Parece que la barriga se esconde.

La única sopa que pude tomarme
Fue de cangrejo
Y la barriga no se dio por enterada.

Mojando un tibio beignet
En una taza de Café Du Monde
La barriga se salió un poquito
Pero nadie la vio.

Ya en el parque sobre la hierba
Goloseando unas toronjas como pelotas de fútbol
Escuché un murmullo de lo alto.

Era Mahalia Jackson
Contándole algún chisme al trompetista:

Legna Rodríguez Iglesias

MY BELLY

Facing the Mississippi,
My belly wasn't noticeable.

In the 75-dollars-a-night Motel
My belly wasn't noticeable.

Next to the statue of José Martí
That we bumped into by accident
My belly wasn't noticeable.

In William Faulkner's house
Where I was left cold and stunned
My belly was nothing.

At 7 degrees centigrade
It seems that bellies hide.

Crab soup
Was the only thing I could have
And my belly didn't even notice.

Dipping a tepid beignet
In a cup from Café Du Monde,
My belly stuck out a little
But nobody saw it.

And on the grass at the park
Savouring grapefruits as big as footballs
I heard a murmur from on high.

It was Mahalia Jackson
Telling some gossip to the trumpet player:

"¿Viste eso, Louis?
La muchacha que acaba de pasar
En vez de uno, tiene dos corazones."

"Did you see that, Louis?
The woman who just passed
Has two hearts instead of one."

Tanya Shirley

SWEET SWEET JAMAICA

We cannot find our little girls
we cannot find our little boys

We search all day
we search all night

for their dangling plaits and rainbow beads
for their bobby socks and superman briefs

What are little girls made of?
Sugar and spice and army knives
bullets and broken glass

What are little boys made of?
Mongrel dog tails, slimy snails,
belt buckles and barbed wire wounds

Have you looked in the sewer?
Have you searched in the swamp?

Where daddies and mistresses and mommies
and neighbours stuff decapitated corpses
of little brown girls and little black boys

who can't play anymore on swings or in trees
in lanes or in puddles, in back rooms or front rooms

No marbles or dandy shandy
jump rope or bull in the pen
no hide and seek or

Tanya Shirley

LA DULCE DULCE JAMAICA

No encontramos a nuestras niñas
No encontramos a nuestros niños

Buscamos todo el día
buscamos toda la noche

sus trenzas volanderas y cuentas arco iris
sus medias cortas y calzoncillos de superman

¿De qué están hechas las niñas?
Azúcar y especias y navajas
balas y pedacitos de cristales rotos

¿De qué están hechos los niños?
Colas de perro sato, caracoles babosos,
heridas de hebilla de correa y de alambre de púas

¿Han mirado en la cloaca?
¿Han mirado en la charca?

Donde los papis y las queridas y las mamis
y los vecinos dejan cadáveres decapitados
de niñas morenas y niños negros

que ya no pueden jugar en columpios o en árboles
en callejones o en charcos, en cuartos o en salones

Ni canicas, ni *dandy shandy*
ni saltan a cuerda, ni *bull in the pen*
ni escondite ni

                    big bird big bird
                    in and out the window
                    big bird big bird in and out the window

Our little girls are stuffed in small spaces
coming up on shore in plastic bags
burning in safe houses
hanging from burglar bars

Our little girls are lying in blood, their legs pried open

Our little boys lie in blood, butchered like cattle
Our little boys hang from street corners
Our little boys are on fire at our feet

When we find them, it is always too late
We hurl stones into the wind
We blow steam up media asses
We stand outside government houses

                    and then we grow quiet
                    like dust on the tombstones
                    of little bones

pájaro grande, pájaro grande
entras y sales de la ventana
pájaro grande pájaro grande entras y sales de la ventana

Nuestras niñas están enclaustradas en espacios pequeños,
emergen en bolsas de plástico en las orillas
quemadas en refugios
colgadas de las rejas

Nuestras niñas yacen ensangrentadas, las piernas de par en par forzadas

Nuestros niños yacen ensangrentados, descuartizados como ganado
Nuestros niños cuelgan de las esquinas
Nuestros niños están en llamas a nuestros pies

Cuando los encontramos, siempre es demasiado tarde
Lanzamos piedras al viento
Insuflamos el culo de los medios con vapor caliente
Nos paramos enfrente de edificios del gobierno

        y entonces nos volvemos silenciosos
        como el polvo en las lápidas
        de pequeños huesos

Tanya Shirley

THE MERCHANT OF FEATHERS II

is the mother whose son is found
in a *compromising position* with a man
in a university bathroom
and is beaten by security guards
who police anuses
while girls walk unguarded in the night
and a mob of educated fools chant
for more blood, more fire;
this is the mother who must put her son back together,
paint his wounds with gentian violet,
ice swollen tendons, protuberant eyes,
find the scars deeper than skin,
and like a seamstress mend what's broken within,
and when his father, who isn't worth two dry stones
or a shilling, sees his son on the news and appears
at her door to beat her son some more,
she will turn herself into serrated edges,
stand sharp and poised to kill,
for her son is her only gold,
and if the father's thirst for blood is too great
she will pacify him with what he needs
to prove he is not like his son;
in her, he will bury the fear.
And in the morning she will stir soft words
into the cornmeal porridge, carry it to her son's bed,
blow a benediction into each spoonful she brings
to his bruised and beautiful lips.

Tanya Shirley

LA MERCADER DE PLUMAS II

es la madre cuyo hijo es encontrado
en una *posición comprometedora* con un hombre
en un baño de la universidad
y es golpeado por los guardas de seguridad
que patrullan los anos
mientras las chicas caminan desamparadas de noche
y una horda de tontos educados claman
más sangre, más fuego;
esta es la madre que tiene que recomponer a su hijo,
pintar sus heridas con violeta de genciana,
poner hielo en los tendones hinchados, los ojos protuberantes,
encontrar las cicatrices más profundas que la piel,
y como una costurera remendar los rotos internos,
y cuando su padre, que no vale dos piedras secas
ni un chavo, ve a su hijo en las noticias y aparece
en la puerta de ella para golpearle un poco más,
ella se convertirá en filo dentellado,
afilada, de pie y a punto de matar,
porque su hijo es su único oro,
y si la sed de sangre del padre es demasiada
le calmará con lo que él necesita
para probar que no es como su hijo;
en ella, él enterrará su miedo.
Y en la mañana ella mezclará tiernas palabras
en la crema de harina de maíz, la llevará a la cama a su hijo,
soplará una bendición en cada cucharada que lleve
a sus amoratados y bellos labios.

Tanya Shirley

NEGOTIATION

> *Big dick cyaan go a supermarket*
> Anonymous proverb

Yes, I know,
I am beautiful.
My mother tells me frequently.

Yes, I know,
I am one of the smartest women you have met.
I learned to read when I was two.

Yes, I know,
the way I move my waist is magic.
I am from the Caribbean.

Yes, it does excite me,
that you promise to perform cunnilingus.
I hear I am sweet like mango.

But what else will you bring to the table?

Is your debt more than you are worth?
Do you mow your mother's grass?
How soundly do you sleep
when a baby is crying?
Do you have a baby
you are yet to claim
because you are waiting
to see if he looks like you?

Do you know your father?
How far has the chip fallen

Tanya Shirley

NEGOCIACIÓN

Pinga grande no va al supermercado
Proverbio anónimo

Sí, lo sé,
soy bella.
Mi madre me lo dice a menudo.

Sí, lo sé,
soy una de las mujeres más brillantes que has conocido.
Aprendí a leer cuando tenía dos años.

Sí, lo sé,
mi manera de mover la cintura es mágica.
Soy del Caribe.

Sí, sí que me excita,
que prometas hacerme un cunnilingus.
Dicen que soy dulce como el mango.

Pero ¿qué más vas a poner sobre a la mesa?

¿Debes más de lo que vales?
¿Cortas el césped de tu madre?
¿Cuán profundo duermes
cuando un bebé llora?
¿Tienes un bebé
al que todavía has de reconocer
porque estás esperando
a ver si se te parece?

¿Conoces a tu padre?
¿Cuán lejos saltó la astilla

311

from the block?
Have you ever raised your hand
and made it land on a woman's face
to remind her of her place in this world?

Do you give to the indigent?
Do you know the meaning of that word?
Do you work? Do you dream?
Do you know how to pray?

Can you go to the grocery store
at midnight to buy super-sized tampons
or will you bring me back a bag of cotton
and a string?

If I start crying at the sight of a full moon,
a starving child, a dead rose, a lizard
over my front door, will you appease me
without condescension?

And don't think I forgot,
do you have a big dick?

del palo?
¿Has alzado alguna vez la mano
y hecho que cayera sobre la cara de una mujer
para recordarle cual es su lugar en el mundo?

¿Das a los indigentes?
¿Conoces el significado de esta palabra?
¿Trabajas? ¿Sueñas?
¿Sabes rezar?

¿Irías a la tienda a comprarme
tampones extra grandes a medianoche?
¿O me traerías una bolsa de algodón
y una cuerda?

Si me pongo a llorar al ver una luna llena,
un niño hambriento, una rosa muerta, una lagartija
encima de mi puerta, ¿me calmarás
sin condescendencia?

Y no creas que me olvidé,
¿tienes una pinga grande?

Safiya Sinclair

GOOD HAIR

> Only God, my dear,
> Could love you for yourself alone
> And not your yellow hair.
> — W.B. Yeats, "For Anne Gregory"

Sister, there was nothing left for us.
Down here, this cast-off hour, we listened
but heard no voices in the shells. No beauty.

Our lives already tangled in the violence of our hair,
We learned to feel unwanted in the sea's blue gaze,
Knowing even the blond lichen was considered lovely.

Not us, who combed and tamed ourselves at dawn,
cursing every brute animal in its windy mane –
God forbid all that good hair being grown to waste.

Barber, I can say a true thing or I can say nothing;
meet you in the canerows with my crooked English,
coins with strange faces stamped deep inside my palm,

ask to be remodelled with castaway hair, or dragged
by my scalp through your hot comb. The mirror takes
and the mirror takes. I've waded there and waited in vanity;

paid the toll to watch my wayward roots foam white,
drugstore formaldehyde burning through my skin.
For good hair I'd do anything. Pay the price of dignity,

send virgins in India to daily harvest; their miles
of glittering hair sold for thousands in the street.
Still we come to them yearly with our copper coins,

314

Safiya Sinclair

PELO BUENO

> Solo Dios, querida,
> Te podría amar solo por ti misma
> Y no tu pelo amarillo.
>> — W.B. Yeats, "Para Anne Gregory"

Hermana, no nos quedó nada.
Aquí abajo, esta hora extraviada, escuchamos
pero no oímos voces en los caracoles. Ninguna belleza.

Nuestras vidas ya enredadas en la violencia de nuestro pelo,
aprendimos, en la mirada azul del mar, a sentir que nadie nos quiere,
sabiendo que hasta el liquen rubio era considerado lindo.

Nosotras, no, que nos peinábamos y amansábamos al amanecer,
maldiciendo cada animal bruto de crines sopladas por el viento –
Dios nos libre de que todo ese pelo bueno crezca para nada.

Barbero, puedo decir una verdad o puedo no decir nada;
con mi inglés torcido, te encuentro en los cañaverales de mis trenzas,
monedas con caras extrañas timbradas en lo profundo de mi palma,

te pido ser remodelada con pelo sacrificado, o arrastrada
por mi cuero cabelludo a través de tu peine caliente. El espejo toma
y el espejo toma. He vadeado allí y he esperado en vanidad;

he pagado la tarifa para ver mis raíces rebeldes en espuma blanca,
formaldehído de farmacia quemándome la piel.
Para tener pelo bueno haría cualquier cosa. Pagaría el precio de la dignidad –

a diario, enviaría a las vírgenes en la India a la cosecha; sus millas
de cabello resplandeciente vendido por miles en la calle.
Aun así acudimos a ellos anualmente con nuestras monedas de cobre,

whole nights spent on our knees, our prayers whispered
ear to ear, hoping to wake with soft unfurling curls,
black waves parting strands of honey.

But how were we to know our poverty?
That our mother's good genes would only come to weeds,
that I would squander all her mulatta luck.

This nigger-hair my biggest malady.
So thick it holds a pencil up.

pasamos noches enteras de rodillas, nuestras oraciones murmulladas
de oreja a oreja, esperando despertar con suaves rizos desplegándose,
olas negras dividiendo mechas de miel.

¿Pero cómo íbamos a saber de nuestra pobreza?
Que de los genes buenos de nuestra madre solo saldrían malas hierbas,
que yo derrocharía toda su suerte de mulata.

Este pelo de negrita mi peor desgracia.
Tan grueso que sostiene un lápiz erguido.

Safiya Sinclair

CRANIA AMERICANA

The Caucasian skull is large and oval, with well-proportioned features. The nasal bones are arched, the chin full, the teeth vertical. This race is distinguished for the facility with which it attains the highest intellectual endowments.

> *Lusus Naturae*
>   n o u n   (*rare*)
>   A f r e e k o f n a t u r e.

Black body burns itself
                to b u s h f i r e −
spurned husk that I am. Skinned viscous,
daughtering fever. Grief knifes its slow lava

through my fluorescent, gnarled
as if a neon viper, as if singed animus.
Gaslamp-hot for necking, lit oceanliners
                    g u l p e d i n.

Such is our ambush. Spore of my peculiar −
Even the sea derails full-throttle at every turn.

What scurvy thrush unmoors   this boiled
microbial   as spite besots my humid mouth.

Storm, hag-seed and holy.
Come dusk, a rumbottle sky
                I a m s i p p i n g.
My preening tongue, the guillotine.

Safiya Sinclair

CRANIA AMERICANA

El cráneo caucásico es grande y ovalado, con rasgos bien
proporcionados. Los huesos nasales son arqueados, la barbilla plena,
los dientes verticales. Esta raza se distingue por la facilidad con la que
alcanza las más altas dotes intelectuales.

    Lusus Naturae
            nombre (*inusual*)
            Engendro.

Cuerpo negro se quema a sí mismo
                    a incendio forestal –
desdeñada cáscara que soy. Despellejada viscosa,
engendrando fiebre. El dolor apuñala su lenta lava

a través de mi fluorescente, retorcida como
una víbora de neón, como animadversión chamuscada.
Caliente como lámpara de gas para besuqueo,
iluminados barcos transatlánticos
                            engullidos.

Esa es nuestra emboscada.   Espora de mi peculiar –
Hasta el mar descarrila en plena aceleración a cada paso.

Qué escorbuto candidiasis desamarra   este nacido
microbiano   mientras el rencor embrutece mi boca húmeda.

Tormenta, semilla de bruja y sagrada.
Al anochecer, sorbo el cielo
                    desde una botella de ron.
Mi lengua atusadora, la guillotina.

Know nothing here will grow politely.
Such is our nature.
Such lurid rains sedate us villainous low:

This eel-eye screws to dazzling fright
        what slowly turns to vapour,
and another hot light spoils me
                        for grotesquerie.

Sibling, Sisyphean.   Howl of my unusual, ﹀
now we have reclassified the very
                        a p e o f u s .

Half fish   and Half monstrous.
Drowned spine of toothache take us
and barnacled,   all crippled filaments
                all jawbone.

Already plucked   of cruder blooms,
brined hippocampus
                unzipped with germ.

My dropsied and unteachable.
Lo, this Indigene. Hissing into madness
this infrared. All night

our dark carousel haphazards,
        churning to house our many jargon,
masked congenital, and cloven in.

Diagram and mooncalfed.   Even I.
How sometime I am wound with solitude.

        Enough a Negress all myself.

Sepan que nada crecerá aquí con cortesía.
Tal es nuestra naturaleza.
Tales lluvias espeluznantes nos sedan, los malvados de abajo:

Hasta un miedo hipnótico, este ojo de anguila atornilla
                lo que lentamente cambia a vapor,
y otra luz caliente me pudre
                    en grotesquería.

Consanguíneos. Sisíficos. Aullido de mi inusual,
ahora, hemos reclasificado el propio
                  simio en nosotros.

Medio pez   y Medio monstruosidad.
Espina ahogada del dolor de muelas nos derrota
y cubiertos de percebes, todo filamentos paralizados
           todo mandíbula.

Ya arrancado   de flores más crudas,
hipocampo en salmuera
           su cremallera desabrochada por gérmenes.

Mi hidropésica e ineducable.
He aquí, esta Indígena. Siseando hasta la demencia
esta infrarroja. Toda la noche

nuestro carrusel oscuro galopando al azar
    se revuelve para albergar nuestra mucha jerga,
enmascarada congénita, y hendida.

Diagrama y lunática becerra abortada.   Incluso yo.
Cómo a veces estoy enrollada por soledad.

    Suficiente, yo misma, una Negra.

Scorn, one golliwog-bone knots the black
mock of me, naked and denouncing
          us artless.

Vexed skinfolk. Unfossiled, hence.
What a brittle world is   man.
Self inflammable, I abjure you.

And wear your gabble like a diadem,
this flecked crown of dictions,
                    this bioluminescence.

Predator coiled eager   at the edge
                    of these maps.

Master, Dare I

               unjungle it?

Desprecio, un hueso de *golliwog* está atado a la burla negra
de mí misma, desnuda y denunciándonos
      sin arte.

Vexed skinfolk. Desfosilizada, por tanto.
Qué mundo quebradizo es el   del hombre.
Autoinflamable, yo de ti abjuro.

Y me visto de tu balbuceo como una diadema,
esta corona moteada de dicciones,
       esta bioluminiscencia.

Ávido depredador enroscado   al borde
                de estos mapas.

Amo, ¿Puedo osar a

       desenjunglarlo?

Safiya Sinclair

MERMAID

Caribbean thyme is ten times stronger than the English variety – just ask Miss Queenie and her royal navy, who couldn't yank a Jamaican weed from her rose-garden that didn't grow back thick, tenfold, and blackened with the furor of a violated man. The tepid American I sank with my old shoes over the jaws of the Atlantic could never understand the hard clamour of my laugh, why I furrowed rough at the brow, why I knew the hollow points of every bone. But dig where the soil is wet and plant the proud seed of your shame-tree; don't let them say it never grew. Roll the saltfish barrel down the hill, sending that battered thunder clanging at the seaside moon, jangled by her long earrings at our sea, ten times bluer than the bluest eye. That mint tea whistling in the Dutch pot is stronger than liquor, and takes six spoons of sugar, please – what can I say, my great-grandfather's blood was clotted thick with sugar cane and overproof rum; when he bled it trickled heavy like molasses, clotted black like phlegm in the throat. Every red ant from Negril to Frenchman's Cove came to burrow and suckle at his vein, where his leg was honeyed with a diabetic rot, and when he caught my grandmother in his wide fishing net, he served her up cold to his wild-eyed son: "Mermaid on the deck."

Safiya Sinclair

SIRENA

El tomillo caribeño es diez veces más fuerte que la variedad inglesa
– solo pregúntele a la Reinita Miss Queenie y su marina real, quiénes
no pudieron arrancar una sola hierba jamaicana de su jardín de rosas
que no volviera a crecer diez veces más gruesa, y ennegrecida con el
furor de un hombre violentado. El americano tibio que hundí con
mis zapatos viejos sobre las mandíbulas del Atlántico jamás pudo
entender el duro clamor de mi risa, porqué fruncía el ceño
bruscamente, porqué conocía las partes huecas de cada hueso. Pero
cava donde la tierra está mojada y siembra la orgullosa semilla de tu
árbol de la vergüenza; no dejes que digan que jamás creció. Lanza el
barril de bacalao salado colina abajo, enviando el tantán de ese
atronador batidero hasta la luna costera, que con sus largos aretes
tintinea sobre nuestro mar, diez veces más azul que el ojo más azul.
Ese té de menta que silba en el caldero es más fuerte que el licor, y
añadan seis cucharadas de azúcar, por favor – qué puedo decir, la
sangre de mi bisabuelo estaba coagulada por azúcar de caña y ron
overproof; cuando sangraba goteaba duro como la melaza, coagulada
negra como flema en la garganta. Cada hormiga colorada desde
Negril hasta Frenchman's Cove venía a escarbar y amamantarse de su
vena, donde su pierna estaba caramelizada por una podredumbre
diabética, y cuando capturó a mi abuela en su ancha red de pesca, se
la sirvió fría a su hijo de mirada enloquecida: "Sirena en la cubierta
del bote".

Dorothea Smartt

JUST A PART: A DISTANT LOT

My family are a distant lot.
Some I've met, maybe once,
many never at all.
I do not know their likes or dislikes,
I struggle to recall their names.
They do not surround me
at significant times of the year.

My family are a distant lot.
Their faces do not spring to mind,
I do not see shared gestures or
ways of saying.

My family are a distant lot,
scattered around migratory paths: from Barbados
landing up in London, Birmingham, New York,
Panama City, Nassau, Miami, Havana.

My family are a distant lot,
people whose names I write down
to remember, interrogate my mother
to make connections on paper –
my family extending across the page –
great uncles and aunts on their travels.
Mum remembers letters arriving
in Bridgetown with news of babies born,
cousins to know.

My family are a distant lot.
Cousin Sherry and I, excavating names,
make mention of a place
with the same address in Bridgetown.
Her grand-aunt's board-house is my grandmother's,

Dorothea Smartt

SOLO UNA PARTE: UN GRUPITO DISTANTE

Mi familia es un grupito distante.
A algunos les he conocido, puede que una vez,
a muchos jamás.
No sé qué les gusta o les disgusta,
me cuesta recordar sus nombres.
No me rodean
en momentos señalados del año.

Mi familia es un grupito distante.
Sus caras no me surgen a la mente,
no veo gestos o
maneras de decir compartidos.

Mi familia es un grupito distante
desperdigado a lo largo de rutas migratorias: desde Barbados,
desembarcaron en Londres, Birmingham, Nueva York,
Ciudad de Panamá, Nassau, Miami, La Habana.

Mi familia es un grupito distante,
gente cuyos nombres escribo
para recordarlos, interrogo a mi madre
para establecer conexiones sobre el papel –
mi familia extendiéndose por la página –
sobre los viajes de tías y tíos abuelos.
Mamá recuerda la llegada de cartas
en Bridgetown con noticias de nacimientos,
primos que conocer.

Mi familia es un grupito distante,
la prima Sherry y yo, excavando nombres,
hacemos mención de un lugar
con la misma dirección en Bridgetown.
La casita de madera de su tía abuela es la de mi abuela,

its sole occupant now the grand-daughter,
providing a link for scattered family.

My family are a distant lot.
Sherry and I find each other, cautious,
each behind a video camera,
smiling at our visceral need to record,
sitting in a room of her family, my family
of not so distant cousins.

For the first time,
at twenty-something, in a room full of
faces holding familiar fragments
of my mother, my sisters, my own,
here, in this living room, I see
my cousin smile my mother's smile.
See her mother's long fingers equal my own.
With diverse kin extending around the room
my sense of self opens out.

This one time we meet – maybe never again –
I ask their likes and dislikes.
Ask them to recall names my mother told me.
As they surround me, aunts become sisters-
in-law, uncles become fathers.
Faces spring from old photos; I see
shared gestures and hear our ways of saying.

My family and I are just apart.
And this distant lot are just
a part I could not see, do not live around.

And I wonder if blood is thicker than water,
even when the bloodline's vague and unknown.

And I wonder if the family I'm born to
is the family that will make me whole.

su única ocupante ahora la nieta,
que sirve de vínculo para la familia repartida.

Mi familia es un grupito distante,
Sherry y yo nos encontramos, cautelosas,
cada una detrás de una cámara de video,
sonriendo a nuestra necesidad visceral de grabar,
sentadas en una sala de su familia, mi familia
de primos no tan lejanos.

Por primera vez,
a los veinte y pico, en una sala llena de
caras compuestas de facciones parecidas
a las de mi madre, mis hermanas, mías,
aquí, en esta sala de estar, veo
a mi prima sonriendo con la sonrisa de mi madre.
Veo los dedos alargados de su madre iguales a los míos.
Con familiares diversos congregados alrededor de la sala
el sentido de mí misma se extiende.

Esta única vez que nos reunimos — quizás nunca más —
les pregunto qué les gusta y qué les disgusta.
Les pido que recuerden nombres que me dijo mi madre.
Mientras me rodean, las tías se vuelven cuñadas,
los tíos se vuelven padres.
Las caras saltan de las fotos viejas; veo
gestos compartidos y oigo nuestras maneras de decir.

Mi familia y yo solo estamos aparte.
Y este grupito distante solo es
una parte que no podía ver, de la que no vivo cerca.

Y me pregunto si la sangre llama, incluso cuando
los lazos de sangre son inciertos y desconocidos.

Y me pregunto si la familia en la que nací
es la familia que me completará.

Dorothea Smartt

LOVING WOMEN

It's a dangerous joy,
well-travelled all the same
in spite of threats.
We have been here before
hidden in stories of back-home
Caribbean women, *more than frens.*

My father knew, my mother knows,
of women *like that*
telling no names –
is only after she gone
her childhood friend tells

of our *macommère* Great Aunt
living with she *fren.*

Dorothea Smartt

AMAR A MUJERES

Es una peligrosa alegría,
aun así un camino concurrido
a pesar de las amenazas.
Hemos estado aquí antes
escondidas en cuentos de allá
de mujeres caribeñas, *más que amiguitas*.

Mi padre sabía, mi madre sabe,
de mujeres *así*
sin decir nombres —
solo cuando ella ya no está
su amiga de infancia cuenta que

nuestra *macommère,* tía abuela,
vivía con su *amiguita*.

Dorothea Smartt

READER, I MARRIED HIM

Reader, I married him.
A son with his father's name,
loving a man twice his age,
hiding from dem men that kill
he las' "fren" – and chop-he
widda a machete! Slice scarring he face
impairing he eyes (like a Mr. Rochester)
but not mine. I could see a way, clear-clear.

Reader, I married him
so he could lef outta JA. Take refuge
in my British citizenship,
my redundant heterosex right
to marry any man. So I flew to Bim,
to do it beachside, tropical style –
at least in the photos
that would serve as proof.

Reader, I married him.
My best man? His lover, gave me away,
was wedding planner, witness,
and his wedding night delight,
man enough to cover every detail
of our act. Rehearsing Junior
in his role. For this was a political act:
I was the lifeboat, love boat.

Reader, I married him,
this young guy half my age.
The Bajan registrar looked weary
at another "rent-a-dread" giving
"Stella-her-groove-back".

Dorothea Smartt

LECTOR, ME CASÉ CON ÉL

Lector, me casé con él.
Un hijo con el nombre de su padre,
que ama a un hombre que le dobla la edad,
que se esconde de esos hombres que mataron
a su último "amigo" — ¡y a él le cayeron
a machetazos! Un corte dejó una cicatriz en su cara
dañando sus ojos (como un Mr. Rochester)
pero no los míos. Yo pude ver el camino, bien claro.

Lector, me casé con él
para que pudiera salir de Jamaica. Refugiarse
en mi ciudadanía británica,
mi superfluo derecho heterosexo
de casarme con cualquier hombre. Así que volé a Bim,
para hacerlo estilo playero, tropical —
al menos en las fotos
que servirían de prueba.

 Lector, me casé con él.
¿Mi padrino? Su amante, me llevó al altar,
fue organizador de la boda, testigo,
y su deleite de noche de bodas,
lo suficientemente hombre para ocuparse de cada detalle
de nuestro acto. Ensayando con Junior
su papel. Porque esto era un acto político:
yo era el bote salvavidas, el barco del amor.

Lector, me casé con él,
este chico que tiene la mitad de mi edad.
La funcionaria barbadense parecía harta
de otro "rasta-en-aquiler" dando a
"Stella-her-groove-back".

I was a politically incorrect act:
bewitch, turn-head tourist trapped
by his honey eyes, glazed by my island man.

Reader, I married him.
I was confident, self-assured, but
still feigning new love coyness.
He was all fingers and thumbs,
dumb in the face of her authority.
Me, the blushing brown-skin bride,
who produced the rings, asked
his lover for the wedding bands.

Reader, I married him – for love
of our humanity. Arms entwined,
we sipped each other's champagne,
clutching me between Sandy Lane's columns –
our photographer sneaking kisses.
Reader, I married him, played a part
for a JA brother. Reader I, married him.
With our *tainted love* we said, "I do."

Yo era un acto políticamente incorrecto:
turista hechizada, con la cabeza dándole vueltas atrapada,
por sus ojos color miel, glaseada por mi isleño.

Lector, me casé con él.
Tenía confianza, estaba segura de mí misma, pero
todavía estaba simulando esa timidez de nuevo amor.
Él parecía incómodo,
embobado ante la autoridad de ella.
Yo, la trigueña novia sonrojada,
que había traído los anillos, pedí
a su amante las alianzas de matrimonio.

Lector, me casé con él – por amor
a nuestra humanidad. Brazos entrelazados,
bebíamos champán los unos de la copa de los otros–
me abrazaban entre las columnas en Sandy Lane –
mientras nuestro fotógrafo iba robando besos.
Lector, me casé con él, hice mi papel
para un hermano de Jamaica. Lector, me casé con él.
Con nuestro *tainted love* nos dimos el "sí, quiero".

Karol Starocean

TOALLAS SANITARIAS

Los restos de empaques de toallas sanitarias son representaciones adustas de arte moderno, en las papeleras de los baños en estos bares de la zona colonial donde vamos a escuchar a Clash y Janis Joplin desgalillarse sobre un escenario a través de una pantalla plana pegada a una pared infestada de humedad y recuerdos. Porque estamos cansados de las bachatas que se suceden de puerta a puerta en las calles, no nos importa la letra de los yanquis que vemos cantar en un festival porque están todos muertos de sobredosis pero eran *cool* y de alguna manera las pobres luces del bar nos hacen sentir bohemios, somos una raza aparte que pretende leer a Camus parados frente a una alcantarilla llena de basura, a los que les toca los límites de los ojos una lagrimita de nostalgia al pasar por un edificio en ruinas. Somos una tela que se rasga, que antes, hace muchos años pintaron a mano para cubrir la terraza del sol y que hoy una voz con ternura susurra en los oídos: No pasa nada, es el salitre. Hay que pretender, te digo con mis dotes de telepatía, hay que pretender que podemos todavía cruzar el malecón de Santo Domingo sin ser aplastados y tú me escuchas y entiendes, mueves la cabeza como si te persiguiera una abeja.

Pedimos cervezas en la barra porque los cocteles son muy caros y detrás de nosotros justo en el muro donde nos recostamos para seguir dentro del bar pero no hablar con nadie, hay un pedazo de cemento a punto de caer y me recuerda, creo que a ti también, que tengo cigarrillos en los bolsillos. Salimos a fumar, nos colocamos a unos centímetros de la entrada, los tipos que se sientan en los muros de los edificios cerrados a ver pasar la vida me hacen preguntarme a mí misma como si te lo preguntara a ti: ¿por qué en estos bares todo el que sale de los baños te mira con odio? Tú no dices nada, tal vez tus niveles de alcohol o aguantarte las ganas de orinar para no atravesar el bar lleno de gente te ha dejado aturdido. Mientras tanto yo, aún de pie fumando, me dejo hipnotizar por aquello que hay allá

Karol Starocean

SANITARY PADS

The remains of sanitary pad packages are grim representations of modern art, in the trash bins of the bathrooms in these bars in the colonial zone where we go to listen to Clash and Janis Joplin detonate on a stage through a flat screen attached to a wall infested with moisture and memories. Because we are tired of the bachatas that play out, door after door, in the streets, we don't care about the lyrics of the *yanquis* that we see sung at a festival because they're all dead of an overdose but they were *cool,* and somehow the poor bar lights make us feel like bohemians, we are a race apart that pretends to read Camus standing in front of a sewer full of garbage, for whom a little tear of nostalgia wells up in the corner of the eyes when passing by a ruined building. We are a fabric that shreds, that before, many years ago they hand-painted to cover the terrace from the sun, and today a voice filled with tenderness whispers in our ears: It's okay, it's the saltpetre. We have to pretend, I tell you, with my telepathic skills we have to pretend that we can still cross the Malecón de Santo Domingo without being crushed and you listen to me and understand, you move your head as if you were being chased by a bee.

We order beers at the bar because the cocktails are very expensive and behind us right on the wall where we lean back to stay inside the bar but not talk to anyone, there's a piece of cement about to fall and it reminds me, I think you, too, that I have cigarettes in my pockets. We go out to smoke, we stand a few centimeters from the entrance, the guys who sit on the walls of closed buildings to watch life go by make me ask myself as if I were asking you: why is it that in these bars, everyone who comes out of the bathroom looks at you with hate? You don't say anything, maybe your alcohol levels or holding your urge to urinate to avoid going through the crowded bar has left you stunned. Meanwhile, still standing smoking, I let myself be hypnotized by what's at the end of the street and I sing: "This street finally has its name"; you don't sing or anything, because of your face I know that

al final de la calle y canto: "Esta calle al final tiene su nombre", tú no cantas ni nada porque sé por tu rostro, que tú también sabes que aquí fuera, debajo del farol de la calle y los tipos con pinta de antecedentes Elamitas que vienen y van con sus chaquetas importadas a pesar del calor, llevando a mujeres del brazo, que siempre van mirando el suelo pero perfumadas, vemos el metraje de nuestra vida en una noche más buscando desesperadamente un *soundtrack* perfecto, la toma concreta de una escena real, biográfica, viva, que nos permita poder llegar a casa y dormir en calma.

Tú no estás de acuerdo, lo noto por el temblor de tu mano, te sientes violento y lanzas la colilla al piso que se envuelve en un abrazo erótico con la mugre de la acera mientras comienzas tu discurso mirando al cielo: hay en medio de nuestro subconsciente ansias y deseos sociales mezclados con la desidia, ese secreto, escondido, ese deseo incontenible, desmesurado a sentir que por unas cuantas horas ser el oyente casi espectador de la distimia cotidiana de Hendrix, por corto tiempo nos permitirá dejar de pertenecer a esta isla.

you also know that here outside, under the street lamp and with the guys that look like descendents of Elamites who come and go with their imported jackets despite the heat, women on their arm, who always look at the floor but are perfumed, we see the footage of our life on one more night of looking desperately for a perfect sound-track, the concrete take of a real, biographical, alive scene, that allows us to be able to come home and sleep calmly.

You don't agree, I notice it by the shaking of your hand, you feel violent and you flick the butt to a floor that's wrapped in an erotic embrace with the grime of the sidewalk while you start your speech looking at the sky: there is in the middle of our subconscious social anxiety and desires mixed with apathy, that secret, hidden, that uncontrollable, disproportionate desire, to feel that for a few hours to be the listener almost spectator of Hendrix's daily dysthymia, for a short time will allow us to stop belonging to this island.

Karol Starocean

ELLA CASI NO LLEGA A SER FLOR

Tan linda, tan roja, tan idiota. Siempre quiso llegar un día corriendo desde la calle, entrar a un café, detenerse de golpe ante una mesa y decirle a quien estuviera ocupando esa mesa:
"Tu amor es el puerto donde anclan todos mis barcos".
Pero en vez de eso se conformaba con correr las cortinas los domingos y desnudarse para soportar el calor, tenderse en el suelo junto al sofá, cerrar los ojos y decirse a sí misma que había cosas peores que estar rodeada de mar y soñar con ver el mar. Porque en algún lugar del mundo algún marinero alguna vez se ahogó en una bañera y se consolaba, porque dentro de su corazón el demonio que la aprisionaba, le recordaba en navidad cuando las pequeñas luces decoraban los balcones de las casas y los árboles artificiales pululaban por la ciudad, que a pesar de tanto plástico y los cientos de luces que prenden y apagan ni una sola vez había podido decirle mirándole la cara a alguien: "¿Sabías que las luces de navidad se reflejan en tus ojos?"

Karol Starocean

SHE ALMOST DIDN'T BECOME A FLOWER

So lovely, so red, so idiotic. She always wanted to arrive one day,
running from the street, to enter a café, abruptly stop in front of a
table and say to someone who was occupying that table:
"Your love is the port where all of my boats anchor".
But, instead of that, she stuck with drawing the curtains on Sundays
and getting naked to stand the heat, lying on the ground next to the
sofa, closing her eyes and saying to herself there had to be worse
things than being surrounded by the sea and dreaming of seeing the
sea. For somewhere in the world, some sailor once drowned in a bath
tub, and she was consoled, because inside her heart the demon that
imprisoned her reminded her of Christmas when the small lights
decorated the balconies of the houses and the artificial trees swarmed
over the city, that despite so much plastic and the hundreds of lights
that blinked on and off, she had never even once been able to say,
looking into someone's face: "Do you know that the Christmas lights
are reflected in your eyes?"

Karol Starocean

EN SANTO DOMINGO HAY TÚNELES

En Santo Domingo hay túneles, muchos túneles, muy largos, que se extienden en una amplitud desparramada incalculable de extremo a extremo de la isla, desde el mar Caribe hasta el Océano Atlántico. Cuando llueve, la mitad del mar Caribe sube a la superficie a saludar a la lluvia y la otra mitad del agua que nace de las nubes se exprime como la mitad de una naranja sobre las calles, las casas, las palmeras desplumadas del malecón, las cañadas de los infelices felices, las estaciones de policía y los postes con aroma a orinales gracias a los perritos alegres sin dueño. Los hombres se quitan las camisas y las mujeres se cubren el cabello con fundas de supermercado para que no se les rice el pelo, los niños se bajan los pantalones para deslizarse por las cañerías hasta el enorme charco del final de la calle. Hay quien piensa en salvavidas y chalecos naranja, pero ellos salen presurosos a cubrirse la cabeza con jabón de cuaba y enjugarse los cabellos con los caños que bajan de los techos de las casas, los caños de afuera, porque adentro los caños son más discretos, no da para bañarse, pero inundan las casas, entonces hay que barrer el agua hacia la calle inundada, con escobas de las hojas secas caídas de las palmeras y suspirar, por mojarse siempre los pies, dentro o fuera de una casa. Los coches no sienten vergüenza al empinarse, se elevan hasta la superficie del agua y comienzan a flotar como los patitos amarillos de hule en la bañera, semejando marionetas de hilos invisibles, autónomos, sin dirección. Los conductores se saludan con la boca llena de espuma, por la rabia. Cuando cae la noche un manto oscuro se cierne más allá de la vista, hasta la oscuridad es húmeda, se puede tocar, se siente la ropa mojada pegada del cuerpo, pero nadie la ve, ni nadie la evita, como si fuera inherente a la vida, por el principio aquel de que la lluvia moja y no se pierde tiempo pensando en ello.

En Santo Domingo los huracanes son fenómenos sociales de gran intensidad y voluntad, aunque en su viaje a veces su euforia disminuya o incluso desaparezca en sus inicios, están decididos a pasar a saludar,

Karol Starocean

THERE ARE TUNNELS IN SANTO DOMINGO

In Santo Domingo there are tunnels, many tunnels, very long, that extend with incalculable amplitude, spreading from one extreme of the island to the other, from the Caribbean Sea to the Atlantic Ocean. When it rains, half of the Caribbean Sea rises to the surface to greet the rain and the other half of the water produced by clouds is squeezed out like half of an orange over the streets, the houses, the plucked palm trees of the boardwalk, the gullies of the lucky unfortunates, the police stations and the poles urine-scented thanks to happy, ownerless dogs. Men take off their shirts and women cover their hair with supermarket bags so that they don't frizz it up, children pull down their pants to slide down the pipes to the huge puddle at the end of the street. Some people think of life jackets and orange vests, but they hurry to cover their heads with *cuaba* soap and rinse their hair out with the rain-spouts from the roofs of the houses, the rain-spouts outside, because inside the rain-spouts are more modest, there's not enough for bathing, but they flood the houses; then, you have to sweep the water towards the flooded street, with brooms made from the dried leaves of the palm trees, and sigh, over always getting your feet wet, inside or outside of a house. Cars don't feel shame when they lift up, rise to the surface of the water and begin to float like yellow rubber duckies in the bathtub, looking like marionettes with invisible strings, autonomous, directionless. Drivers greet each other with their mouths full of spit, because of the rage. When night falls, a dark mantle hangs in the air as far as the eye can see, even the darkness is damp, you can touch it, you feel the wet clothes sticking to your body, but nobody sees it, nor does anyone avoid it, as if it were inherently part of life, following the principle that rain gets things wet so don't waste time thinking about it.

In Santo Domingo hurricanes are social phenomena of great intensity and volition, although in their journey sometimes their euphoria diminishes or even disappears at its beginnings, they are determined

se sienten solos y buscan tierra, objetos y personas, cuando desean observar de cerca, en los contornos de sus ojos todo permanece en calma, como el encuadre que un fotógrafo sin angustias buscaría para captar sus mejores ángulos, captar por un instante la realidad y luego imprimirla para su conciencia ilimitada o la de todo el mundo.

Es cuando los huracanes pasan a saludar a Santo Domingo debajo de los túneles grandes, muy grandes y largos cuando aparece el fantasma de la Carabela Santa María, todos pensaron desde 1492 que con los restos del naufragio se había erigido un fuerte, pero he aquí que mintieron todos y como nadie estuvo ahí, no pueden comprobarlo, porque lo que sí se puede comprobar es el fantasma de la Carabela que surge desde los acantilados en la desembocadura del río Ozama. Es una visión espantosa, aquella sombra fantasmagórica que se va moviendo con todas las señas de querer dirigirse a alguna parte, mientras la gente agita las tazas para que el azúcar se mezcle con el chocolate, toda la ciudad a oscuras, dándose puntitos de luminosidad con velas encendidas encima de la nevera apagada, de las mesas con manteles de plástico chino, las puertas abiertas para que entre un poco de la brisa de una calle sin alumbrado eléctrico, pero que abraza a todos, los que hacen los mismos cuentos, los que se pelean lanzando botellas de cerveza y los que cantan debajo de los árboles que también parecen sombras, como la carabela esa que sigue intentando salir más allá del puerto por el mar. Y cuando vuelve a desaparecer entre la agonía de la noche, el miedo a los mosquitos cede ante el cansancio y el sueño, por reacción natural todos se encierran en sus casas.

Al otro día las sirenas de pánico no dejan de sonar, haciendo que los niños lloren. No hay peces ni pescadores porque entre el huracán que desea saludar hasta los huesos y la carabela fantasma la lluvia es insoportable. Mientras tanto, los corales dejan de nadar y de los edificios sale humo. No se respira, no se siente. Encima de los túneles la ciudad duerme, naufraga, se queja y se espanta de mis ojos abiertos.

to pass by to greet us, they feel alone and look for land, objects and people, when they want to observe up-close, at the rims of their eyes everything remains calm, like the framing of a photographer who would, without anguish, seek to capture its best angles, capture for an instant the reality and then print it for its limitless consciousness or that of the whole world.

It's when the hurricanes come to greet Santo Domingo under the large tunnels, very large and long, that the phantom of the Caravel Santa María appears, everyone has thought since 1492 that with the shipwreck remains, a fort had been erected, but lo and behold, they all lied and since no one was there, it can't be proven, for what can be proven is the phantom of the caravel that surges up from the cliffs at the mouth of the Ozama River. It's a frightful vision, that phantasmagorical shadow that moves with all the signs of wanting to go somewhere, while people stir cups so that sugar mixes with chocolate, the whole city in the dark, giving off small points of luminosity with lit candles on top of the non-working fridge, on tables with Chinese oilcloth covers, the doors open to let a little breeze enter from a street with no electrical lighting, but which embraces everyone, those who tell the same tales, those who fight among themselves, throwing beer bottles, and those who sing under the trees that also look like shadows, like that caravel that keeps trying to move beyond the Port to the sea. And when it disappears again admidst the agony of the night, the fear of mosquitos relinquished on account of fatigue and being sleepy, naturally, all react by staying shut up in their houses.

The next day, the emergency sirens don't stop blaring, causing the children to cry. There are no fish or fishermen because between the hurricane that wishes to salute us down to the bone and the phantom caravel, the rain is unbearable. Meanwhile, the corals quit swimming, and vapour rises from the buildings. No one breathes, no one feels. On top of the tunnels, the city sleeps, shipwrecks, complains and is frightened of my open eyes.

Ariadna Vásquez Germán

UNA MUJER PUEDE PERDER LA FALDA EN UN BAÑO

Una mujer puede perder la falda en un baño. Puede entrar con ella puesta y antes de salir, perderla. Una mujer puede dejar ir la falda por uno de sus huecos, extender el vacío de la prenda, abrir esa puerta. Una mujer es capaz de irse, camino hacia el desagüe de su falda. Después de todo es suya la ropa, es aquello que ella puede quitarse si quiere, desprenderse sin intervenciones ajenas. La falda puede ser su narrativa negativa, su forma de demorarse. Ella puede decir: aquí me detengo. Es decir, la falda es elevada para que ocurra la orina y puede que no regrese a su sitio tras completarse el acto. Se puede, por ejemplo, integrar al cuerpo, volverse demasiado útil para las costillas. Subir y bajar la falda es una forma del tiempo; es abierta la falda, su eternidad está arriba y abajo, también en el instante de su fuga. Es que es ahuecada la falda, se escapa por ambos lados, por ello se pierde, es fácil su extravío.

Ariadna Vásquez Germán

A WOMAN COULD LOSE HER SKIRT IN A BATHROOM

A woman could lose her skirt in a bathroom. She could enter with it on and before getting out, lose it. Through one of its openings, a woman could let her skirt go, expanding the emptiness of the garment, opening that door. A woman is capable of leaving, through the drain of her skirt. After all, it's her clothes, it's something she can take off if she wants to, get rid of without outside interventions. The skirt can be her negative story, her manner of detaining herself. She can say: I am stopping myself here. In other words, the skirt is raised for peeing and it can be that it doesn't return to its place after the act is completed. It could, for example, be integrated into the body, so usefully clinging to the ribs. Raising and lowering the skirt is a form of time; the skirt is open, its eternity is up high and down low, also in the instant of its escape. It's that the skirt is hollow; it escapes from both ends, that's why it gets lost, it's easy for it to go missing.

Ariadna Vásquez Germán

DE *SI HUBIERA TENIDO UN DIÁLOGO EN CASABLANCA*...

1
esta marca de agua que compartimos en la mirada
corriente adentro
la agitación de los pulmones
que se estremecen en una danza de ahogado
es solamente ahora
que parece que somos una casa
aunque nunca lo pedimos
estas manos agarradas
el hilo delgado que nos ata
y no podemos darnos la espalda o avanzar
cada uno con su umbral
a otra casa
estamos dentro
y es así ¿es así? ahora
y no será así después
tantas noches entre inundaciones
con la cabeza náufraga y los cuerpos
y las ramitas húmedas sobre el colchón hundido
resistiendo
y quizás es imposible la casa
y no somos
sino un adentro de paredes altas
donde bailamos cálidos
arropados por el agua
tan juntos
que el tiempo nos persigue para ver
que si somos una casa
si no somos
tendremos que caer como si no pudiéramos saberlo
habremos de salir y respirar
con los pulmones quietos

Ariadna Vásquez Germán

FROM *SI HUBIERA TENIDO UN DIÁLOGO EN CASABLANCA…*

1
this watermark we share in our gaze
a current within
our distressed lungs
that shudder in a dance of drowning
it's only now
that we seem to be a house
even though we never asked for this
this holding of hands
the thin thread that binds us
and we can't turn our backs or move forward
each of us with our own threshold
to another house
we're inside
and that's how it is, isn't it?
later it's not going to be how it is now
so many nights of flooding
with our shipwrecked heads and our bodies
and wet twigs all over the sunken mattress
resisting
and maybe the house is impossible
and we are only
the interior essence of high walls
where we dance warmly
cloaked in water
so close together
that time chases us down to see
whether we are a house
if we aren't
we'll have to fall away from here like we can't grasp it
we'll have to get out and breathe

cabizbajos
disimulando
el agua estancada en el añoro
como si hubiéramos perdido
como si fuera real
una casa

with calm lungs
heads bowed
concealing
the stagnant water of our longing
as if we had lost
a house
as if it were real

5

ir hacia algún lado
como ir hacia un destino donde la ganancia espera
como tener los ojos para esa luz que recompensa
y si hubiera el camino
¿a qué lado nos llevaría?
será algún borde o una planicie
quizás un acantilado donde el mar deslumbra en las mañanas
una ventana desde donde la ola se enmarca como ese deseo
al que cada día vigilaremos

ir hacia ese lado
que es un lado distinto de muchos otros
donde llegábamos antes
descalzos delgados
con un olor a herrumbre y lodazal
la ropa destejida sobre la piel
imaginando siempre ese otro lado
cuya idea yace más lejos
mucho más allá de lo lejos
como si la errancia anidara una fe violenta hacia el añoro

ir a ese lado y realmente llegar
pero ¿será convincente ese hallazgo?
encontrar nuestros pies recién nacidos
sobre aquel manto de arena que todo lo sostiene
¿qué silueta haría la luz delante de la enorme roca?
y los caracoles
¿qué estuvieron haciendo por tanto tiempo
antes de que llegáramos a levantarlos?

ir hacia ese lado donde la claridad se asienta sobre el caminante
y al arribar
¿de cuál otro lado nos distanciaríamos?
¿olvidaríamos a nuestra llegada
que hubo un final fallido en cada antiguo viaje?

5

to go somewhere
like going to a destination where profits await
like having eyes for the rewarding light
and if there were a path
where would it lead us?
will it be some border or plain,
maybe a cliff where the sea dazzles in the mornings
a window where the wave is framed like
that desire we safeguard everyday

to go to that somewhere
someplace distinct from all those places
we arrived at before
barefoot thin
smelling of rust and muck
threadbare clothes over our skin
always imagining that other side
the idea of which lies far away
so much further away
as if wandering embedded a violent faith in longing

to go to that somewhere and really arrive
but will this be a convincing discovery?
finding our recently-born feet
on that mantle of sand that sustains everything
what silhouette does the light make in front of the enormous rock?
and the seashells
what were they doing for the long time
before we arrived and picked them up?

to go to that somewhere, a place of clarity settling over the walker
and upon arrival
what other somewhere will we distance ourselves from?
on arriving, will we forget
there was a failed ending to every old journey?

será que sólo era necesario aprehender
que ninguno fue nunca nuestro lado
aunque hubiéramos llegado a tiempo
tantas veces
ardiendo porque la desesperación es el principio de todos los incendios

ir hacia algún lado
¿y en cuál otro nos aguardaría la falta?
¿desde cuál norte escucharíamos al relámpago?

it could be that it was only necessary to perceive
that none of them were ever our somewhere
even if we had arrived on time
so many times
burning because desperation is the beginning of all fires

to go somewhere
And in what other place will failure await us?
From what compass heading will we hear the thunder?

Donna Aza Weir-Soley

ROOTS

I come from hard-packed red dirt
yielding coffee, cocoa, pimento, butter ackees and soft white yam
(bright white and sweet like the smile of my first boyfriend).

I come from hardworking
tough-loving, tenderhearted dark men
and tall, statuesque healer women,
midwives, priestesses, dreamers and seer women
with skin shades ranging from
common mango yellow to
blue-black star-apple purple.

I am packed hard, impervious,
softly yielding fruit in and out of season,
like the earth that nurtured me.

Donna Aza Weir-Soley

RAÍCES

Vengo de una dura y sólida tierra colorada
que da café, cacao, pimento, *butter ackee*, suave ñame blanco
(de un blanco brillante y dulce como la sonrisa de mi primer novio).

Vengo de hombres prietos que trabajan duro,
de fuerte querer y corazón tierno
y mujeres altas, monumentales, sanadoras,
comadronas, sacerdotisas, soñadoras y adivinas
con tonos de piel que van del
amarillo común del mango al
azul tirando a negro del caimito morado.

Endurecida, soy sólida y resistente.
Doy frutos delicadamente dentro y fuera de temporada,
como la tierra que me crio.

Donna Aza Weir-Soley

AN ON-GOING CONVERSATION

Daily we must fight
for the same crumbs
knowing neither rest nor respite,
breaking the same stones
to build the same road
to journey on without end,
lugging the same old loads
avoiding the same cracks
(that broke our mothers' backs).

And yes…
even in sleep
we must keep
that third eye open
listen for the approach
of the white-bellied rat
that blows first
to numb the spot
before it bites

bites and blows
bites and blows

numbing us further into sleep…
till we awake to bleeding heels
a gnawed-off knuckle
a frayed spine
that cannot support
our own familiar weight.

We must keep a steady vigil
have our grigris prepared

Donna Aza Weir-Soley

UNA CONVERSACIÓN EN CURSO

A diario debemos luchar
por las mismas migas
sin conocer tregua ni respiro,
rompiendo las mismas piedras
para construir el mismo camino
por el que viajar sin fin,
arrastrando las mismas viejas cargas
sorteando las mismas grietas
(que rompieron las espaldas de nuestras madres).

Y sí...
incluso durante el sueño
debemos mantener
ese tercer ojo abierto
escuchar en caso que llegue
la rata de vientre blanco
que primero sopla
para adormecer el sitio
antes de morder

muerde y sopla
muerde y sopla

adormeciéndonos hasta caer más profundamente en el sueño...
hasta despertarnos con talones ensangrentados
un nudillo roído
un espinazo deshilachado
que no puede soportar
nuestro propio peso.

Debemos velar atentamente
tener nuestros *grigris* preparados

to ward off creeping evil
We must grow ears
in the soles of our feet
(the better to hear the earth's counsel)
eyes in the back of our throats
so we do not swallow
poisoned words
from smiling, well-meaning lips.

Sometimes we have to lie still
in a dark, quiet place
and listen to our inside voices
and the voices of our ancestors
warning us of danger,
teaching us how to proceed,
reminding us that though
we will emerge battle-scarred and tired,
and often sick and tired of always
being sick and tired,
we cannot, must not give in,
or only pass the baton when we have to,
must claim the right to defend the selves
we fight daily to preserve.

For Barbara Christian, with love and nuff positive light.

para ahuyentar el mal que avanza acechante
Debemos dejarnos crecer orejas
en las plantas de los pies
(para oír mejor el consejo de la tierra)
ojos en el fondo de nuestras gargantas
para no tragarnos
palabras envenenadas
de labios sonrientes, bien-intencionados.

A veces tenemos que permanecer inmóviles
en un lugar tranquilo, oscuro
y escuchar nuestras voces interiores
y las voces de nuestros ancestros
advirtiéndonos del peligro,
enseñándonos cómo proceder,
recordándonos que aunque
resurgiremos con cicatrices de batalla y cansados,
y a menudo hartos de siempre
estar hartos,
no podemos, no debemos ceder,
o solo pasar el testigo cuando tengamos que hacerlo,
debemos reclamar el derecho de defender los seres
que luchamos a diario por preservar.

Para Barbara Christian, con amor y nuff *luz positiva*

Donna Aza Weir-Soley

GATEKEEPER

Meet me where the four roads cross
where all paths open, close at your whim
Meet me at the crossing
where little feet dance the fates of kings
and small axes fell giant oaks and cypresses
Meet me inbetween the cycles of seasons
dancing in time to the beat of hearts and heads

Spirit knows the road
before and after
beyond what can be seen,
so meet me at the crossroads
where blood and fire lick the knife's blade
and it doesn't matter who eats first
as long as everyone gets fed
and no bread's wasted,
while somewhere there's a hungry-belly child.

Meet me in the clearing at twilight
when night eclipses day
and fates give way to faith
Meet me twixt tomorrow,
yesterday and today

Donna Aza Weir-Soley

EL GUARDIÁN DE LAS ENCRUCIJADAS

Encontrémonos donde se entrecruzan los cuatro caminos
donde todas las sendas se abren, se cierran a tu antojo
Encontrémonos en el cruce
donde pies menudos bailan la suerte de los reyes
y hachas pequeñas hacen caer enormes robles y cipreses
Encontrémonos en medio de los ciclos de las estaciones
bailando al compás del latido de los corazones y las cabezas

El espíritu conoce el camino
antes y después
más allá de lo que puede verse,
así que encontrémonos en la encrucijada
donde la sangre y el fuego lamben la hoja del cuchillo
y no importa quien come primero
siempre que todo el mundo se alimente
y no se desperdicie pan,
mientras en algún lado hay un niño con la barriga hambrienta.

Encontrémonos en el claro cuando llegue el ocaso,
cuando la noche eclipse el día,
el destino ceda a la fe
Encontrémonos entre mañana,
ayer y hoy.

Tiphanie Yanique

DICTIONARY

wife – (European origins) a married woman. As in slave in the house. As in chef, maid, nanny and prostitute. But unpaid for these services. A woman defined in relation to her spouse, generally a man. In the colloquial, wife means woman: as in "Old wives' tale" meaning a story passed down by ignorant old women. As in "She's my wife, not my mistress and so did not receive a fur for Christmas. Instead, I bought her a vacuum cleaner, which she loved."

wifey – (American Negro origins) diminutive of wife but more desirable. Girl who cooks, cleans, fucks and gives back massages. As in, "I took this girl home to my moms and she brought potato salad instead of a bottle of wine – because she's a good wifey and knows better." Woman to have sex with but to whom you are not married, and probably never will marry. Or might marry if she gets pregnant – and then she will become WIFE. If she is not wed at the time of giving birth she will become a "baby mama". A diminutive less desirable for all parties.

get wife – (Caribbean origins) to have sex, to fuck a human female, to be on a mission to have sex. As in "You get wife last night? That must be why you in such a good mood." Or "My woman vex with me and ain give me wife in a week." A man might say to a whore: "I'll give you twenty dollars for the wife." Meaning, I will pay you an inadequate sum to fuck you. "Get" translates loosely to "have". "Wife" is a direct translation of "sex".

to wife – (origins unknown) a feminine specific verb suggesting a woman has convinced a man that she is worthy of romantic and sexual commitment. As in "He promised to wife me but I'm still waiting on the ring." Once the woman has the ring, being wifed may be elevated to "being ringed", as in lassoed, as in good enough that

364

Tiphanie Yanique

DICCIONARIO

wife: esposa – (origen europeo) una mujer casada. Como en esclava de la casa. Como en chef, criada, niñera y prostituta. Pero no remunerada por estos servicios. Una mujer definida en relación a su esposo, generalmente un hombre. En su uso coloquial, esposa significa mujer: como en "*Old wives' tale*" – cuento de esposas viejas – que en inglés significa una historia transmitida por viejas ignorantes. Como en "Es mi esposa, no mi amante y por eso no le regalé un abrigo de pieles en Navidad. En lugar de eso, le compré una aspiradora, que le encantó".

wifey: esposita – (origen negro americano) diminutivo de esposa pero más deseable. Chica que cocina, limpia, chinga y da masajes de espalda. Como en "Llevé a una chica a casa de mi mamá y trajo ensalada de papas en lugar de una botella de vino – porque ella es una buena esposita y ella sabe–". Mujer con la que tener sexo pero con quien no estás casado, y con quien probablemente nunca te vas a casar. O puede que te cases con ella si se queda embarazada – y entonces ella se convierte en *WIFE*–. Si ella no está casada cuando da a luz se convierte en una "*baby mama*". Un diminutivo menos deseable para todas las partes.

get wife: conseguir esposa – (origen caribeño) tener sexo, chingarse una hembra humana, ir en misión de tener sexo. Como en "¿Conseguiste esposa anoche? Debe ser por eso que estás de tan buen humor". O "Mi mujer está enfogona' conmigo y no me da esposa desde hace una semana". Un hombre podría decirle a una puta: "Te doy veinte dólares por esposa". Lo que significa te pagaré una suma inadecuada por chingarte. "Conseguir" se traduce aproximadamente como "tener". "Esposa" es una traducción directa de "sexo".

to wife: esposarse – (origen desconocido) un verbo específicamente femenino que sugiere que una mujer ha convencido a un hombre de que ella es merecedora de un compromiso romántico y sexual. Como en "Él prometió tomarme como esposa pero aún estoy esperando el

a man would swing a rope around you. Preferably the rope is made of gold and has a diamond at the knot.

anillo". Una vez la mujer tiene el anillo, "ser esposada" podría subir a categoría "ser anillada", como en ser lazada, como en ser lo suficientemente buena para que un hombre lance una cuerda alrededor de ti. Preferiblemente la cuerda está hecha de oro y tiene un diamante en el nudo.

Tiphanie Yanique

MY BROTHER COMES TO ME

They are at the red gate
of my grandmother's white house
The gate is taller than them both
The mother, who is my mother, is holding her son's hand
The boy, who is my brother, is only four years old
She, our mother, is going crazy
She wants to take him with her
A blood stain has spread permanently on my brother's white shirt
I am at the steps of the house, like a bride
I am fifteen and calling to my brother, "Come to *me*"
Her teeth are bared They are not pearls
"*I* am your mother," she shouts
We are all crying and all our tears are all different
Our mother's hair is a flame above us

Tiphanie Yanique

MI HERMANO VIENE A MÍ

Están en el portón rojo
de la casa blanca de mi abuela
El portón es más alto que ellos dos
La madre, que es mi madre, está agarrando la mano de su hijo
El niño, que es mi hermano, solo tiene cuatro años
Ella, nuestra madre, se está volviendo loca
Ella se lo quiere llevar
Una mancha de sangre se ha extendido permanentemente
    en la camisa blanca de mi hermano
Estoy en las escaleras de la casa, como una novia
Tengo quince años y estoy llamando a mi hermano, "Ven *conmigo*"
Ella, amenazante, enseña los dientes No son perlas
"*Yo* soy tu madre," grita ella
Todos estamos llorando y nuestras lágrimas son todas distintas
El pelo de nuestra madre es una llama por encima de nosotros

Tiphanie Yanique

DANGEROUS THINGS

This is the island.
It is small and vulnerable,
it is a woman, calling. You love her
until you are a part of her
and then, just like that,
you make her less than she was
before – the space
that you take up
is a space where she cannot exist.
It is
something in her history
that does this,
don't mind
her name. The island
is a woman, therefore
dangerous things live below,
beautiful things, also – which can be the most dangerous.
True, we will never be
beyond our histories.
And so I am the island.
And so this is a warning.

Tiphanie Yanique

COSAS PELIGROSAS

Esta es la isla.
Es chiquita y vulnerable,
es una mujer, llamando. La amas
hasta que formas parte de ella
y entonces, así como así,
la haces más pequeña de lo que era
antes – el espacio
que tú ocupas
es un espacio donde ella no puede existir.
Es
algo en la historia de ella
que provoca esto,
no importa
el nombre de ella. La isla
es una mujer, por tanto
abajo viven cosas peligrosas,
además de cosas bonitas – que pueden ser las más peligrosas.
Verdad, jamás dejaremos atrás
nuestras historias.
Y pues yo soy la isla.
Y pues esto es una advertencia.

NOTES AND GLOSSARY

Gloriann Sacha Antonetty Lebrón
"Gloria" refers to the Cuban dance and musical genres of "sones", "boleros" and "danzones". The Cuban "son" is recognized by a distinctive singing style, a clave beat, a call-and-response structure, a percussion section using bongos and maracas, and frequently, the "*tres*" (a six-stringed guitar-like instrument). The slow-tempo "boleros" of Cuba are related to the 19th century "trova" tradition. The "danzón" is a formal 2/4 time, partner dance music, the result of a fusion of many musical influences, traditionally played by musical groups that include brass and wind instruments. "Dama de barrio" translates as "Lady of the neighbourhood".

"Barbershop" mentions "biuti", a term often used in conversation for a hair salon or beauty shop. The "soneo" is the improvisation part of a salsa song. "Maelo" was the nickname of Puerto Rican composer and salsa singer Ismael Rivera (1931-1987), called "el Sonero Mayor", who was known for his "soneos".

Nicole Cecilia Delgado
"Murders": "Bésame mucho" translates to English as "Kiss me a lot". It is the title of a popular song written in 1940 by the Mexican pianist and composer Consuelito Velásquez.

Thaís Espaillat
"La Virgen de la Cueva Always Has Work": "La Virgen de la Cueva" translates to English as "The Virgin of the Cave". The phrase is from a children's song about rain "Que llueva, que llueva, la Virgen de la Cueva".

Sonia Farmer
"Sirenomelia" and "The Other Woman" refer to pirates Anne Bonny (1697?-1782?), Mary Read (1685-1721) and John "Jack" Rackham, known as Calico Jack (1682-1720).

Khadijah Ibrahiim

"The Attic Is a Silent Place": "We speak to you by parables" are words from the Rosicrucian manifesto, which continues: "We speak to you by parables, but would willingly bring you to the right, simple, easy, and ingenuous exposition, understanding, declaration, and knowledge of all secrets." Rosicrucianism has its roots in alchemical and hermetic philosophy dating from the sixteenth century. In the twentieth century it had followers of esoteric Christianity, connections with masonry and the Golden Dawn (of which W. B. Yeats was a member). Rosicrucianism spread to the Caribbean, probably in the late nineteenth century, where there are still lodges in most islands.

"Rock Against Racism": The "poll-tax" refers to Margaret Thatcher's hugely unpopular attempt to switch the cost of property rates onto individuals, penalising poorer families; it was abandoned after poll-tax riots. The phrase "Maggie snatched milk" refers to her actions, as Minister for Education, to cut free school milk for children over seven years of age. The cry was "Maggie Thatcher, Milk Snatcher". Neville Staple of the Specials at the 1981 Rock Against Racism Concert in Potternewton Park, Leeds, reportedly said the words "like a zebra crossing".

Cindy Jiménez-Vera

"Still Life": This text formed part of an artistic performance by Elizabeth Magali Robles titled "Still Life: Quietud Movil", which consisted in posting poems about death in the metropolitan area of San Juan as a manner of bearing the collective mourning that impacted Puerto Rico after the deaths resulting from Hurricane María.

Ann-Margaret Lim

"At the Karaoke Bar, 21st Century Hotel": *Fung Fung Yen*: biscuits; *Fa Chung:* sausage.

Canisia Lubrin

"Village Crescendos": The word "Massav" refers to a giant Saman tree, which is thought to be more than 400 years old and is located in Derek Walcott Square in the city of Castries in Santa Lucia. The "mabouya" is a skink found in the Caribbean. The poem mentions the expression "bookie bucktooth", which is related to "bush-fool" and "country bookie", used, according to *Dictionary of Caribbean English Usage* by Richard Allsopp, to refer to foolish or uncouth person, in particular one who has come from the country and goes to the city, where he is easily tricked. In this case, the "bookie" has bucked-teeth.

Jamila Medina Ríos

"Fur(n)ia" refers to the "damajuana", a round, smooth, light-grey seed used in Cuba for beading jewellery.

Mara Pastor

"Rust": The scientific name for the "yagrumo" is *Cecropia peltata*. In English, it is called the "trumpet tree" or "snakewood".

Esther Phillips

"Birthday Visit to Cuba": The "George" referenced in this poem, as well as the other two by the same poet, is the Barbadian writer and cultural activist George Lamming, the author of several novels and collected essays and lectures.

Legna Rodríguez Iglesias

"It Would Be Strange, So Strange for Me to Forget": The flowering "flamboyán" tree's scientific name is *Delonix regia*. Although, we chose to translate the word as "flamboyant", the tree is known throughout the Caribbean by other names in English, as well, such as the "royal poinciana" and the "flame tree".

Safiya Sinclair

"Crania Americana": In this poem, Sinclair constructs a sense of womanhood in response to Caliban. The poem re-appropriates all of the words spoken by Caliban and the lines spoken about him in William Shakespeare's play *The Tempest*. Sinclair distills the feminine from the "impolite body" of Caliban and his rebellion.

Dorothea Smart

"Reader, I Married Him": "Stella-her-groove-back" refers to Terry McMillan's 1996 novel *How Stella Got Her Groove Back* and the 1998 film adaptation. "Tainted love" refers to a pop song written by Eric Cobb, first recorded by Gloria Jones in 1964, and popularized in Britain by the band Soft Cell in 1981.

Karol Starocean

"Sanitary Pads" refers to the Malecón de Santo Domingo. "Un malecón" is "a pier" in English. The word is also used to describe a long walkway for strolling along the edge of the seawall.

"There are Tunnels in Santo Domingo" refers to "cuaba" soap, which is made from the essential oils extracted from the resin of cuaba pine wood, *Pinus occidentalis*.

Ariadna Vásquez Germán

"Excerpts From *Si hubiera tenido un diálogo en Casablanca...*": The title of the manuscript from which these poems were taken may be translated to English as "If I had had a dialogue in *Casablanca*".

Marion Bethel

"Domingo en el Fuerte Charlotte": La expresión en inglés británico "a jolly good chap" se podría traducir como "un tipo alegre y agradable".

"En la plaza del mercado": La expresión "guh mornin" recrea la pronunciación caribeña de "good morning" que significa "buenos días". "Calypso" se refiere a una música satírica sincopada, de ritmo optimista, de comentario social, y en ocasiones de insinuación, realizada por un cantante y una sección de ritmo, una banda o una guitarra. "Níspero" es la fruta del chicozapote, árbol de la familia de las *Sapotaceae*.

"Vinagre, abejas y cabras": En el Caribe, los "jumbeys" son fantasmas de una persona o animal muerto, o espíritus malignos.

Malika Booker

"El blues de mi madre" menciona "obeah", una práctica material y espiritual del Caribe, que se puede usar para curar, dañar o lograr un resultado deseado.

Vahni Capildeo

"Investigación de zapatos del pasado": El poema menciona un "swoosh" en los zapatos. El "swoosh" es el logo de Nike, por ejemplo.

Sonia Farmer

"Sirenomelia" y "La otra mujer" mencionan a las piratas Anne Bonny (1697?-1782?) y Mary Read (1685-1721), y al pirata John "Jack" Rackham, conocido como Calico Jack (1682-1720).

Millicent A. A. Graham

"Catadupa": "Chainey root" y "raw-moon bush" son hierbas usadas en Jamaica para hacer tónicos saludables que se cree que mejoran la circulación, combaten la anemia, limpian la sangre, aumentan los niveles de energía, alivian la artritis y el reumatismo, aumentan la resistencia y actúan como afrodisíacos.

Khadijah Ibrahiim

"El desván es un lugar silencioso": "Le hablamos en parábolas, pero con gusto lo llevaremos a la simple, fácil e ingenua exposición, comprensión, y declaración correcta y el conocimiento de todos los secretos" es un fragmento del manifiesto rosacruz. El rosacrucismo tiene sus raíces en la filosofía alquímica y hermética que data del siglo XVI. En el siglo XX tenía seguidores del cristianismo esotérico, conexiones con la masonería y la Aurora Dorada (de la que W. B. Yeats era miembro). El rosacrucismo se extendió en el Caribe, probablemente a fines del siglo XIX, donde todavía hay logias en la mayoría de las islas.

"Rock contra el racismo": El término "poll-tax" se refiere al enormemente impopular intento de aplicación, por parte de Margaret Thatcher, de un impuesto que pretendía cambiar el costo del impuesto de propiedad a individuos, penalizando así a las familias más pobres; el impuesto fue eliminado debido a los graves disturbios que se produjeron. La frase "Maggie snatched milk" se refiere a la medida llevada a cabo por Thatcher, como Ministra de Educación, de eliminar la leche escolar gratuita para niños mayores de siete años. El grito era "Maggie Thatcher, Milk Snatcher" que se podría traducir como "Maggie Thatcher, ladrona de leche". Neville Staple de The Specials en el concierto Rock Against Racism de 1981 en Potternewton Park en la ciudad de Leeds, según se dice, dijo las palabras "como un paso de cebra".

Cindy Jiménez-Vera

"Still Life": Este texto forma parte del performance artístico de Elizabeth Magali Robles titulado Still Life: Quietud móvil, que consistía en pasquinar poemas sobre la muerte en el área metropolitana, como manera de llevar el duelo colectivo que nos arropa tras los muertos del huracán María.

Ann-Margaret Lim

"En el bar de karaoke, Hotel 21st Century": Fung Fung Yen: pancitos o panecillos; Fa Chung: salchicha.

"Al leer el diario de Thistlewood, parte III": La palabra "Syvah" se refiere a un baile popularizado por el deejay jamaicano Ding Dong.

Canisia Lubrin

"Crescendos de aldea": La palabra "Massav" se refiere a un enorme árbol Saman, que se cree que tiene más de 400 años de antigüedad, que se encuentra en la Plaza Derek Walcott en la ciudad de Castries de Santa Lucía. El "mabouya" es un escinco que se encuentra en el Caribe. El poema menciona la expresión "bookie bucktooth" que a su vez se podría relacionar con la expresión "bush fool" o "country bookie", utilizada, según el *Dictionary of Caribbean English Usage* de Richard Allsopp, para referirse a una persona ignorante e inculta, en particular una del campo que va a la ciudad y a la que engañan con facilidad. En este caso, el "bookie" tiene dientes desmesurados.

Shara McCallum

"Lo que te cuento": "Whitey gal" se podría traducir como "blanquita".

Monica Minott

"Sister Bernice": "Kumina" se refiere a una práctica religiosa y espiritual jamaicana con raíces centroafricanas. "Roll, Jordan, Roll" es el título de una canción espiritual de la diáspora africana ampliamente conocida. La canción hace referencia al río Jordán, un río de gran relevancia para el judaísmo y el cristianismo, ya que en la Biblia se explica que los israelitas lo cruzaron para llegar a la Tierra Prometida y que en él Jesús de Nazaret fue bautizado por Juan el Bautista. Para algunos, la canción hace referencia al camino de huida hacia los estados del norte de los Estados Unidos, siguiendo los ríos (Mississipi y Ohio) que llevaban a los esclavos hacia la libertad; otros creen que hace referencia al tránsito del mundo terrenal al espiritual, al más allá; y para otros alude al fluir constante del agua como filosofía de vida, al fluir a pesar de las dificultades. Los versos que cierran el poema *"Roll Jordan, roll. My soul arise in heaven Lord / Roll Jordan, roll"* se podrían traducir como "Corre, Jordán, corre. Mi alma subirá al cielo Señor / Corre, Jordán, corre" o "Fluye, Jordán, fluye. Mi alma subirá al cielo Señor / Fluye, Jordán, fluye" según su interpretación.

"Ahuyentar duppies": En Jamaica, un "duppy" es un espíritu o fantasma ancestral.

Esther Phillips

"Visita de cumpleaños a Cuba": El "George" que se menciona en este poema, así como en los otros dos de la misma autora, es el escritor y activista cultural barbadense George Lamming, autor de diversas novelas y recopilaciones de ensayos y discursos.

Jennifer Rahim

"Estimada poesía": "At last my love has come along" se traduce como "Al fin mi amor llegó".

Shivanee Ramlochan

"El ciclo del hilo rojo:1. En el tercer aniversario de la violación": En Trinidad y Tobago, el "dingolay" es un baile espontáneo, alegre, y libre.

"Cling cling": "Scotch bonnet" es una variedad de pimiento rojo picante. "Dhal", en este contexto, se refiere a lentejas amarillas partidas. "Silver bera" se traduce como "joyería de plata".

"Vivek escoge sus maridos": "Phagwa" se refiere a un festival de primavera en la India, Trinidad y Tobago y otras regiones de la diáspora india, en el que los participantes embadurnan su ropa y cuerpo con líquido colorido y polvo pigmentado. La palabra "abeer" se refiere a este tinte.

Tanya Shirley

"La dulce dulce Jamaica": El término "dandy shandy" se refiere a un juego infantil jamaicano; "bull in the pen" es una canción y un juego para niños en el que los participantes juegan a ser gallinas que protegen a sus polluelos de un toro y un halcón.

Safiya Sinclair

"Crania Americana": En este poema, Sinclair construye un sentido de femineidad en respuesta a Caliban. El poema se reapropia de todas las palabras pronunciadas por Caliban y los versos pronunciados sobre él en la obra teatral *La tempestad* de William Shakespeare. Sinclair condensa lo femenino en el "cuerpo grosero" de Caliban y su revolución.

El término "vexed" se traduce como "enfadado", "polémico", o "controvertido", dependiendo del contexto. "Skinfolk" es una expresión afroamericana para los parientes en términos de raza y no solamente en términos de relaciones de parentesco.

"Sirena": El ron "overproof" tiene un contenido de alcohol que va del 57.5% al 75.5%. Generalmente, la palabra inglesa "overproof" se usa en textos en español.

Dorothea Smartt

"Amar a mujeres": El término "macommère" se podría traducir como "comadre". Este puede hacer referencia a una buena amiga que ayuda a la madre a cuidar de sus niños (como si fuera otra madre). En el contexto caribeño, también puede tener otros significados relacionados con la identidad sexual.

"Lector, me casé con él": "Stella-her-groove-back" hace referencia a la novela de Terry McMillan *How Stella Got Her Groove Back* que en 1998 fue llevada al cine con el mismo nombre. En español el título se tradujo como *La nueva vida de Stella* en su versión para Latino América, y *Cómo Stella recuperó la marcha* en su versión para España. "Tainted love" hace referencia a la canción pop escrita por Eric Cobb que popularizó el grupo británico Soft Cell en 1981.

Karol Starocean

"En Santo Domingo hay túneles" menciona el "jabón de cuaba". Este es un jabón hecho aceite extraído de la resina de la madera del pino, *Pinus occidentalis*.

Donna Aza Weir-Soley

"Raíces" menciona "butter ackee", una fruta suave, cremosa y de color amarillo. Su nombre científico es *Blighia sapida*.

"Una conversación en curso" menciona "grigris", un amuleto o un talismán usado para proteger al usuario. En inglés criollo jamaicano, "nuff" significa "suficiente", "mucho", "muchos" o "muchísimo".

CONTRIBUTORS

Gloriann Sacha Antonetty Lebrón is a Puerto Rican writer and educator. Her first poetry collection, *Hebras* (2015) received an honourable mention for the Gautier Benitez Award in 2014. She is the founding editor of the journal *Étnica,* the first online journal in Puerto Rico dedicated to people of African descent and diversity. She has published her work in *Maraña de las Tejedores de Palabras, Palenque: Antología puertorriqueña de temática negrista, antirracista, africanista y afrodescendiente,* as well as *Afroféminas y Atrementum: Voces Subversivas.* She has also published in several journals, including *Revista Boreales*, *Revista Cruce* (UMET), and *Revista Académica* (EDP University).

Marion Bethel lives in The Bahamas. She has published two books of poetry, *Guanahani, My Love,* which won the Casa de las Américas Award in 1994, and *Bougainvillea Ringplay*. She is working on a third manuscript of poetry.

Jacqueline Bishop is a writer and visual artist with six books to her name, including *The Gymnast and Other Positions,* which won the 2017 OCM Bocas Award for Caribbean Literature, in the category of non-fiction.

Danielle Boodoo-Fortuné is a poet and visual artist from Trinidad and Tobago. She is the 2015 winner of the Hollick-Arvon Caribbean Writer's Prize and the 2016 Wasafiri New Writing Prize. Danielle's first poetry collection, *Doe Songs*, was published by Peepal Tree Press in 2018.

Malika Booker is a British poet of Guyanese and Grenadian parentage. *Breadfruit* (pamphlet, flippedeye, 2007) was a Poetry Book Society Recommendation, and her collection *Pepper Seed* (Peepal Tree Press, 2013) was longlisted for the OCM Bocas Prize and shortlisted for the Seamus Heaney Centre Prize for first full collection (2014). She is published with poets Sharon Olds and Warsan Shire in *The Penguin Modern Poet Series: 3 Your Family: Your Body* (2017). She is a fellow of Cave Canem and The Complete Works and was inaugural Poet in Residence at the Royal Shakespeare Company.

Malika is currently Poetry Lecturer at Manchester Metropolitan University.

Vahni Capildeo is a Trinidadian Scot whose seven books and four pamphlets extend from prose poetry into immersive theatre, including Midnight Robber material inspired by traditional masquerade. Their DPhil in Old Norse literature and translation theory underpins a multi-layered, multilingual approach. Capildeo's work has been honoured by the Cholmondeley Award and the Forward Prize for Best Collection. They write a regular column for *PN Review*. Capildeo's non-fiction, on topics such as microtravel and citizenship, is widely published. Capildeo was the Douglas Caster Cultural Fellow at the University of Leeds. Their new projects include responses to the *Odyssey* and the *Windrush*.

Nicole Cecilia Delgado (Puerto Rico, 1980) is a poet, editor, translator, and book artist. She is the founder of La Impresora, an experimental Risograph print shop and publishing studio in Santurce, Puerto Rico. A collection of her poetry, *Apenas un cántaro, poemas 2007-2017,* was recently released (Ediciones Aguadulce). She has published several other collections. Some of her work has been translated into English, German, Polish, Portuguese, Catalan, and Galician. She has kept a blog since 2005: http://nicolececilia.blogspot.com

Thaís Espaillat (Santo Domingo, 1994) is a poet and visual artist of the Dominican Republic. She edits and designs zines in her small literary press, Hacemos Cosas. Her first poetry collection *Pudo haberse evitado* was published by Ediciones Cielonaranja in 2018. Her poems have been published in Argentina, the Dominican Republic and Mexico. Her work often deals with the absurd and the search for poetry in weird and small places. Thaís sometimes remembers to update her blog, saltedeaqui.wordpress.com, with freshly picked poems from the tamarind tree.

Sonia Farmer is a writer, visual artist, and founder of Poinciana Paper Press, a small and independent press located in Nassau, The Bahamas. Poinciana Paper uses letterpress printing, bookbinding, hand-papermaking, and digital to publish chapbooks of Caribbean literature. Farmer's artwork has been exhibited at the National Art Gallery of The Bahamas. Her poetry won the 2011 Small Axe Literary Competition. Her poetry collection *Infidelities* (Poinciana Paper Press, 2017) was longlisted for the 2018 OCM Bocas Award for Caribbean Literature. In 2019, she published the poetry collection *The Best Estimation in the World* (Poinciana Paper Press). She holds a BFA in Writing from Pratt Institute and an MFA in Book Arts from the University of Iowa.

Gelsys García Lorenzo (1988) received her doctorate degree in Filología Hispánica from the Universidad Complutense de Madrid, in 2016, and her Licenciatura en Letras from the Universidad de La Habana in 2010. She has published the poetry collections *No te afeitarás en vano* (Hypermedia Ediciones, 2016) and *La Revolución y sus perros* (Leiden, 2016), among others. She has also compiled an anthology about theatre inspired by the Bible, *Anuncia Freud a María* (Leiden, 2017).

Millicent A. A. Graham lives in Kingston, Jamaica. She is the author of two collections of poetry. *The Damp in Things* (Peepal Tree Press, 2009) and *The Way Home* (Peepal Tree Press, 2014). A fellow of the University of Iowa's International Writing Program, 2009, and an awardee of the Michael and Marylee Fairbanks International Fellowship to Bread Loaf Writer's Conference, 2010, she has had work published in: *So Much Things to Say 100 Calabash Poets*; the *Jamaica Journal*; *Caribbean Writer*; *BIM*; *City Lighthouse*. She recently contributed to *Yonder Awa,* an anthology of Scottish and Caribbean writers for the Empire Cafe Project.

Zulema Gutiérrez Lozano was born in Holguín, Cuba, in 1982. She is a poet, story teller and promoter of literature. She is a graduate of the Centro de Formación Literaria Onelio Jorge Cardoso, and she is a member of AHS. She is also a writer of children's literature. She has received various poetry prizes, including the Premio Portus Patris (2018), the Premio Nacional for *Adelaida del mármol* (2018), and the Premio de la Ciudad de Holguín. Her poetry collections *Danza alrededor del fuego* and *Metralla* are forthcoming. She has also been published in anthologies and journals within Cuba and elsewhere.

Khadijah Ibrahiim was born in Leeds of Jamaican parentage. She is a writer, literary activist, researcher, educator, theatre-maker, and artistic director of Leeds Young Authors. Educated at the University of Leeds, she has a B.A. in Arabic and Middle Eastern Studies and a M.A. in Theatre Studies. Her poetry collection *Another Crossing* (2014) was published by Peepal Tree Press, and her performance based on the collection premiered at the West Yorkshire Playhouse (2014). She has been a trustee of the Leeds Studio and a Geraldine Connor Foundation Creative Associate Artist, serving as the GCF project producer for the performance 'Windrush: an Influential Force on British Culture' (2018). She has performed widely.

Yaissa Jiménez is a writer, poet and screenplay writer from the Dominican Republic. She has worked in Santo Domingo as a ghost writer, editor, reviewer and content developer. Her essays and opinion articles explore themes of African descendants, Caribbean identity, feminism, culinary arts and environmental protection. *Encuentro con inmortales*, a collection of erotic poetry, was published in 2014. *Ritual Papaya* (Zemi Publicaciones, 2018) is her second poetry collection.

Cindy Jiménez-Vera is the author of four poetry collections: *No lugar* (2017), *Islandia* (2015), *400 nuevos soles* (2013), and *Tegucigalpa* (2012). She has also published a non-fiction book chronicling her trip to El Salvador entitled *En San Sebastian, su pueblo y el mio* (2014), and a collection of children's poetry, *El gran cheeseburger y otros poemas con dientes* (2015). Her work has been translated into English, Italian, and Portuguese, and published in literary and academic journals, anthologies, textbooks, and newspapers across Latin America, the Caribbean, the US, Europe and elsewhere. *I'll Trade You This Island* is a bilingual anthology of a selection of her poetry with English translations by Guillermo Rebollo-Gil (2019). She is the founder, Director and Editor in Chief at Ediciones Aguadulce, an independent press in Puerto Rico, dedicated to poetry books.

Ann-Margaret Lim has two published books of poems, *The Festival of Wild Orchid* and *Kingston Buttercup*, and was featured in *Ebony Magazine* after her 2014 debut at the Calabash Lit Fest. She has represented Jamaica in poetry festivals in Latin America, and her work is published in UK, Caribbean and US anthologies.

Hannah Lowe's first poetry collection *Chick* (Bloodaxe, 2013) won the Michael Murphy Memorial Award for Best First Collection and was short-listed for the Forward, Aldeburgh and Seamus Heaney Best First Collection Prizes. In September 2014, she was named as one of 20 Next Generation poets. She has also published three chapbooks: *The Hitcher* (Rialto, 2012); *R x* (sine wave peak, 2013); and *Ormonde* (Hercules Editions, 2014). Her family memoir *Long Time, No See* was published by Periscope in July 2015 and featured as Radio 4's Book of the Week. Her second collection, *Chan,* is published by Bloodaxe (2016). A new chapbook The *Neighbourhood,* was published in January 2019 (Outspoken Press). She is the current poet in residence at Keats House and a commissioned writer on the Colonial Countryside Project with the University of Leicester and Peepal Tree Press.

Canisia Lubrin is a writer, editor, critic and teacher with work published widely in North America and forthcoming in the UK. She is the author of the awards-nominated poetry collection *Voodoo Hypothesis* (Wolsak & Wynn, 2017), named a 2017 CBC Best Book and *augur* (Gap Riot Press, 2017) finalist for the 2018 bpNichol Chapbook Award. Her poetry collection *The Dyzgraphxst* (2019) is published by Penguin Random House Canada. Lubrin's fiction appears in *The Unpublished City: Volume I*, finalist for the 2018 Toronto Book Award. She is co-director and host of *Pivot Readings* in Toronto and teaches writing at Humber College and the University of Toronto's School of Continuing Studies.

Shara McCallum, from Jamaica, is the author of five books of poetry, published in the US and UK, most recently *Madwoman*, winner of the 2018 OCM Bocas Prize for Caribbean Poetry and the 2018 Sheila Margaret Motton Book Prize. Her work has appeared widely in the US, the Caribbean, and Europe, has been translated into several languages, and has received such recognition as a Witter Bynner Fellowship from the US Library of Congress and a Poetry Fellowship from the National Endowment for the Arts. McCallum is a Liberal Arts Professor of English at Penn State University.

Jamila Medina Ríos (Holguín, 1981) has published the poetry books *Huecos de araña* (Premio David, 2008), *Primaveras cortadas* (2012), *Del corazón de la col y otras mentiras* (2013), *Anémona* (2013, 2016), and *País de la siguaraya* (Nicolás Guillén Award, 2017). Her poetry has also been anthologised in *TrafficJam* (2015), *Para empinar un papalote* (2015) y *JamSession* (2017). Her fiction and essays have been published in *Ratas en la alta noche* (2011) and *Diseminaciones de Calvert Casey* (Alejo Carpentier Award, 2012). She is a philologist and an editor of such publications as *Tres escotillas al mar* (2017).

Monica Minott is a Chartered Accountant. She has received two awards in the Jamaican National Book Development Council's annual literary competitions for book-length collections of her poetry. She was awarded first prize in the inaugural *Small Axe* poetry competition. Her poems have been published in *The Caribbean Writer*, *Small Axe*, *IC*, *Cultural Voice Magazine*, *SX Salon*, *Jubilation*, *The Squaw Valley Review*, *BIM: Arts for the 21ˢᵗ Century*, and *Coming Up Hot*, an anthology of poems featuring eight emerging poets from the Caribbean. An entry entitled 'Spirits' was named in the top ten entries for the Hollick-Arvon Caribbean Writers prize 2015. Her poems have been aired on Power 106 in Jamaica. Her first collection, *Kumina Queen,* was published by Peepal Tree Press in 2016. In 2018, Peekash Press featured four poems in an anthology titled *Thicker Than Water.*

Mara Pastor (1980) is a Puerto Rican poet, editor and translator. She lives in Ponce, Puerto Rico, where she teaches literature. Her works include the chapbooks *As Though the Wound Had Heard* (Card Board House Press, 2017) and *Children of Another Hour* (Argos Books, 2013). She is also the author of several books in Spanish, including *Falsa heladería* (2019), *Sal de magnesio* (2015), *Arcadian Boutique* (2014), *Poemas para fomentar el turismo* (2011), *Candada por error* (2009) and *Alabalacera* (2006).

Some of her poems have been translated into English and, recently, to German. She has performed in the Festival de Poesía de Rosario, Argentina; Latinale, Berlin (2016); Festival de la Palabra, San Juan (2015); Festival de la Lira, Ecuador (2015); La Habana International Book Fair, Cuba (2014) and Festival del Caracol, Tijuana (2013). She is also the coeditor of the anthology of Puerto Rican poetry *Vientos Alisios*. Her most recent editorial work was *A toda costa* (Mexico City, 2018), an anthology of contemporary Puerto Rican fiction.

Esther Phillips is the author of *When Ground Doves Fly*, *The Stone Gatherer,* and *Leaving Atlantis*. She is the editor of the journal *BIM: Arts for the 21st Century*, founder of the Bim Literary Festival and Book Fair, and was appointed first Poet Laureate of Barbados in February 2018.

Jennifer Rahim is a widely published poet and fiction writer. She lives in Trinidad. Her poetry collections include *Approaching Sabbaths,* which won a 2010 Casas de las Americas Prize. *Curfew Chronicles: a fiction* won the 2018 OCM Bocas Award for Caribbean Literature.

Shivanee Ramlochan is a Trinidadian book blogger, poet and critic. Her debut collection, *Everyone Knows I Am a Haunting,* was a 2018 People's Choice T&T Book of the Year finalist, and was shortlisted for the 2018 Forward Prize for Best First Collection.

Legna Rodríguez Iglesias (Camagüey, Cuba, 1984) received the Premio Iberoamericano de Cuentos Julio Cortázar in 2011, and she was the recipient of the Casa de las Américas award in Theatre (2016) for the play *Si esto es una tragedia yo soy una bicicleta*. In 2016 she also received the Paz Prize, from The National Poetry Series, *Miami Century Fox* (Akashic Books, 2017). She is the author of various other poetry collections, including *Transtucé* (Editorial Casa Vacía, 2017); *Hilo + Hilo* (Editorial Bokeh, 2015); *Dame Spray* (Hypermedia Ediciones, 2016); and the bilingual edition of *Chicle (ahora es cuando)* (Editorial Letras Cubanas, 2016). Her published fiction includes the novels *Mi novia preferida fue un bulldog francés* (Editorial Alfaguara, 2017); *Las analfabetas* (Editorial Bokeh, 2015); and *Mayonesa bien brillante* (Hypermedia Ediciones, 2015). She has also published two short story collections: *No sabe/no contesta* (Ediciones La Palma, 2015) and *La mujer que compró* *el mundo* (Editorial Los Libros de la Mujer Rota, 2017). Ediciones Aguadulce published her book of poetry for children, *Todo sobre papá,* in 2016. She is the mother of a precious baby. She once had the same number of tattoos as years, but now she doesn't.

Tanya Shirley has published two poetry collections: *She Who Sleeps With Bones* (Peepal Tree Press, 2009) and *The Merchant of Feathers* (Peepal Tree Press, 2014). She is a featured poet on www.poetryarchive.org and has read her poems and conducted writing workshops in Venezuela, Canada, the U.S.A., England, Scotland and the Caribbean. She was awarded an MFA in Creative Writing from the University of Maryland, USA. She taught at The University of the West Indies, Mona, Jamaica, for over ten years and has been writer-in-residence twice at Sierra Nevada College, Lake Tahoe. Shirley is also a proud Cave Canem Fellow. Her second poetry collection, *The Merchant of Feathers,* was longlisted for the OCM Bocas Prize for Caribbean Literature and shortlisted for the Guyana Prize for Literature, Caribbean Award. In 2017 she was awarded a Silver Musgrave Medal from The Council of the Institute of Jamaica for her outstanding contribution in the field of Literature.

Safiya Sinclair was born and raised in Montego Bay, Jamaica. She is the author of *Cannibal*, winner of a Whiting Writers' Award, the Addison M. Metcalf Award from the American Academy of Arts and Letters, the OCM Bocas Prize for Caribbean Poetry, and the Prairie Schooner Book Prize in Poetry. Her work has appeared in *The New Yorker*, *Granta*, *The Nation*, *Poetry*, and elsewhere. Sinclair's other honours include a Pushcart Prize, fellowships from the Poetry Foundation, Yaddo, and the Bread Loaf Writers' Conference.

Dorothea Smartt is a poet/ live artist published by Peepal Tree Press. She was appointed a Fellow of the Royal Society of Literature in Britain in 2019.

Karol Starocean was born in Santo Domingo in 1981. She is both a writer and an artist. Her work *The Big Vaina* (2016), which combines painting, poetry and art journals, won the 26th Eduardo León Jiménez Art Competition. Her books include the limited edition *Saltacharcos* (2016), a collection of poems and drawings, as well as *Dramamine* (Ediciones Cielo Naranja, 2017) and *Forgotten* (Papá Bocó, Argentina, 2018). Her poems have also been included in the project *Liberoamericanas +100 poetas contemporáneas* (Argentina, España, 2018).

Ariadna Vásquez Germán has published the books of poetry *Una Casa Azul* (Editorial Angeles de Fierro, 2002, RD), *Cantos al hogar incendiado* (Praxis, 2007, México), *El libro de las inundaciones* (Atarraya Cartonera, 2011, Puerto Rico and Proyecto Literal, 2012 México), *Debí dibujar el mar en alguna parte* (Editora Nacional, 2013, RD, recipient of the Premio Nacional de Poesía Salomé Ureña de Henríquez, 2012), and the short novel *Por el desnivel de la acera* (Praxis, 2005, México).

Donna Aza Weir-Soley was born in St. Catherine, Jamaica and migrated to the United States at the age of 17. Currently, she is an Associate Professor of English, and affiliate faculty in African and African Diaspora Studies, Women's Studies and the Latin American and Caribbean Center at Florida International University. Dr. Weir-Soley is also the Vice President of the Association of Caribbean Women Writers and Scholars. She won the Woodrow Wilson Career Enhancement Fellowship in 2004-2005 to complete her scholarly work, *Eroticism, Spirituality and Resistance in Black Women's Writings* (University Press of Florida, 2009, reprinted in 2017). Weir-Soley is a frequent invited speaker at the annual Woodrow Wilson Foundation Career Enhancement Fellowship Conference where she mentors new Woodrow Wilson Fellows. She is co-editor (with Opal Palmer Adisa) of the anthology *Caribbean Erotic* (Peepal Tree Press, 2010), and the author of two books of poetry: *First Rain* (Peepal Tree Press, 2006, reprinted 2011) and *The Woman Who Knew* (chapbook, Finishing Line Press, 2016). She is the mother of three wonderful young men and lives in Miami.

Tiphanie Yanique, from the Virgin Islands, is the author of the poetry collection, *Wife*, which won the 2016 Bocas Prize in Caribbean poetry and the United Kingdom's 2016 Forward/Felix Dennis Prize for a First Collection. Her novel, *Land of Love and Drowning*, won the 2014 Flaherty-Dunnan First Novel Award from the Center for Fiction, the Phillis Wheatley Award for Pan-African Literature, and the American Academy of Arts and Letters Rosenthal Family Foundation Award, and was listed by NPR as one of the Best Books of 2014. It was a finalist for the Orion Award in Environmental Literature and the Hurston-Wright Legacy Award. Her short story collection, *How to Escape from a Leper Colony*, won her a listing as one of the National Book Foundation's 5Under35. Her writing has also won the Bocas Award for Caribbean Fiction, the Boston Review Prize in Fiction, a Rona Jaffe Foundation Writers Award, a Pushcart Prize, a Fulbright Scholarship and an Academy of American Poet's Prize. She has taught at The New School and is now the Director of the Creative Writing at Wesleyan University.

ABOUT THE EDITORS AND TRANSLATORS

Loretta Collins Klobah has an M.A. in creative writing, M.F.A. in poetry writing, and a doctoral degree in English, with an emphasis on Caribbean literature. For two decades, she has been a professor at the University of Puerto Rico main campus in San Juan, where she teaches courses in Anglophone Caribbean literature, creative writing, and the medical humanities. She is also a poet with two collections published by Peepal Tree Press, *The Twelve-Foot Neon Woman* (2012) and *Ricantations* (2018). Her debut collection received the OCM Bocas Award for Caribbean literature in the category of poetry and was short-listed for the 2012 Felix Dennis Prize for Best First Collection, offered by the Forward Prizes. The second book was designated a Summer Recommendation by the Poetry Book Society in Britain. It was long-listed for the 2019 OCM Bocas Award for Caribbean literature. In 2018, she served as a judge for the OCM Bocas Award for Caribbean Literature, in the area of poetry. She has also been awarded the Pushcart Prize for Poetry, the Earl Lyons Award from The Academy of American Poets, a scholarship at Breadloaf Writers' Conference, a Fulbright for research in Jamaica, and a grant from the National Endowment for the Humanities. Her poems have appeared in *The New Yorker, BIM, Caribbean Beat Magazine, The Caribbean Writer, The Caribbean Review of Books, Live Encounters, PN Review, Poui: The Cave Hill Literary Annual, Susumba's Book Bag, Moko: Caribbean Arts and Letters, WomanSpeak, Simple Past, Smartish Pace, Ekphrastic Review, A Congeries of Poetry at Connotation Press: An Online Artifact, Stand, TriQuarterly Review, Quarterly West, Black Warrior Review, The Missouri Review, The Antioch Review, Cimarron Review,* and *Poet Lore.* Poems have been anthologized in *Best American Poetry 2016,* edited by David Lehman and Edward Hirsch; *New Caribbean Poetry,* edited by Kei Miller; *Under the Volcano/bajo el volcán,* edited by Magda Bogin; *Puerto Rico en mi Corazón,* edited by Erica Mena, Raquel Salas-Rivera, and Ricardo Maldonado; *TriQuarterly New Writers,* edited by Reginald Gibbons and Susan Hahn; and *How Much Earth,* edited by Christopher Buckley. She has published many articles and book chapters on Caribbean literature and culture and frequently reviews new publications and interviews authors. She has lived in Jamaica and other locations of the Caribbean Diaspora(s) in London and Toronto. She has also travelled extensively throughout the Caribbean region as a writer and academic.

Maria Grau Perejoan, holds a doctoral degree in Cultural Studies with an emphasis on Caribbean Literature and Literary Translation from the University of Barcelona, and an MPhil in Cultural Studies from the University of the West Indies, Trinidad and Tobago. She was visiting lecturer at the UWI, St Augustine Campus for three academic years, she then moved on to lecture courses in Caribbean Literature and Translation at the University of Barcelona, and since 2020 she is a lecturer at the Department of Spanish, Modern and Classical Languages at the University of the Balearic Islands. She has been awarded the scholarship Becas Iberoamérica: Santander Investigación (2016-2017), and The Fulbright Commission, Spain, selected her to be part of the Fulbright Visiting Scholar Program (2017-2018), enabling her to work on this project in Puerto Rico. She has lived and taught in the Caribbean islands of Trinidad and Puerto Rico, and has also travelled to other locations in the Caribbean and its Diaspora(s) to attend conferences and interview authors. Her translations of Caribbean authors are informed by her linguistic and cultural knowledge of the region. She has previously translated Trinidadian writers Earl Lovelace and Jennifer Rahim into Spanish, and has also theorised on translating Anglophone Caribbean authors into Spanish. Among her publications on literary translation are "The Role of Literary Translators in the West Indian Literary Field and the Importance of Creole" in *Translation and Translanguaging in Multilingual Contexts* (2016), and "West Indian Writers Who Do Not 'Translate As Well': The Case of Trinidadian Writer Earl Lovelace" in *Tusaaji: A Translation Review* (2014).

PERMISSIONS

Our acknowledgments of and gratitude to the authors and book publishers who have given us permission to reprint the original versions of the poems, along with our translations:

Gloriann Sacha Antonetty Lebrón, "La cajita", "Gloria", "Barbería", previously published in *Hebras*, © 2015 Editorial EDP University. Used by permission of the author.

Marion Bethel, "Sunday in Fort Charlotte", "Vinegar, Bees & Goats", "In the Marketplace", previously published in *Bougainvillea Ringplay*, © 2010 Peepal Tree Press. Used by permission of the publisher.

Jacqueline Bishop, "Snakes", "Ixora", previously published in *Fauna*, © 2006 Peepal Tree Press. Used by permission of the publisher.

Jacqueline Bishop, "Hasan Talking to Himself in the Mirror of a Cheap Hotel Room", previously published in *Snapshots from Istanbul*, © 2009 Peepal Tree Press. Used by permission of the publisher.

Danielle Boodoo-Fortuné, "Portrait of My Father as a Grouper", "Boa Gravida", "A Hammer to Love With", previously published in *Doe Songs*, © 2018 Peepal Tree Press. Used by permission of the publisher.

Malika Booker, "My Mother's Blues", "Pepper Sauce", "Cement", previously published in *Pepper Seed*, © 2013 Peepal Tree Press. Used by permission of the publisher.

Vahni Capildeo, "Investigation of Past Shoes", "Slaughterer," previously published in *Measures of Expatriation*, © 2016 Carcanet Press. Used by permission of the publisher.

Vahni Capildeo, "Into Darkness/Plus que Noir", previously published in *Utter*, © 2013 Peepal Tree Press. Used by permission of the publisher.

Nicole Cecilia Delgado, "Asesinatos", "Hombre nuevo", "Lecciones chinas", previously published in *Apenas un cántaro*, © 2018 Ediciones Aguadulce. Used by permission of the publisher.

Thaís Espaillat, "La Virgen de la Cueva siempre tiene trabajo", "Invadirnos sería perder el tiempo", "Residencial Bolivar", previously published in *Pudo haberse evitado,* © 2018 Thaís Espaillat, Ediciones Cielonaranja. Used by permission of the author.

Sonia Farmer, "Sirenomelia", "The Trial", "The Other Woman," previously published in *Infidelities,* © 2017 Poinciana Paper Press. Used by permission of the publisher.